Praise for *Latinx/a/os in Higher Education*

"Batista, Collado, Pérez, and associates have done a tremendous service by filling a major gap in the higher education literature. Through both personal narratives and policy papers, this ground-breaking volume makes visible the challenges and triumphs of Latinx/a/o students, faculty, and administrators as they navigate the professional pathways to educational success. It will undoubtedly inspire the next generation of higher education leaders!"

—**Beverly Daniel Tatum**, President Emerita,
Spelman College

"This book provides valuable insights from foremost thought leaders on best practices for expanding opportunities for Latinx/a/o students, faculty, and staff in higher education. Too often we hear language and make assumptions about this population without fully understanding its rich diversity of backgrounds, perspectives, challenges, interests, and strengths."

—**Freeman A. Hrabowski III**, President,
University of Maryland, Baltimore County

"*Latinx/a/os in Higher Education* is timely and a much needed resource in providing an important voice to the pathways of success for Latinx/a/o student affairs professionals, faculty, and students. An essential contribution to the field, this compelling culmination of personal narratives supported by research and data provides an authentic view to the lived experiences of Latinx/a/os in higher education."

—**SARA MATA,** National Science Foundation National Research Traineeship Program Coordinator, University of Oklahoma; cochair, NASPA Latinx/a/o Knowledge Community

"If ever there was a moment in time within higher education for a book that examines the broad experience of Latinx/a/os within the academy, from multiple perspectives and through both personal and professional lenses, this is the moment and this is the book. *Una lectura obligada!* (A must read!)"

—**ELLEN HEFFERNAN,** President, Spelman Johnson

"This impressive collection of contributors highlights the importance of collaborative learning and programming. As the U.S. population becomes more and more diverse, where Latinx/a/os will represent the largest ethnic majority, institutions of higher education need to guarantee campus communities that are inclusive and supportive of everyone. This book offers valuable insight into the importance of including all constituent groups, but especially student voices, in the development of programmatic pathways to success."

—**DEBORAH BIAL,** President and Founder, The Posse Foundation

LATINX/A/OS
IN HIGHER EDUCATION

Exploring Identity, Pathways, and Success

100 ◆ YEARS

1919 ▽ 2019

NASPA®

Student Affairs
Administrators in
Higher Education

LATINX/A/OS
IN HIGHER EDUCATION

Exploring Identity, Pathways, and Success

Angela E. Batista, Shirley M. Collado, and David Pérez II

EDITORS

Foreword by Nichole M. Garcia and Daniel G. Solórzano

NASPA®

Student Affairs
Administrators in
Higher Education

Published by
NASPA–Student Affairs Administrators in Higher Education
111 K Street, NE
10ᵗʰ Floor
Washington, DC 20002
www.naspa.org

Additional copies may be purchased by contacting the NASPA publications department at 202-265-7500 or visiting http://bookstore.naspa.org.

NASPA does not discriminate on the basis of race, color, national origin, religion, sex, age, gender identity, gender expression, affectional or sexual orientation, or disability in any of its policies, programs, and services.

Library of Congress Cataloging-in-Publication Data

Names: Batista, Angela E., 1971- editor. | Collado, Shirley M., 1972- editor. | Perez, David, II, 1974- editor.
Title: Latinx/a/os in higher education : exploring identity, pathways, and success / Angela E. Batista, Shirley M. Collado, and David Perez II, editors.
Description: First edition. | Washington, DC : NASPA-Student Affairs Administrators in Higher Education, [2018] | Includes bibliographical references.
Identifiers: LCCN 2018003197 (print) | LCCN 2017052009 (ebook) | ISBN 9780931654664 (eBook) | ISBN 9780931654749 (pbk.) | ISBN 9781948213011 (hbk.)
Subjects: LCSH: Hispanic Americans--Education (Higher)--United States. | Hispanic American college students--United States. | Hispanic American college administrators--United States.
Classification: LCC LC2670.6 (print) | LCC LC2670.6 .L48 2018 (ebook) | DDC 378.008968--dc23
LC record available at https://lccn.loc.gov/2018003197

Printed and bound in the United States of America

FIRST EDITION

CONTENTS

**PART V: LOOKING TO THE FUTURE
AND ADVANCING THE LATINX/A/O
EXPERIENCE IN HIGHER EDUCATION**

FOREWORD

Nichole M. Garcia and Daniel G. Solórzano

My trenzas [braids] and school uniform were a culture disguise. They were also a precursor for the more elaborate mask [mascaras] I would later develop. Presenting an acceptable face, speaking without a Spanish accent, hiding what we really felt—masking our inner selves—were defenses against racism passed on to us by our parents to help us get along in school and in society. (Montoya, 1999, pp. 6–7)

Margret Montoya (1999) described *mascaras, trenzas, y greñas* (masks, braids, and tangles) as the weaving together of academic voice with personal narrative to subvert dominant discourse. As the Latinx/a/o[1] community makes sense of our stories, our ideas are (re)braided, creating generations of difference and

---

[1] We, the authors, acknowledge *Latinx* as a political term used to challenge the social construction of gender and sexual identities. The suffixes "a/o" denote our positionality in acknowledging our privilege as heterosexuals who work in solidarity with the LGBTQIA Latinx community.

similarity that are woven together to tell our stories as well as those of our parents and grandparents. These blended stories draw on experience as a source of strength, which we use as we navigate institutions of higher education that were not necessarily built with people of color in mind (Solórzano & Yosso, 2002). As a Chicano senior scholar, Daniel Solórzano pushes his mentees to tell their stories, giving name to and honoring their experiences. Nichole Garcia, as a Chicana Riqueña emerging scholar and Solórzano's mentee, learned that "[a] woman who writes has power, and a woman with power is feared" (Anzaldúa, 2015, p. 170). We often find ourselves in conversations about how to ground our scholarship in telling stories not just to academics but to the generations before us that labored so that we could pursue higher education. Latinx/a/o faculty, student affairs professionals, and policymakers must acknowledge our presence within higher education as well as the experiences of preceding generations; by interweaving our stories—*máscaras, trenzas, y greñas*—we can advance who we are as a people.

Angela Batista, Shirley Collado, and David Pérez II put *trenzas* into praxis and reveal the multiple *máscaras* Latinx/a/o communities occupy in higher education. This groundbreaking edited volume is one of the first to combine perspectives on Latinx/a/o graduate students, student affairs professionals, and faculty. As Sylvia Hurtado, Joseph Ramirez, and Katherine Cho note in chapter 1, demographic shifts have resulted in the Latinx/a/o community becoming the largest ethnic group in the United States, yet Latinx/a/o higher education attainment is among the lowest. Solórzano and Villalpando (1998) predicted that "even though the absolute numbers of students of color on college campuses will increase during the next decade, it appears that they will continue to have proportionately lower levels of college entrance and graduation rates" (pp. 211–212). While this may be true, "numbers do not speak for themselves" (Covarrubias & Velez, 2013, p. 271). In their narratives in this book, Anesat León-Guerrero, Lorena Jirón, Juan Carlos Matos, and Jacob Diaz share powerful counter-stories, giving voice to numbers and exposing their *greñas y mascaras*. We must remind ourselves—and others—that Latinx/a/os are in the best position to explain their professional and academic experiences. In turn, faculty and student affairs practitioners must be held accountable for meeting the needs of these Latinx/a/o students.

Statistics on education can be misleading: data are often aggregated, erasing the complex lived realities within each group. We need to be acutely aware that Latinx/a/o students prior to entering institutions of higher education are tracked and pushed out—often limiting their pathways into and through four-year institutions (Contreras, 2011; Solórzano, Villalpando, & Oseguera, 2005). Over the years, we have come to learn that the majority of Latinx/a/o students attend community colleges, where they experience high attrition rates. Regardless of institutional type or level, a majority of Latinx/a/o students are not exposed to a college-going culture, a rigorous academic curriculum, high-quality teaching, and high expectations for student success (Contreras, 2011; Oakes, Rogers, Lipton, & Morrell, 2002; Solórzano & Solórzano, 1995). In chapter 7, Edward Martinez and Ignacio Hernández detail how Latinx/a/o student experiences at community colleges can inform successful student affairs practices at four-year institutions. For example, the Puente Community College Program fosters learning environments that are culturally relevant and supportive of underserved students. Latinx/a/os have benefited greatly from the Puente Program's culturally relevant curriculum (Solórzano, Datnow, Watford, & Park, 2013). Puente has improved the persistence and transfer rates for many Latinx/a/o students. We know that Puente works, and a future direction would be to create similar programs in developmental math—a Puente program for math.

Latinx/a/o students' underperformance in education has been a point of contention among scholars who often perpetuate deficit perspectives and do not hold institutions accountable for failing to meet the needs of this student population. Valencia and Solórzano (1997) detailed how deficit thinking theory and practice undermine the success of vulnerable populations: "Given the high likelihood that deficit thinkers will not develop workable school success programs for low-SES [socio-economic status] minority students the responsibility will indubitably rest with those who espouse anti-deficit thinking views" (p. 199). In chapter 6, David Pérez II, Claudia García-Louis, Tracy Arámbula Ballysingh, and Eligio Martinez advance an anti-deficit framework, which accounts for contextual forces that determine Latinx/a/o undergraduates' precollege socialization and readiness, college achievement, and postcollege success. In doing so, they offer a counter-narrative that shifts attention from Latinx/a/o failure to success and provides a framework to increase pathways to and through higher education. That said, we still need to explore the following questions:

- How do we frame and complicate narratives of achievement in the face of institutional racism?

- How can we redefine success and achievement that centers on the lived experiences of Latinx/a/o students in and out of educational institutions?

- How can we honor and build on the assets that Latinx/a/o students bring with them to college from their homes and communities?

Latinx/a/o students have a historical legacy of resistance and advancements in higher education. The 1960s to 1970s proved to be a turning point with the Chicana/o Student Movement and the Puerto Rican Student Movement (Gómez-Quiñones, 1978; Marquez & Jennings, 2000; Solórzano & Villalpando, 1998; Torres & Velázquez,

1998). These movements, simultaneously taking place on the east and west coasts of the United States were acts of resistance intended to improve K–12 schools and higher education. Based on these movements, Chicana/o studies and Puerto Rican studies as academic disciplines were birthed, holding institutions of higher education accountable to the students they served. Activist-based interventions opened the door for many Latinx/a/o students to be admitted and to hold professional positions in higher education. In fact, Solórzano was directly involved with the Chicana/o antiwar movement, and his involvement with student and community activism had a positive impact on his ability to graduate from college, go on to graduate school, and work in academia to serve others. Over the past 44 years, Solórzano has established a pipeline of students of color through his caring and critical race mentorship. Dimpal Jain, a former advisee, shared:

> [Danny] begins by asking about your and your family's well-being. To this day, I've never had another mentor consistently begin with this question. As a first-generation student who comes from a low-income family with immigrant parents, I instantly feel at ease by this welcome question. This is a clear example of Danny's praxis and importance he puts on the inclusion of family and community. (Jain & Solórzano, 2015, p. 126)

Solórzano's mentorship has been crucial to many individuals and their pathways to and through the PhD. This edited volume represents the intergenerational approach of mentorship that Solórzano and many others share. Mentorship for Latinx/a/o students is critical in achieving intergenerational persistence and retention in higher education.

There is still a need for hiring initiatives geared toward Latinx/a/o faculty and student affair professionals, as "higher education must recognize the cultural resources that we bring to academia and must welcome, engage, and encourage our perspectives and our scholarship, for the benefit of all students" (Delgado Bernal & Villalpando, 2002, p. 177). In their respective chapters in Part IV, Anthony Cruz, William Luis, and Mildred García share their journeys to student affairs senior leadership, the professorate, and the presidency, imparting lessons along the way and acknowledging our ability to succeed in higher education. Nevertheless, as Angela Batista and Shirley Collado highlight in chapter 15, fostering new pathways through the power of cohorts, mentors, professional development, and leadership participation is critical for expanding ways for Latinx/a/o individuals to practice authentic leadership.

It is important that members of the Latinx/a/o community adopt our own terminology to describe who we are as a people. As Brianna Carmen Sérráno notes in chapter 5, an example is the recent emergence of *Latinx* as a political term, created by the Latinx/a/o lesbian, gay, bisexual, transgender, queer, intersex, and asexual (LGBTQIA) community to challenge constructs of gender and sexuality. Much like the terms *Chicano* and *Boricua*, we must acknowledge nomenclature that encases historical eras and reflects the heterogeneity within our population (Comas-Diaz, 2001). Language can render our community invisible or hyper-visible. In various presidential administrations, immigrant and undocumented students are hyper-visible with the elimination of Deferred Action for Childhood Arrivals, which has an impact on financial aid, campus climates, and deportation. As faculty and student affairs professionals, we have to be mindful of our students who are negotiating literal and metaphorical borders within the ivory tower, which Joel Pérez and Gerardo Ochoa in chapter 3 seek to dismantle for undocumented students. We are asking that institutions of higher education develop policies and practices to protect this population. Throughout Latinx/a/o history, students have utilized their education to advance liberation and reject colonialism. In reclaiming our identities and naming ourselves, we inherently demonstrate time and time again that we are *presente* in higher education. More important, our respective positions as Latinx/a/o faculty, as student affairs professionals, and as students create bridges where "our conceptual *trenzas* . . . may appear unneat or *greñudas* to others . . . [but] the *trenzas* of our multicultural lives offer personally validating interpretations for the *mascaras* we choose to wear" (Montoya, 1999, p. 207).

REFERENCES

Anzaldúa, G. (2015). Speaking in tongues. In C. Moraga & A. Anzaldua (Eds.), *This bridge called my back* (pp. 163–173). Albany, NY: SUNY Press.

Comas-Diaz, L. (2001). Hispanics, Latinos, or Americanos: The evolution of identity. *Cultural Diversity and Ethnic Minority Psychology, 7*(2), 115–120.

Contreras, F. (2011). *Achieving equity for Latino students: Expanding the pathway to higher education through public policy.* New York, NY: Teachers College Press.

Covarrubias, A., & Velez, V. (2013). Critical race quantitative intersectionality: An anti-racist research paradigm that refuses to "let the numbers speak for themselves." In A. Dixson & M. Lynn (Eds.) *Handbook of critical race theory in education* (pp. 270–285). New York, NY: Routledge.

Delgado Bernal, D., & Villalpando, O. (2002). An apartheid of knowledge in academia: The struggle over the" legitimate" knowledge of faculty of color. *Equity & Excellence in Education, 35*(2), 169–180.

Gómez-Quiñones, J. (1978). *Mexican students por la raza: The Chicano student movement in Southern California, 1967–1977.* Los Angeles, CA: CAL Editorial La Causa.

Jain, D., & Solórzano, D. G. (2015). A critical race journey of mentoring. In C. S. V. Turner & J. C. González (Eds.), *Modeling mentoring across race/ethnicity and gender: Practices to cultivate the next generation of diverse faculty* (pp. 125–143). Sterling, VA: Stylus.

Marquez, B., & Jennings, J. (2000). Representation by other means: Mexican American and Puerto Rican social movement organizations. *PS: Political Science & Politics, 33*(3), 541–546.

Montoya, M. (1999). Mascaras, trenzas, y grenas: Un/masking the self while un/braiding Latina stories and legal discourse. In D. L. Galindo (Ed.), *Speaking Chicana: Voice, power, and identity* (pp. 1–10). Tucson, AZ: University of Arizona Press.

Oakes, J., Rogers, J., Lipton, M., & Morrell, E. (2002). The social construction of college access. In W. G. Tierney & L. S. Hagedorn (Eds.) *Increasing access to college: Extending possibilities for all students* (pp. 105–122). Albany, NY: SUNY Press.

Solórzano, D., Datnow, A., Watford, T., & Park, V. (2013). *Pathways to postsecondary success: Maximizing opportunities for youth in poverty.* Final report produced by the Pathways to Postsecondary Success Project at UC/ACCORD (All Campus Consortium on Research for Diversity), University of California, Los Angeles.

Solórzano, D. G., & Solórzano, R. W. (1995). The Chicano educational experience: A framework for effective schools in Chicano communities. *Educational Policy, 9*(3), 293–314.

Solórzano, D. G., & Villalpando, O. (1998). Critical race theory, marginality, and the experience of students of color in higher education. In C. A. Torres & T. R. Mitchell (Eds.), *Sociology of education: Emerging perspectives* (pp. 211–224). Albany, NY: SUNY Press.

Sólorzano, D. G., Villalpando, O., & Oseguera, L. (2005). Educational inequities and Latina/o undergraduate students in the United States: A critical race analysis of their educational progress. *Journal of Hispanic Higher Education, 4*(3), 272–294.

Solórzano, D. G., & Yosso, T. J. (2002). Critical race methodology: Counter-storytelling as an analytical framework for education research. *Qualitative Inquiry, 8*(1), 23–44.

Torres, A., & Velázquez, J. E. (1998). *The Puerto Rican movement: Voices from the diaspora.* Philadelphia, PA: Temple University Press.

Valencia, R., & Solórzano, D. (1997). Contemporary deficit thinking. In R. R. Valencia (Ed.), *The evolution of deficit thinking: Educational thought and practice* (pp. 160–210). New York, NY: RoutledgeFalmer.

INTRODUCTION

Angela E. Batista, Shirley M. Collado, and David Pérez II

At a time when many students in the United States still face considerable barriers to education and career opportunities, the changing demographics of Latinx/a/o college students have begun to shift campus culture and priorities. Along with new challenges regarding admission, financial aid practices, and cultural competency, the increased representation of Latinx/a/o students also brings with it new opportunities for collaboration and innovation between academic and student affairs departments. The need to develop promising pathways within success-oriented environments for Latinx/a/o individuals in higher education is now more important than ever. It is clear that conditions along the pathway—such as point of entry, support and resources, and more—need to change for everyone and that, as higher education leaders, we must focus on the conditions necessary for Latinx/a/o students, faculty, and professionals to thrive.

DEMOGRAPHICS

It is projected that the United States will have a majority-minority population by 2043, with Latinx/a/o becoming the largest ethnic minority (U.S. Census Bureau, 2016). This development represents a change in the landscape, bringing with it major implications for higher education, for students, and for colleges and universities throughout the country. According to the U.S. Census Bureau (2016), the Hispanic population of the United States reached 56.6 million as of July 1, 2015, with Hispanics constituting 17.6% of the nation's total population. This figure represents an increase in the Hispanic population of 2.2% between 2014 and 2015. By 2060, the Hispanic population in the United States is projected to rise to 119 million, making it 28.6% of the nation's total population.

TERMINOLOGY

In order to understand the issues discussed throughout the book, it is important to address terminology and how Latinx/a/o individuals identify. As a group, Latinx/a/os represent a mixture of racial/ethnic and other intersecting identities and "for many U.S. Latinos, mixed-race identity takes on a different meaning—one that is tied to Latin America's colonial history and commonly includes having a white and indigenous, or 'mestizo,' background somewhere in their ancestry" (Gonzalez-Barrera, 2015, para. 2). Latinx/a/o individuals in the United States, in particular, continue to experience change in how their identity is characterized, as the labels used to identify members of the group have continued to evolve (see explanations on the following pages). Generally, this book examines and explores issues affecting people whose ethnic background is from Latin American and Spanish-speaking countries. However, within Latinx/a/o communities in the United States, most people identify with their country of origin (e.g., Dominican, Puerto Rican, Mexican). It is also critical to understand that Hispanics or Latinos are considered an ethnic, not racial, group. Indeed as a group, their racial identity is a mix of European Whites, Black slaves, and indigenous communities from the Caribbean and other parts of Latin America.

Hispanic vs. Latino

As discussed by Sofia Pertuz in chapter 4, the term *Hispanic* was first used by the U.S. government in the 1970s. Prior to that year, the census did not have an all-inclusive category for people from different countries in Latin America. Thus, the U.S. government created the new term *Hispanic* in an attempt to bring all members of these groups under one descriptor. Eventually, as the Hispanic community grew and diversified in the United States, the term *Hispanic* was rejected by the Latinx/a/o community and the new term *Latino* began to be used to refer to anyone of Latin American origin or ancestry, including Portuguese and Brazilian. Though the U.S. government still uses the term *Hispanic* today, the term *Latino* was added with the 2000 census.

Latina and Latin@

In chapter 5, Brianna Carmen Sérráno addresses the gender binary that results from the inherent gendering of words to either masculine or feminine in the Spanish language. As the author notes, the Spanish language defaults to the masculine ending "o" when referring to an entire group. As a result, women challenged the use of the term *Latino* and eventually began to embrace the term *Latina* to describe themselves. As Sérráno explains, the term *Latina* was ultimately deemed as not inclusive of the fluidity of gender identity within the Latino community and the new and more inclusive *Latin@* term began to be utilized.

Latinx

More recently, the term *Latinx* has been adopted to be more inclusive of lesbian, gay, bisexual, transgender, queer, intersex, and asexual (LGBTQIA) individuals. Initially, this new term was adopted mainly by the LGBTQIA community, but many others have adopted it as a way to more inclusively describe all members of the community. This has led to national debate within the entire community and resulted in disagreement about its use, as Sérráno discusses in chapter 5. During the past few months, this wave of national conversations has included the idea of expanding the original *Latinx* term to include both traditional female and masculine endings in an effort to include all members of the community—*Latinx/a/o*. This is still very much a conversation in process, and Sérráno examines it more deeply in her chapter.

As editors, we have intentionally chosen to utilize the more inclusive *Latinx/a/o* term and to honor that self-identity is a personal choice. The term *Latinx/a/os* is used throughout this book to refer to people and communities of Latin American origin or ancestry who live in the United States. While the term is herein intended to be inclusive of all the diverse cultures that comprise the groups from different Latin American ancestry and gender identity, the editors acknowledge that self-identity is a very individualized process for people of Latinx/a/o heritage. Therefore, the writers featured in this book have chosen their own identifiers as well as those of the community and issues under their discussion. Consequently, the terms *Hispanic, Latino, Latina, Latin@, Latinx*, and *Latinx/a/o* all intentionally appear in this volume as a way to honor the multi descriptors used in the literature, existing research, and within the community still. This variation is especially noted in the literature when citing previous works, and the terminology used by the original author has been retained.

MISSION AND OVERVIEW

The overall premise of this book is to provide a forum for contributors to share their perspectives and experiences in higher education. This publication will explore topics relevant to the experience of Latinx/a/o students and professionals and will illustrate key elements that should be considered in the development of varied pathways for success. While there are many publications that focus on topics related to the Latinx/a/o experience in education, there is very limited theoretical and practical literature about best practices—especially with regard to innovation and expansion of opportunities for Latinx/a/o students and professionals in higher education. This publication will respond to the needs of higher education professionals, institutions, and leadership organizations, such as NASPA–Student Affairs Administrators in Higher Education, which is working to respond proactively and effectively to demographic trends that center the experience of Latinx/a/os.

We hope this publication will also serve as a key resource and guide to both Latinx/a/o individuals and allies who pursue excellence in terms of new professional pathways, learning in higher education and student affairs preparation programs, and ongoing professional development. We seek to showcase the journey and experiences of current Latinx/a/o students, faculty, and staff as a way to relate the complexity of Latinx/a/o identity, increase understanding of the experience of Latinx/a/o students and professionals in higher education, and highlight major considerations for diversifying pathways to success.

Because we feel that it is critical to highlight and celebrate some of the sharpest and most engaged Latinx/a/o minds around these issues, we have committed to featuring Latinx/a/o writers and those working to advance the success of Latinx/a/o students and professionals in higher education. To that end, our work includes eminent Latinx/a/o scholars as well as many first-time writers who are actively engaging on important issues in higher education. In addition to their particular areas of work and interest, these scholars and practitioners represent a rich illustration of the diversity, commitment, and talent that exists within the Latinx/a/o community. Their stories exemplify the many ways in which Latinx/a/os enter higher education and are changing the landscape and experience of students and other professionals through teaching, advocacy, and leadership.

THEMES AND TOPICS

To help readers examine the experience of Latinx/a/o students and professionals in higher education, we have organized this work in five sections. Part I helps readers to understand the current landscape of Latinx/a/os in higher education. Part II explores Latinx/a/o identity in the United States. Part III examines best practices and models for developing pathways to Latinx/a/o student success. In Part IV, student affairs administrators and faculty reflect on their personal and professionals journeys. Part V looks to the future with considerations for advancing the Latinx/a/o experience in higher education.

In addition to scholarly chapters focused on important issues that affect the experience of Latinx/a/o students and professionals, personal narratives from students, faculty, and administrators are showcased throughout, illustrating the complexity of identity and its many intersections, the influence of cultural values and norms, and the importance of being guided and supported in order to succeed in higher education. Undergraduate student Anesat León-Guerrero, for example, writes about "living between two worlds" and coming of age as a Chicana in higher education. Third-year law student Lorena Jirón reflects on the importance of guidance while "swimming upstream" throughout her academic journey. Juan Carlos Matos explores how identity, involvement, and intentionality have influenced his experiences as a student and professional. Jacob Diaz discusses the experience of "being an insider-outsider" as a senior student affairs administrator. Professor William Luis details his personal and professional journey from early schooling in New York City to becoming a leading literary scholar. Mildred García shares how her passion and commitment to equity in higher education led her to the university presidency.

Other authors interlace their scholarly work with descriptions of their personal, educational, and professional journeys, revealing how their pathways to success in higher education came together and how they have navigated cultural differences and institutional politics to overcome barriers. Their experiences exemplify the courage, strength of spirit, and strong work ethic that is typical of the Latinx/a/o community. As higher education works to address the needs of a changing student population and to find new ways to increase Latinx/a/o leadership, we need to look to these role models—as well as revere and celebrate their contributions to higher education.

It has been our honor as an editing team to bring this particular group of Latinx/a/o thought leaders together and to collaboratively create a way to share ourselves and our community with you. We invite you to join us in this journey and to work with us to create new and innovative pathways for Latinx/a/o students and professionals to continue to succeed in higher education.

REFERENCES

Gonzalez-Barrera, A. (2015). *"Mestizo" and "mulatto": Mixed-race identities among U.S. Hispanics.* Retrieved from Pew Hispanic Center website: http://www.pewresearch.org/fact-tank/2015/07/10/mestizo-and-mulatto-mixed-race-identities-unique-to-hispanics

U.S. Census Bureau. (2016). *FFF: Hispanic heritage month 2016.* Retrieved from https://www.census.gov/newsroom/facts-for-features/2016/cb16-ff16.html.

PART I

CURRENT STATUS OF LATINX/A/OS IN AMERICAN HIGHER EDUCATION

CHAPTER 1

THE CURRENT LATINX/A/O LANDSCAPE OF ENROLLMENT AND SUCCESS IN HIGHER EDUCATION

Sylvia Hurtado, Joseph Ramirez, and Katherine Cho

Although Latinx/a/o students currently account for approximately one in six students (16.5%) participating in higher education, many colleges and universities enroll a much smaller percentage of Latinx/a/o students and employ few Latinx/a/o faculty and staff (National Center for Education Statistics [NCES], 2016). National statistics mask the extent to which Latinx/a/o students are concentrated in specific geographic areas and institutions; more detailed analyses are needed to understand equity issues across the higher education system (Hatch, Uman, & Garcia, 2016). More than 63% of all Hispanic students enrolled in higher education attend college in one of four states: California, Florida, New York, and Texas. In 14 states, Hispanic students account for less than 5% of the state's college population, further emphasizing enrollment disparities across the nation (NCES, 2015). Such variations highlight how key institutions are responsible for a majority of Latinx/a/o participation in higher education, and that in many areas, Latinx/a/o students remain severely underrepresented on college campuses. This shapes student experiences: Their identities become more salient in contexts where these students are the numerical minority, as negative experiences with the institutional climate—due to a lack of understanding among faculty, staff, and peers about the background of Latinx/a/o students— makes these students aware of cultural distinctiveness (Ruiz Alvarado & Hurtado, 2015). The purpose of this chapter is to provide a broad overview of Latinx/a/o students, faculty, and staff as well as to discuss developments in research and theory that can promote agency and action for advancing student success based on an identity-centered model for diverse learning environments.

For decades, scholars have noted the overrepresentation of Latinx/a/o students at public institutions and at community colleges (Fry, 2002; Ganderton & Santos, 1995; Núñez, Sparks, & Hernández, 2011; Villalpando, 2010). This portrait is changing: Among 18- to-24-year-olds in college, Hispanics are now the largest minority group at four-year colleges (Fry & Lopez, 2012; Fry & Taylor, 2013; Hurtado, 2015). Similarly, Hispanic students were the largest minority group earning baccalaureate degrees as of spring 2014, with Hispanic students earning 11.2% of conferred bachelor's degrees (NCES, 2015). While representation at two-year institutions remains high—with more than half of Hispanic undergraduate students (51.3%) enrolling in two-year colleges—Hispanic students account for a growing proportion of students at four-year colleges and universities, particularly at public institutions, where they comprise nearly one in five undergraduates (NCES, 2015). Many first-generation students began college in two-year colleges and require support as transfers to four-year institutions. Hispanic participation in private four-year colleges continues to lag behind—10.5% of undergraduates identify as Hispanic—and so these campuses must consider improving efforts to address such underrepresentation. At private, for-profit institutions, Hispanic students represent 17.2% of all undergraduates (NCES, 2015), a percentage that is comparable to their overall participation in higher education. However, those institutions are typically more expensive than public institutions, have higher student loan default rates, and offer relatively fewer student support programs (Looney & Yannelis, 2015; NCES, 2015).

In contrast, Hispanic-serving institutions (HSIs) have been critical for Latinx/a/o enrollment. These institutions receive federal designation if they enroll an undergraduate student body where at least 25% of the full-time equivalent students are Hispanic and eligible for Title V funding for student support plans. According to the Hispanic Association of Colleges and Universities (HACU; 2016), the number of HSIs has increased rapidly, nearly doubling in the past decade to 435 institutions as of 2014. These institutions, which account for a fraction of all degree-granting institutions in the United States, enroll more than 60% of all Hispanic students in higher education (HACU, 2016). Although only a handful of HSIs are defined by a historical mission to serve Hispanic students, most serve large numbers of racially/ethnically diverse, first-generation, and low-income students (Núñez, Hurtado, & Calderón Galdeano, 2015). The rapidly changing nature of these institutions makes their success inseparable from notions of Latinx/a/o student success.

While public institutions and HSIs enroll a majority of Latinx/a/o students, there are notable differences between the undergraduate and graduate populations. Whereas 83.3% of Hispanic undergraduates attend a public college or university, less than half of Hispanic graduate students (49.1%) are enrolled in public institutions (NCES, 2015). Major policy trends—such as the free community college initiatives in San Francisco and Tennessee (Berndtson, 2017; Carruthers, 2016) as well as the proposal to make all of New York's two- and four-year public institutions free for low- and middle-income families (McKinley, 2017)—will further encourage Latinx/a/o undergraduates to enroll at public institutions. In this context, advancing economic and social mobility for Latinx/a/o students will depend on a collective focus on degree completion and preparation for graduate and professional school careers, particularly at public institutions.

In addition to the distinct patterns of where Latinx/a/o students[1] go to college, it is important to consider *who* goes to college. Since the early 1980s, there have been more Latina students attending college than Latino students (Hurtado, Sáenz, Santos, & Cabrera, 2008; Villalpando, 2010). Recent data show that among young adults—those between 18 and 24 years old—40.4% of Hispanic women were enrolled in higher education compared with 30.8% of their male peers. While differences in college participation by gender have been noted (NCES, 2016), it is also important to emphasize the substantial variation within Latinx/a/o subpopulations. Among young adults, 33.4% of Mexicans and 32.5% of Salvadorans participate in college compared with 45.7% of Cubans and nearly 60% of Colombians and Venezuelans (NCES, 2016). Students with college-educated parents are more

---

[1] Although often presented as a single, homogenous group, students who identify as Latinx/a/o have widely varied backgrounds, traditions, immigration histories, and cultures—a fact that contributes to different experiences in higher education (Fergus, Noguera, & Martin, 2010; Page, 2013; Villalpando, 2010). While this chapter focuses on broad enrollment trends, we acknowledge the limitations of this approach and that important distinctions are lost when statistics about Latinx/a/o students are aggregated.

likely to attend and succeed in college, but more than half of Mexican Americans entering four-year colleges are likely to be first-generation college students, and that figure has increased in recent years (Hurtado, 2015). This is significantly higher than all other racial/ethnic groups. Such disparities emphasize the wide variation in Latinx/a/o social identities and the participation and success of these individuals in higher education. The important point is to learn to recognize distinct racial/ethnic Latinx/a/o identities that will inform effective pedagogy and programming within classrooms and learning environments outside the classroom.

LATINX/A/O STUDENTS' COLLEGE ACCESS AND SUCCESS

Access: College Choices

In examining Latinx/a/o student participation in higher education and the need to further expand access, it is crucial to consider how students learn about college options, navigate the college application requirements, and decide where to begin or continue their educational journey. As scholars have noted, the college-going process for Latinx/a/o students is complex, as issues of ethnicity, gender, geography, socioeconomic standing, generational and immigrant status, high school opportunity structures, and many other influences contribute to their enrollment decisions (Loya, Hwang, & Oseguera, 2015; Núñez et al., 2011; Pérez & Ceja, 2015; Pérez & McDonough, 2008; Rios-Aguilar & Kiyama, 2012). Similarly, scholars argue that "rational" economic models are inadequate to explain Latinx/a/o students' enrollment decisions and new approaches are needed to understand the college-going process (Núñez, et al., 2011). New models, such as the Latina/o Student and Parent College-Going Negotiation Model (Alvarez, 2015), are promising developments that more fully outline students' pathways to higher education. As scholarship on Latinx/a/o students' college choice has grown more nuanced, recent studies have revisited issues of family (Alvarez, 2015; Ceja, 2006; Martínez & Cervera, 2012; Pérez & McDonough, 2008; Rios-Aguilar & Kiyama, 2012) and finances (Kim, 2004; Montalvo, 2013), and how the two influence Latinx/a/o students' decision-making and college-going processes. This culturally responsive research informs college recruitment and retention efforts.

Today, Hispanic students are transitioning from high school to college at historically high rates, with 68.9% of recent high school completers in 2015 enrolling in postsecondary institutions; compare this figure to that of two decades prior, when just over half of Hispanic students were immediately transitioning into college (NCES, 2016). High school support systems and opportunity structures for college information and guidance have become increasingly important, given students' more immediate transitions. However, prior studies have shown that Latina/o students are less likely to get college information—or rely on the guidance—from school agents such as counselors or teachers (Hurtado et al., 2008; Martínez & Cervera, 2012). As a result, scholars have sought to understand how high schools provide information to students and families as well as the role that other individuals, including family and peers, play in Latinx/a/o students' college choice process.

The Role of Family and Peers

Past literature framed family and ties to locality as rationales for attending less selective institutions than students are qualified for and enrolling in two-year institutions versus four-year institutions (Grodsky, 2002; Kurlaender, 2006). Or, in the case of early retention models, families were seen as external commitments that distracted from, not enhanced, students' educational success (Tinto, 1987). As a result, student affairs professionals and high school administrators, especially college counselors, developed more programs to reorient families in order to increase the "college-going" opportunities, even if that meant Latino students were selecting institutions that were farther away from their families (Auerbach, 2004). This deficit-lens framework is rooted in the myth that Latina/o families do not value or support the path for higher education (Torrez, 2004; Valencia & Black, 2002). Remnants of this idea are seen in the common rhetoric around Latinx/a/o families' lack of understanding of college demands—without recognizing the effects of class differences or cultural values (Tornatzky, Cutler, & Lee, 2002; Torrez, 2004; Zambrana & Hurtado, 2015).

In contrast, more recent literature has delved deeper into the strength that family members model and communities provide as students embark on college pathways (Alvarez, 2010; Matos, 2015; Valencia & Black, 2002). Within the framework of cultural community wealth, the theories of social and cultural capital (Bourdieu & Passeron, 1977) have been expanded to include such concepts as aspirational capital or hope in the midst of barriers, linguistic capital through communicating in multiple languages, navigational capital in negotiating larger social institutions, familial capital that encompasses many forms of support, and resistance capital or taking a critical view of existing norms (Yosso, 2005). Thus, these types of Latinx/a/o culturally relevant capital add more dimensions that reflect how families interact with their college-age children. Similarly, concepts like *familismo*, which posits that Hispanic students in the college-choice process prioritize family obligations and responsibilities (Marín & Marín, 1991), introduce additional complexity as students negotiate between the multiple contextual demands of college, community, and family. While some studies reflect lack of cultural and social capital as a default rationale for Latina/o failure, these new frames encapsulate more complex relationships of support, responsibility, and selection decisions (Alvarez, 2010; Hernandez & Lopez, 2005).

Although families are important in fostering educational aspirations and commitments, Martínez and Cervera (2012) found that more than one third of Latina/o students in a national sample did not go to a family member for information about colleges during their senior year of high school. Similarly, Ceja's (2006) work focusing on Chicana undergraduates found that while parental roles were limited, siblings were particularly crucial in providing information and advocating for their success. Peers are also primary sources of information and continued support in Latina/o transition during the first few years of college (Hurtado, Carter, & Spuler, 1996). Utilizing knowledgeable peers is a powerful source of information about college—especially in terms of academic and social adjustment.

Finances and Financial Concerns

The Great Recession had a pronounced effect on students' college selection, making many applicants more sensitive to cost, financial aid, and potential debt obligations. Data from the Higher Education Research Institute reveal that students are increasingly more likely to weigh issues of college costs and financial aid when deciding where to enroll (Eagan et al., 2016). Although a substantial proportion of Latinx/a/o students are enrolled in lower-cost institutions, it is important to note that many remain concerned about financing college. For example, Hispanic first-year students at four-year colleges and universities were about 2.5 times more likely than non-Hispanic White students to express a major concern about financing college, and came from families that earned 54 cents for every dollar earned by the parents of non-Hispanic White students (Santos & Sáenz, 2013). Amid these concerns, many Hispanic undergraduates receive financial aid in the form of grants and scholarships that ease the costs of their education, with nearly two thirds (62.7%) of full-time students receiving Pell Grants in 2011–2012. Even with grant aid, a majority of full-time, Hispanic undergraduates (51.2%) still assumed a loan during the same time frame, with the average amount borrowed totaling approximately $10,000. Additionally, more than one quarter (27.4%) of part-time students borrowed an average of nearly $7,000 (NCES, 2015). Although Hispanic households may be less likely to carry education debt (Fry, 2014) and often attend less expensive institutions, Latinx/a/o students continue to face challenges in meeting the costs of their education and opt to work during college.

Student Enrollment Mobility

While Latinx/a/o student enrollment and college choice provide key information regarding students' entry into higher education, examining student mobility and transfer between institutions provides a more complex and accurate view of students' experiences. With more than half of Hispanic students enrolled in two-year colleges, college transfer must be built into the planning for those aspiring to a baccalaureate degree, or many will not realize their goal (Fry, 2002; NCES, 2016).

Yet transfer and college mobility is not simply movement from a community college to a four-year institution. A recent study using National Student Clearinghouse data found that nearly one in five Latinx/a/o students experienced "reverse transfer"—transfer from a four-year institution to a two-year institution (Ruiz Alvarado, 2014). This may occur for financial reasons, to obtain unavailable but required courses, or to pursue remedial coursework necessary to continue in the four-year college. A more comprehensive and accurate picture of Hispanic college participation and mobility is emerging because scholars have recently examined enrollment in the context of persistence and transfer (including lateral and reverse transfer) (Kim, Saatcioglu, & Neufeld, 2012). These types of analyses are important given the increasing pressure for campuses to boost graduation rates and move more students to a degree. Additionally, such research can help improve the systems and processes that facilitate students' frequent movement between institutions.

Moreover, a quarter of Latinx/a/o students entering four-year colleges and universities *began* college in fall 2016, indicating there was either "some" or a "very good" chance of transferring to another institution (Eagan et al., 2016). Research has shown that first-year students who indicate a likelihood of transfer are significantly less likely to complete a degree within six years at their initial four-year institution (DeAngelo, Franke, Hurtado, Pryor, & Tran, 2011). With Latinx/a/o students entering college already willing to transfer or stop-out, higher education institutions must pay closer attention to student experiences if they want to reverse the chances of these students dropping out and support the success of those who do transfer.

Latinx/a/o Student Success

There is a pressing need to improve the rate at which Latinx/a/o students earn a degree or certificate. For many years, scholars have examined the rate at which Latina/o students complete their educational goals, making note of the differences by Latina/o ethnicity, generation status, and institutions attended (Fry, 2002; Villalpando, 2010). Recent data highlight how Latinx/a/o degree completion continues to fall below national averages; without improvements in institutional practice, Latinx/a/o students may not realize or leverage the full benefits of a college education. Recent completion statistics show that for Hispanic students entering two-year colleges in 2011, less than one third (29.9%) earned a degree or certificate within three years, including only 17.5% who attended public institutions. For those at four-year institutions,

30.4% of Hispanic students completed their degree in four years, with one quarter (24.8%) of students at public institutions compared with nearly half (47.2%) of students at private, nonprofit institutions earning their degree in four years. While overall six-year graduation rates are more encouraging (53.5%), they vary considerably depending on the selectivity and type of the institution (NCES, 2015).

When considering dynamic enrollment patterns, studies that track students' completion across all institutions provide a more encouraging picture of Latinx/a/o student success. In Ruiz Alvarado's (2014) study, the six-year graduation rate for Latina/o students (entering at 2004 and graduating in 2010) at four-year institutions improved from 57.4% (measured at the initial institution) to 72.6% when taking into account transfer and completion at another institution. Given that traditional measures of retention and graduation rates do not account for these different types of pathways, it is important to expand the way Latinx/a/o student success is conceptualized and tracked, particularly as graduation rates and completion metrics become increasingly important measures of educational equity. Student programs and advising can begin to anticipate Latinx/a/o student mobility and help them navigate productive pathways.

Latinx/a/o Faculty and Staff

The extent to which Latinx/a/os are represented within the faculty and staff ranks can provide a more comprehensive picture of Latinx/a/o participation in higher education (Hatch et al., 2016); it can also help to understand how these individuals support student success. In fall 2013, less than 4.8% (1 in 20) of all faculty at degree-granting postsecondary institutions (two- and four-year) identified as Hispanic, including 3.2% of full-time faculty who have earned the rank of "Professor" (NCES, 2015). Although this number had slightly increased from a decade prior, when 3.7% of all faculty identified as Hispanic, inclusion into the faculty ranks has proceeded at a much slower rate than inclusion into the student body. Examining the pipeline to the professoriate—the rate at which Latinx/a/o students serve as graduate assistants or earn doctoral degrees—provides some hope that there will be a continued increase of Latinx/a/o faculty over time, as Hispanic students accounted for 6.8% of graduate assistants and doctoral degree recipients in 2013–2014 (NCES, 2015). However, without substantive changes to faculty recruitment, evaluation, and promotion practices (Ponjuán, 2011), the representational imbalance between student and faculty Latinx/a/o populations in higher education may continue to grow.

Similar to faculty colleagues, Latinx/a/o staff members at colleges and universities comprise a low percentage of the overall staff population. Hispanic student and academic affairs administrators accounted for 8.2% of those working in such positions in fall 2013, with an even smaller percentage of individuals in higher-level management positions (5.3%) identifying as Hispanic (NCES, 2016). Data from fall 2007—when staff were not disaggregated by position—show that of the professional staff classified as executive, administrative, or managerial, less than 5% identified as Hispanic, whereas 10.2% of those in nonprofessional roles identified as Hispanic (NCES, 2008). While the academy certainly has diversified and Latinx/a/o participation has grown over time, data regarding faculty and staff representation reveal how higher education institutions are not as inclusive of Latinx/a/o employees as the national student population figures would suggest. It is important to recognize that even though student enrollment figures continue to reach new heights, there are relatively few Latinx/a/o faculty and staff members employed in higher education, particularly at the highest levels of appointments. This reality suggests that, while improvements in representation must occur, more faculty and staff also must learn how to become advocates and mentors for Latinx/a/o students as well as for junior faculty and staff.

CREATING DIVERSE LEARNING ENVIRONMENTS FOR STUDENT SUCCESS

Enrollment, representation, and degree completion are key issues for Latinx/a/o students; so too are the conditions they encounter throughout their educational journeys. Inclusive environments— ones that affirm students' identities, develop their talents, validate their capabilities, and foster positive interactions—are vital for promoting Latinx/a/o student success. Inclusive colleges and universities are places where Latinx/a/o students, staff, and faculty feel welcomed and empowered to express multiple identities without fear of judgment or discrimination.

For years, scholars have emphasized the importance of the campus climate for racial diversity and its relationship to Latina/o experiences (see, e.g., Hurtado, 1994; Hurtado & Carter, 1997; Hurtado & Ponjuán, 2005). This research has made clear that students benefit from environments that promote positive interactions across difference—where hostilities and tensions are minimized, where Latinx/a/o individuals are visible in all areas within the institution, and where faculty, staff, and administrators value and prioritize equity and inclusion in practice. A substantial body of campus climate literature informed the development of the Multicontextual Model for Diverse Learning Environments (MMDLE; Hurtado, Alvarez, Guillermo-Wann, Cuellar, & Arellano, 2012), which links the climate for diversity with key educational and pluralistic democratic outcomes that are vital to producing a more engaged and empowered college-educated citizen.

The MMDLE posits that we acknowledge multiple dimensions of

the campus climate for diversity (the historical legacy of inclusion/ exclusion, compositional diversity, psychological and behavioral interactions) and place student identity at the center of programming, content, and pedagogical practice (Hurtado et al., 2012). Staff, administrators, and instructors play a key role in promoting student success and achievement. Figure 1.1 depicts the central contexts and processes adapted from the MMDLE to emphasize practice.

Figure 1.1. *Central Contexts and Processes in the Multicontextual Model for Diverse Learning Environments*

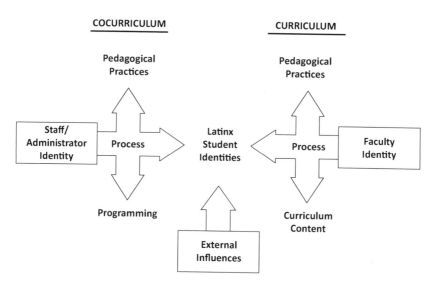

Note. Adapted from "A Model for Diverse Learning Environments: The Scholarship on Creating and Assessing Conditions for Student Success," by S. Hurtado, C. L. Alvarez, C. Guillermo-Wann, M. Cuellar, and L. Arellano, in J. C. Smart and M. B. Paulsen (Eds.), *Higher Education: Handbook Of Theory And Research* (Vol. 27, p. 48), 2012, Dordrecht, Netherlands: Springer. Copyright © 2012 by Springer. Adapted with permission.

The model indicates important parallels between what student affairs professionals do in the cocurricular context and what faculty do in the academic context in educating students. First, placing Latinx/a/o student identity at the center of practice would mean that faculty and staff know students well—their social identities (race, gender, class, sexual orientation), culture, histories, needs, and familial responsibilities. Second, more awareness is needed on how faculty and staff identities inform their daily practice with students. Faculty and staff interactions are informed by their own histories, backgrounds, and perspectives. Third, while conveying content and concepts in programming, pedagogical practices in both curricular and cocurricular spheres involve a variety of ways to actively engage students in the learning process. For example, both student affairs professionals and faculty may use informed peer mentors to convey information and concepts as well as to pose questions that can help advance student learning. At the center of the model are key processes that involve fostering the sense of belonging on campus (psychological), engagement (behavioral), socialization (learning how to become a successful college student), and validation. Validation is defined as "an enabling, confirming, and supportive process initiated by in- and out-of-class agents that foster academic and interpersonal development" (Rendón, 1994, p. 44). Academic and general interpersonal validation from faculty and staff has a significant positive effect on a student's sense of belonging and significantly diminishes the negative impact of experiences of discrimination or bias in college (Hurtado, Ruiz Alvarado, & Guillermo-Wann, 2015).

Role of Faculty and Staff in Creating Diverse Learning Environments

Although it may seem fair to treat students the same, this is not actual educational equity, especially when Latinx/a/o students have overcome significant disparities to get to college and continue to face additional barriers associated with race, class, gender identity, and sexual orientation once they are in college. Instead, it is important to recognize and validate Latinx/a/o student identities and affirm cultural groups, programs, and centers as legitimate spaces for sense of belonging, growth, and development. With relatively few Latinx/a/o faculty and staff to serve as role models, all educators can incorporate family and community cultural wealth dimensions into a more culturally responsive approach to higher education. Campus programs have begun to incorporate the family as a means to help promote opportunities and student success. For example, some are working toward advancing opportunities for students in science research training programs by developing five bundles of assets among students: educational endowments, academic socialization, network development, family expectations, and material resources (Johnson & Bozeman, 2012). An asset-based approach to educating and training Latinx/a/o students helps them to develop their skills and build on their strengths (even when students do not recognize their own strengths). Indeed, recognition from authority figures is central to students' developing competencies and professional identities, especially for first-generation college students. Further professional development may be necessary for staff and faculty to become more adept at fostering diverse learning environments on campuses where Latinx/a/o enrollments are growing, in order to advance student retention to the degree, multicultural competencies, and capacity for life-long learning. Latinx/a/o success holds promise for a more equitable society and sustainable economic future that will benefit all.

REFERENCES

Alvarez, C. L. (2010). Familial negotiation of the Latina college choice process: An exploration of how parents and their daughters obtain and utilize information to navigate the process. *Enrollment Management Journal: Student Access, Finance, and Success in Higher Education, 4*(4), 57–80.

Alvarez, C. L. (2015). A model for understanding the Latina/o student and parent college-going negotiation process. In P. A. Pérez & M. Ceja (Eds.), *Latina and Latino college access and choice: Critical findings and theoretical perspectives for a changing demographic.* New York, NY: Routledge.

Auerbach, S. (2004). Engaging Latino parents in support college pathways: Lessons from a college access program. *Journal of Hispanic Higher Education, 3*(2), 125–145. doi: 10.1177/1538192703262514

Berndtson, D. (2017, February 8). San Francisco becomes first city to offer free community college tuition to all residents. *PBS NewsHour.* Retrieved from http://www.pbs.org/newshour/rundown/san-francisco-becomes-first-city-offer-free-community-college-tuition-residents

Bourdieu, P., & Passeron, J. C. (1977). *Reproduction in education, culture and society.* London, United Kingdom: Sage.

Carruthers, C. (2016, January 20). Tennessee is showing how free community college tuition works. *The New York Times.* Retrieved from http://www.nytimes.com/roomfordebate/2016/01/20/should-college-be-free/tennessee-is-showing-how-free-tuition-community-college-works

Ceja, M. (2006). Understanding the role of parents and siblings as information sources in the college choice process of Chicana students. *Journal of College Student Development, 47*(1), 87–104.

DeAngelo, L., Franke, R., Hurtado, S., Pryor, J. H., & Tran, S. (2011). *Completing college: Assessing graduation rates at four-year institutions.* Los Angeles, CA: Higher Education Research Institute, University of California, Los Angeles.

Eagan, M. K., Stolzenberg, E. B., Ramirez, J. J., Aragon, M. C., Suchard, M. R., & Rios-Aguilar, C. (2016). *The American freshman: Fifty-year trends, 1966–2015.* Los Angeles, CA: Higher Education Research Institute, University of California, Los Angeles.

Fergus, E., Noguera, P., & Martin, M. (2010). Construction of race and ethnicity for and by Latinos. In E. G. Murillo, Jr. et al. (Eds.), *Handbook of Latinos and education: Theory, research, and practice* (pp. 170–181). New York, NY: Routledge.

Fry, R. (2002). *Latinos in higher education: Many enroll, too few graduate.* Retrieved from Pew Hispanic Center website: www.pewhispanic.org/files/reports/11.pdf

Fry, R. (2014). *Young adults, student debt and economic well-being.* Retrieved from Pew Research Center website: http://www.pewsocialtrends.org/2014/05/14/young-adults-student-debt-and-economic-well-being

Fry, R., & Lopez, M. H. (2012). *Hispanic student enrollments reach new highs in 2011.* Retrieved from Pew Hispanic Center website: http://www.pewhispanic.org/2012/08/20/iii-hispanic-college-enrollments

Fry, R., & Taylor, P. (2013). *Hispanic high school graduates pass whites in rate of college enrollment.* Retrieved from Pew Hispanic Center website: http://www.pewhispanic.org/2013/05/09/ii-immediate-entry-into-college

Ganderton, P. T., & Santos, R. (1995). Hispanic college attendance and completion: Evidence from the high school and beyond surveys. *Economics of Education Review, 14*(1), 35–46.

Grodsky, E. (2002). Constrained opportunity and student choice in American higher education. *Dissertation Abstracts International, 63*(8), 3008-A.

Hatch, D. K., Uman, N. M., & Garcia, C. E. (2016). Variation within the 'New Latino diaspora': A decade of changes across the United States in the equitable participation of Latina/os in higher education. *Journal of Hispanic Higher Education, 15*(4), 358–385.

Hernandez, J. C., & Lopez, M. A. (2005). Leaking pipeline: Issues impacting Latino/a college student retention. *Journal of College Student Retention, 6*(1), 37–60.

Hispanic Association of Colleges and Universities. (2016). *2016 fact sheet: Hispanic higher education and HSIs.* Retrieved from http://www.hacu.net/hacu/HSI_Fact_Sheet.asp

Hurtado, S. (1994). The institutional climate for talented Latino students. *Research in Higher Education, 35*(1), 21–41.

Hurtado, S. (2015). Trend analyses from 1971 to 2012 on Mexican American/Chicano freshmen: Are we making progress? In R. Zambrana & S. Hurtado (Eds.), *The magic key: The educational journey of Mexican Americans from K–12 to college and beyond* (pp. 53–75). Austin, TX: University of Texas.

Hurtado, S., Alvarez, C. L., Guillermo-Wann, C., Cuellar, M., & Arellano, L. (2012). A model for diverse learning environments: The scholarship on creating and assessing conditions for student success. In J. C. Smart & M. B. Paulsen (Eds.), *Higher education: Handbook of theory and research* (Vol. 27, pp. 41–122). Dordrecht, Netherlands: Springer.

Hurtado, S., & Carter, D. F. (1997). Effects of college transition and perceptions of the campus racial climate on Latino college students' sense of belonging. *Sociology of Education, 70*(4), 324–345.

Hurtado, S., Carter, D. F., & Spuler, A. (1996). Latino student transition to college: Assessing difficulties and factors in successful adjustment. *Research in Higher Education, 37*(2), 135–157.

Hurtado, S., & Ponjuán, L. (2005). Latino educational outcomes and the campus climate. *Journal of Hispanic Higher Education, 4*(3), 235–251.

Hurtado, S., Ruiz Alvarado, A., & Guillermo-Wann, C. (2015). Thinking about race: The salience of racial identity at two-and four-year colleges and the climate for diversity. *The Journal of Higher Education, 86*(1), 127–155.

Hurtado, S., Sáenz, V. B., Santos, J. L., & Cabrera, N. L. (2008). *Advancing in higher education: A portrait of Latina/o college freshmen at four-year institutions: 1975–2006.* Los Angeles, CA: Higher Education Research Institute, University of California, Los Angeles.

Johnson, J., & Bozeman, B. (2012). Perspective: Adopting an asset bundle model to support and advance minority students' careers in academic medicine and the scientific pipeline. *Academic Medicine: Journal of the Association of American Medical Colleges, 87*(11), 1488.

Kim, D. (2004). The effect of financial aid on students' college choice: Differences by racial groups. *Research in Higher Education, 45*(1), 43–70.

Kim, D., Saatcioglu, A., & Neufeld, A. (2012). College departure: Exploring student aid effects on multiple mobility patterns from four-year institutions. *Journal of Student Financial Aid, 42*(3), 1.

Kurlaender, M. (2006). Choosing community college: Factors affecting Latino college choice. In C. L. Horn, S. M. Flores, & G. Orfield (Eds.), *Special issue: Latino educational opportunity* (New Directions for Community Colleges, No. 133, pp. 7–16). San Francisco, CA: Jossey-Bass.

Looney, S., & Yannelis, C. (2015). A crisis in student loans? How changes in the characteristics of borrowers and in the institutions they attended contributed to rising loan defaults. *Brookings Papers on Economic Activity, 2015*(2), 1–89.

Loya, K. I., Hwang, J., & Oseguera, L. (2015). Latina/o students' college destinations: Gender, generational status, and college sector selectivity. In P. A. Pérez & M. Ceja (Eds.), *Higher education access and choice for Latino students: Critical findings and theoretical perspectives* (pp. 112–129). New York, NY: Routledge.

Marín, G., & Marín, B. V. (1991). *Research with Hispanic populations.* Thousand Oaks, CA: Sage.

Martínez, S., & Cervera, Y. L. (2012). Fulfilling educational aspirations: Latino students' college information seeking patterns. *Journal of Hispanic Higher Education, 11*(4), 388–402.

Matos, J. M. D. (2015). La familia: The important ingredient for Latina/o college student engagement and persistence. *Equity & Excellence in Education, 48*(3), 436–453. doi: 10.1080/10665684.2015.1056761

McKinley, J. (2017, January 3). Cuomo proposes free tuition at New York state colleges and for eligible students. *The New York Times.* Retrieved from https://www.nytimes.com/2017/01/03/nyregion/free-tuition-new-york-colleges-plan.html

Montalvo, E. J. (2013). The recruitment and retention of Hispanic undergraduate students in public universities in the United States, 2000–2006. *Journal of Hispanic Higher Education*, *12*(3), 237–255.

National Center for Education Statistics. (2008). *Digest of education statistics: 2008*. Retrieved from https://nces.ed.gov/programs/digest

National Center for Education Statistics. (2015). *Digest of education statistics: 2015*. Retrieved from https://nces.ed.gov/programs/digest/

National Center for Education Statistics. (2016). *Digest of education statistics: 2016*. Retrieved from https://nces.ed.gov/programs/digest/

Núñez, A.-M., Hurtado, S. & Calderón Galdeano, E. (Eds). (2015). *Hispanic-serving institutions: Advancing research and transformative practice*. New York, NY: Routledge.

Núñez, A.-M., Sparks, P. J., & Hernández, E. A. (2011). Latino access to community colleges and Hispanic-serving institutions: A national study. *Journal of Hispanic Higher Education*, *10*(1), 18–40.

Page, J. (2013). Hispanics: A diverse population of students to influence the landscape of higher education. *Journal of Hispanic Higher Education*, *12*(1), 37–48.

Pérez, P. A., & Ceja, M. (Eds.). (2015). *Higher education access and choice for Latino students: Critical findings and theoretical perspectives*. New York, NY: Routledge.

Pérez, P. A., & McDonough, P. M. (2008). Understanding Latina and Latino college choice: A social capital and chain migration analysis. *Journal of Hispanic Higher Education*, *7*(3), 249–265.

Ponjuán, L. (2011). Recruiting and retaining Latino faculty members: The missing piece to Latino student success. *Thought & Action*, *27*, 99–110.

Rendón, L. I. (1994). Validating culturally diverse students: Toward a new model of learning and student development. *Innovative higher education*, *19*(1), 33–51.

Rios-Aguilar, C., & Kiyama, J. M. (2012). Funds of knowledge: An approach to studying Latina(o) students' transition to college. *Journal of Latinos and Education*, *11*(1), 2–16.

Ruiz Alvarado, A. (2014). *Latina/o pathways through college: Characteristics of mobile students and the institutional networks they create*. (Doctoral dissertation). Retrieved from ProQuest database. (Accession No. 3626169)

Ruiz Alvarado, A., & Hurtado, S. (2015). Salience at the intersection: Latina/o identities across different campus contexts. In D. J. Davis, R. J. Brunn, & J. L. Olive (Eds.), *Intersectionality* in research in education (pp. 48–67). Sterling, VA: Stylus.

Santos, J. L., & Sáenz, V. B. (2013). The eye of the perfect storm: The convergence of policy and Latina/o trends in access and financial concerns, 1975–2008. *Educational Policy*, *28*(3), 393–424.

Tinto, V. (1987). *Leaving college: Rethinking the causes and cures of student attrition*. Chicago, IL: University of Chicago Press.

Tornatzky, L. G., Cutler, R., & Lee, J. (2002). *College knowledge: What Latino parents need to know and why they don't know it*. Claremont, CA: Tomas Rivera Policy Institute.

Torrez, N. (2004). Developing parent information frameworks that support college preparation for Latino students. *The High School Journal*, *87*(3), 54–62. doi: 10.1353/hsj.2004.0006

Valencia, R. R., & Black, M. S. (2002). "Mexican Americans don't value education!"—On the basis of the myth, mythmaking, and debunking. *Journal of Latinos and Education 1*(2), 81–103.

Villalpando, O. (2010). Latinas/os in higher education: Eligibility, enrollment, and educational attainment. In E. G. Murillo Jr., S. A. Villenas, R. T. Galván, J. S. Muñoz, G. Martínez, & M. Machado-Casas (Eds.), *Handbook of Latinos and education: Theory, research, and practice* (pp. 232–249). New York, NY: Routledge.

Yosso, T. J. (2005). *Critical race counterstories along the Chicana/Chicano educational pipeline*. New York, NY: Routledge.

Zambrana, R., & Hurtado, S. (Eds.). (2015). *The magic key: The educational journey of Mexican Americans from K–12 to college and beyond*. Austin, TX: University of Texas Press.

CHAPTER 2

POLICY ACTORS AND PUBLIC POLICY IN HIGHER EDUCATION

*Developing a National Organizational Infrastructure
for Latina/o Postsecondary Advocacy*

Magdalena Martinez and Melissa L. Freeman

ederal policy advocacy on behalf of institutions serving large Latina/o populations dates back to the early 1980s, when Texas leaders created the Hispanic Association of Colleges and Universities (HACU; Calderón Galdeano, Flores, & Moder, 2012). Since the federal designation of Hispanic-serving institutions (HSIs) in 1992, additional national actors have entered the policy and political landscape—with a focus on Latina/o students in education. Simultaneously, researchers have created a robust body of literature on

Latina/o students in higher education (see, e.g., Freeman & Martinez, 2015; Gaitan, 2012; Martinez & Fernández, 2004; Núñez, Hoover, Pickett, Stuart-Carruthers, & Vázquez, 2013; Núñez, Hurtado, & Galdeano, 2015; Perez & Ceja, 2015; Pérez & Cortés, 2011; Sáenz, Ponjuán, & Figueroa, 2016).

Latina/o-focused professional associations, such as the American Association of Hispanics in Higher Education (AAHHE), the National Community College Hispanic Council, and the Alliance of Hispanic Serving Institution Educators, have increased their presence nationally, albeit with an emphasis on professional development for researchers and administrators. To what degree have Latina/o-focused associations, think tanks, organizations, and research had an impact on shaping policy and politics, and at what levels of the policymaking process are their contributions most salient? Who are the primary policy actors in the Latina/o postsecondary policymaking landscape? Do policy actors coalesce around common Latina/o-focused policy priorities or policies that disproportionately affect Latina/o students? If so, is there a national organizational infrastructure that facilitates the coordination, communication, and advocacy of Latina/o-focused policies?

Research on these questions is limited. This chapter identifies prospective research directions that examine how policy actors engage, shape, and advocate for Latina/o-focused postsecondary policies in political environs. First, we frame what a national organizational infrastructure may entail, then provide an overview of public policy frameworks—with a focus on policy actors—that may be instructive in future research; a review of the literature provides a context for prospective study directions. We discuss two policy models, the Advocacy Coalition Framework and a discursive model, Discourse Coalitions, to center our discussion on actors and coalitions. We conclude by proposing recommendations for analysts interested in initiating lines of inquiry, and we then aim to delineate the role of actors and how they leverage assets across organizations to promote a collective Latina/o postsecondary policy agenda.

DEVELOPING A NATIONAL ORGANIZATIONAL INFRASTRUCTURE

The concept of a national organizational infrastructure is based on research by Nicholls (2003), who identified those community-based policy actors who helped to facilitate the coordination, communication, learning, and articulation of multiple organizations in urban movements in Los Angeles, California. Nicholls examined how disparate organizations coalesced around policy priorities. He drew from literature on social movements to understand how individuals in organizations come to develop a collective identity. He also examined the role of interactions that are sustained through networks of institutions and people (Nicholls, 2003). Central to his analysis was how decentralized and fragmented groups or activities came to mobilize the necessary human, intellectual, and financial resources needed to produce significant policy and political change.

Nicholls (2003) found key components used to rally collective resources toward loosely agreed-upon goals. These components included the process of trust-building, learning, and relation-nurturing, or relational frames, which builds or strengthens links between individuals and organizations. He identified three types of mechanisms that shaped and created a dynamic organizational infrastructure: (a) coalitions and collaborations, (b) reflective spaces, and (c) anchor organizations (see Figure 2.1). Coalitions or collaborations were the most common mechanisms for coordinating multisector mobilizations. These required the consensus of a broad range of policy actors. That requirement limited the potential efficacy on public policy issues but facilitated first encounters between policy actors; it also facilitated trust-building and learning processes on how to act collectively. Spaces of reflective interaction were generally neutral secondary associations and institutions (e.g., universities, funding organizations, technical assistance organizations) that provided policy actors with the opportunity to encounter each other. Typically, large-scale meetings, workshops, and research opportunities, these spaces allowed policy actors to build and strengthen relationships, coalitions, and collaborative efforts. Anchor organizations were designed for the purpose of effecting long-term change in one or more policy areas. They had a narrower base of participants than did coalitions, and they had clearly defined divisions of labor, rules, and procedures. They tended to evolve from concerted, long-term interactions, which occurred through personal networks, coalitions, and reflective spaces.

Figure 2.1. *Dynamic Organizational Infrastructure*

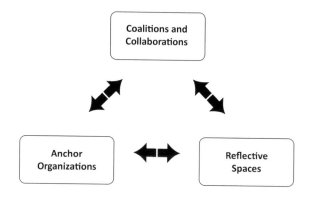

Note. Adapted from "Forging a 'New' Organizational Infrastructure for Los Angeles' Progressive Community," by W. J. Nicholls, 2003, *International Journal of Urban and Regional Research, 27,* p. 895. Copyright © 2003 by John Wiley & Sons. Adapted with permission.

Drawing from Nicholls' (2003) research, we probe if there is a national organizational infrastructure for Latina/o-focused policy in higher education. Through a review of policy analysis frameworks and literature on Latina/o-focused policies, we address the following questions in this chapter: How have Latina/o policy ideas, developments, and implementation moved through a national organizational infrastructure? Are there key policy actors, organizations, or policy movements that define a national organizational infrastructure? If so, who and what are they?

PUBLIC POLICY ANALYSIS FRAMEWORKS AND POLICY ACTORS: A BRIEF OVERVIEW

Researchers have examined the role of policy actors in higher education, public policy change, and politics through the lens of lobbying (Cook, 1998; Parsons, 2004), interest groups (Ness, Tandberg, & McLendon, 2015), communities (Miller & Demir, 2006), and advocacy coalitions (Dougherty, Nienhusser, & Vega, 2010). The role of policy actors has typically been a key component in the study of public policymaking. Initial examination of the public policy process offered rational, linear-based approaches, such as the Policy Stages Approach and Rational-Comprehensive Model (MacRae & Wilde, 1979; Simon, 1957). Understanding policymaking often did not account for the intersection or dynamic process of policymaking, policy actors, and the role of ideology. Subsequent contemporary approaches incorporated and underscored the dynamic process of policymaking (Kingdon, 1994), periods of political stability and conflict (True, Jones, & Baumgartner, 1999), complex internal and external policy and political environments, policy actors and coalitions (Sabatier & Jenkins-Smith, 1988, 1993, 1999), and the role of discursive practices of policy actors and coalitions in shaping policy (Fischer, 2003; Hajer, 1993, 1995).

Broadly speaking, actors seek to influence, frame, and negotiate policy priorities in policymaking arenas. Consider for instance, the impact of policy actors on the Higher Education Act of 1965—perhaps the most influential federal intervention to date—to increase access and completion for low-income students through federal funding. Public policy is a tool used by policy actors to incentivize and prioritize specific behavior in order to produce specific outcomes. For example, Title V, Developing Hispanic-Serving Institutions Program (1999), targets institutions that serve large numbers of Hispanic students, offering incentives to prioritize Hispanic student access and enrollment. The literature describes higher education policy actors as professional associations, organizations, institutions, or key stakeholder groups (e.g., HACU, AAHHE, Excelencia in Education) either tightly or loosely coupled by specific priorities or interests (Cook, 1998; Dougherty et al., 2010; Ortega, 2011). Most notably, researchers have examined the role of policy actors related to higher education funding (Parsons, 2004; Tandberg, 2010), governance decentralization (McClendon, 2003), and the Higher Education Act (Cook, 1998). Research is limited on Latina/o-focused policy in higher education.

Literature on Latina/o-Focused Policy and Higher Education

Literature on higher education and Latina/o-focused policy at the national level has been limited primarily to descriptive accounts on the historical evolution of HSIs (Calderón Galdeano et al., 2012; Gasman, Baez, & Turner, 2008; MacDonald, Botti, & Clark, 2007; Merisotis & O'Brien, 1998), and the researchers do not necessarily situate their analyses in policy analysis frameworks. For instance, Calderón Galdeano et al. (2012) described the legislative history and relationship between HACU, institutions with large Latina/o enrollments, and the subsequent designation of HSI at the federal level. MacDonald et al. (2007) traced the evolution of higher educational opportunities for Latina/

os in the United States from the Higher Education Act of 1965 to the designation of Title V in the Act's 1998 reauthorization. The authors described the evolution through a stages model, which included establishing visibility and legitimacy, self-determination, self-scrutiny, emulation, and autonomy. They compared the evolution with the experiences of African Americans in higher education while recognizing the historical, social, and political differences between historically Black colleges and universities (HBCUs) and HSIs. These authors suggested that the model established by HBCUs inspired Latino educators to found HSIs. Initiatives to influence national policy for Latina/os have occurred beyond the HSI designation (Calderón Galdeano et al., 2012).

Martinez (2008) examined national higher education associations' motivation for joining coalitions using typology from Hula (1999) and Hojnacki (1997). Established in the early 2000s, the Alliance for Equity in Higher Education brought together national organizations such as HACU, the National Association for Equal Opportunity, and the American Indian Higher Education Consortium to represent the interests of HSIs, HBCUs, and TCUs (tribal colleges and universities) as a way to advocate for additional federal resources. Martinez's (2008) analysis confirmed the critical role of political brokers to identify and pursue common goals. In this case, early funding from the W.K. Kellogg Foundation assisted with formation of the Alliance under the auspices of the Institute for Higher Education Policy. Martinez (2008) found support for Hula (1999) and Hojnacki's (1997) typology and concluded that disparate organizations join coalitions for three reasons: (a) to pursue strategic goals and leverage resources; (b) to gather information to strategically position themselves and their organizations; and (c) for symbolic reasons, such as presenting a united front to policymakers.

Ortega (2011) studied 68 national higher education associations and their collective advocacy on the Development, Relief, and Education for Alien Minors (DREAM) Act legislation, a federal policy predicted to benefit significant numbers of undocumented Latina/o students. Ortega (2011) used social capital theory (Coleman, 1988) and Dewey's (1954) communication community to understand the aggregate function of multiple associations working toward common goals. He found that the associations, as a collective, extended social capital and symbolic resources to their policy priorities, such as the DREAM Act (2001). Ortega (2011) found that when higher education associations worked as a collective, their support for the DREAM Act went from 16% in 2006 to 46% in 2009. He attributed the increase to the collective values, shared goals, and coalition building.

The literature on the evolution of HSI designation and coalitions is important for understanding the role policy actors play in advocating for Latino-focused policies. Other topics to examine include the policy process of actors bringing Latina/o-focused policy issues to the forefront of national policymakers' agenda; the context that facilitates or hinders their ability to engage and shape the policy environ; and how policy actors coalesce, communicate, and negotiate among themselves to pursue common policy goals. There are several valuable policy analysis frameworks, but here we will focus on two: the Advocacy Coalition Framework (ACF) and Discourse Coalitions (DC). Both frameworks center their analyses on the role of actors and the dynamic interplay of politics and policy, yet their theoretical underpinnings differ, adding to the models' diversity and richness.

Advocacy Coalition Framework

Building coalitions to leverage collective assets in pursuit of common goals is a common practice in the public policy arena. Sabatier and Jenkins-Smith's (1988, 1993, 1999) ACF centers policy change on the examination of coalitions of actors. At the macro-level, policymaking is affected by factors in the broader political and socioeconomic system. The authors posited that most policymaking occurs in a policy subsystem that is geographically bounded and that encompasses actors from multiple levels of government, interest groups, expert groups, and the media. Sabatier and Jenkins-Smith (1999) assumed that the beliefs of policy participants are stable and major policy change is very difficult. Stable policy subsystems assume a low probability of policy change; however, the authors argue that there are four paths to major policy change: (a) external shocks, (b) internal shocks, (c) policy-oriented learning, and (d) negotiated agreements (Weible & Sabatier, 2007).

External shocks can include changes in socioeconomic conditions, public opinion, systemic governing coalitions, and policy decisions and impacts from other subsystems. An example of an external shock is the rapid growth of the school-aged Latina/o population in the 1990s and the anticipated effect on higher education. This external shock likely opened a window for policymakers and coalitions, like HACU, to advocate on behalf of institutions serving large populations of Latina/os. Internal shocks include events to attract public attention—highlighting policy vulnerabilities, failures, or neglect; bringing new information into the policy process can also occur from within a policy subsystem and lead to major policy change. The model assumes that individuals have a three-tiered hierarchical belief system: deep core values, policy core values, and secondary policy values. Of the three levels of beliefs, secondary beliefs are thought to be the most susceptible to policy-oriented learning and new information. In situations where coalitions have been in policy disagreements for decades, negotiated agreements serve as a pathway to major policy change.

The majority of policymaking occurs within the subsystems and involves detailed negotiations among actors who are typically specialists of a particular policy subsystem. At this micro-level, the ACF draws from social psychology and posits five assumptions about policy actors: (a) individuals are rationally motivated and bounded by their inability to learn about and comprehend a complex world, or they filter information through their beliefs frame; (b) to increase policy success, actors seek out advocacy coalitions with similar core beliefs; (c) when policy disagreements arise, conflicts are mediated by policy brokers; (d) actors and coalitions employ diverse resources (e.g., legal authority, public opinion, mobilization, financial resources) to influence policy; and (e) coalitions attempt to influence policy through strategic use of venues (e.g., courts, legislature, local governing boards, media) in which they have a competitive advantage. Sabatier and Jenkins-Smith (1999) hypothesized that coalition actors' beliefs and behaviors are embedded within informal networks and that actors attempt to translate components of their belief systems into actual policy. In order to increase the probability of policy success, these actors ally, leverage resources, and develop complementary strategies with other organizations. At the meso-level, the ACF assumes that the most efficient way to deal with multiple actors in a subsystem is to aggregate the behavior of hundreds of actors and organizations involved in a policy subsystem over the course of long periods.

The ACF has been employed to examine a variety of policy issues, including nuclear security (Herron & Jenkins-Smith, 2002), air pollution (Zafonte & Sabatier, 2004), domestic violence policy (Abrar, Lovenduski, & Margetts, 2000), and drug policy (Kübler, 2001). Two higher education studies focused on policies that disproportionately affect Latina/os employ the ACF or major components of the model. Nienhusser (2015) examined the policymaking environment for undocumented immigrants in New York. He described the national, state, and local policy environments that shaped in-state tuition for undocumented students. Through a careful analysis of various coalitions, he identified the five political forces—governor, pressure from advocacy groups, Latino policymakers, legislators' geographic affiliations, and legislators' political party membership—that ultimately shaped the passage of New York's in-state resident tuition policy. In an earlier study, Dougherty et al. (2010) also examined the politics of in-state tuition eligibility for undocumented students in Texas and Arizona. They described the coalition movements in both states and highlight how the beliefs, actions, and influence of coalition members shaped two very different outcomes for Texas and Arizona. Texas state policy allowed for in-state tuition for undocumented students, whereas Arizona's policy did not. The authors noted that one limitation of the theories is the lack of recognition that persistent racial, socioeconomic, and gender inequalities play a significant role in the social and political structures, especially when it comes to power. To address this limitation of the ACF, we propose that researchers consider discursive policy models (Fischer, 2003; Hajer, 1993, 1995; Schmidt, 2012).

Discursive Policy Models and Discourse Coalitions

Discursive policy models draw heavily from Habermas's (1985) critical theory and posit that words and language, when combined with power, are important data for political and policy analysis (e.g., Fischer, 2003; Fischer & Gottweis, 2012). These models are concerned with "the substantive content of ideas and the interaction processes of discourse and policy argumentation in institutional context" (Schmidt, 2012, p. 85). In their seminal book *The Argumentative Turn in Policy Analysis and Planning,* Fischer and Forester (1993) urged policy researchers to include the study of language, discourse, and argumentation as essential dimensions of theory and analysis in policymaking. This social constructive approach, they argued, rejects the beliefs that policy analysis is value-free and that the process of policymaking and analysis is a straightforward, rational application of scientific techniques. Fischer (2003) explained that discursive models start "from the assumption that all actions, objects and practices are socially meaningful and that these meanings are shaped by the social and political struggles in specific historical periods"; moreover, "discourses represent specific systems of power and the social practices that produce and reproduce them" (p. 73).

Hajer (1993) proposed to understand policy change through the analysis of discourse coalitions. He suggested that coalitions embody important differences; therefore, aggregating different policy actors and organizations misses key understandings of why and how specific policy changes come about in political environs. He posited that rather than cognitive beliefs about policy, coalitions are held together by narrative storylines that interpret events and courses of action in concrete social contexts (Fischer, 2003). Most coalitions and their members are held together by simplified storylines that symbolically reflect the *concerns* of core beliefs rather than the beliefs themselves. Individual preferences are less well defined through a tiered hierarchical belief system and are more fluid. While policy-relevant facts continue to matter, actors and coalitions follow storylines that offer social orientation, reassurance, or guidance. From this perspective, storylines are the primary dynamic driving the policy process, acting as a window to understanding the coordination and operation of policy coalitions. For instance, storylines often are the instruments to articulate policy problems, solutions, and coalition actions.

Storylines can also identify the presence or absence of social groups and their identities— such as gender, class, and race. In his research on acid rain policy, Hajer (1995) found that storylines were the glue of coalitions. It was not the objective, measurable facts of the policy problems that moved coalition members to action; rather, it was *how* they saw the facts that become important. The stability of coalitions is more a function of trust and credibility—as interpreted through storylines—than of entrenched core beliefs. From this perspective, "stability is the function of successful discursive reproduction of institutions by reliable and trusted members of policy coalitions" (Fischer, 2003, p. 108).

Policy-oriented learning, a component to policy change, is assumed to occur through different disciplinary research and therefore various disciplinary discourses. Disciplines often work from different—and sometimes competing—premises and assumptions, which affect the ways in which policy problems are defined, solutions proposed, and options interpreted. Hajer's (1995) research found that actors' arguments were shaped by their disciplinary orientation, which manifested in the differing and sometimes conflicting policy storylines. He found that reaching an agreement about the nature of a problem was itself problematic because even within science communities, physicists and biologists for example, had very different conceptions of science and its practices. From this perspective, discourse is viewed not only as an instrument to convey learning but also as a way of social regulation and control of specific scientific discourse communities. Emphasis is placed not only on the evidence—vis-à-vis storylines—but also on the role of political credibility, acceptability, and trust. Discursive analysis also centers the political dimensions that influence what comes to be understood and accepted as learning. As Fischer (2003) explained:

> Learning for one person may not be learning for another person with a different political ideology. No amount of data, regardless of how well tested and verified it might be, will convince a person that anything important or useful has been presented if, in his or her view, the findings lead to policy judgments that take him or

her in the wrong direction, or at least down a road he or she is unwilling to travel. (p. 111)

Discourse coalitions and models often focus on the interpretative analysis of policymaking, change, and participants of the policy process. For researchers interested in employing interpretative analysis, Yanow (2000) offered four methodological stages. In brief, she suggested a first stage is to identify the artifacts—language, objects, and acts—that carry meaning for a given policy issue, as defined by policy actors and coalitions. The second is to identify the policy-relevant communities of practice. The third is to identify the relevant discourses and meanings being communicated through artifacts. Finally, she suggested identifying discourses of conflict, their conceptual sources, and differing meanings that coalitions bring to the issue. In addition, there are multiple resources on the process of the collection and analysis of discourse, narrative, and framing data available to researchers interested in discursive models.

In higher education policy research, there is an observable void on the use of discursive theories and models. The limited research that does exist employs feminist theory (e.g., Shaw, 2004) or critical race theory (e.g., Maramba, Sulè, & Winkle-Wagner, 2015), both of which center the analysis on identities. These discursive models are ripe for use to examine higher education policy, with an emphasis on language use and actions resulting from discourses. For analysts interested in Latina/o-focused issues, these models can help unravel policy and the embedded assumptions, values, and beliefs about the role of education, Latina/o populations, and the intersections of race, class, and gender in policy actions.

CONCLUSION

In this chapter we introduce the idea of a national organizational infrastructure and ask whether such a construct exists and how researchers might define and investigate its role in the policy land-scape with a focus on Latina/o students. We provide a brief review of policy analysis models, with an emphasis on the role of actors and coalitions. A literature review of research on Latina/o-focused higher education policy confirms a stark lack, yet there appears to be an interest, based on the descriptive case studies and state policy analysis that exist. Two policy analysis models are discussed: ACF and DC. Both center their analysis on the roles of actors and coalitions. We suggest that these frameworks, distinct in theoretical assumptions, offer researchers two different entry points to examine Latina/o-focused higher education policy.

For analysts interested in exploring Latina/o-focused policies, we suggest the following initial steps. First, identify the unit of analysis: Is it a local, state, or federal policy issue? Second, identify the over-arching policy focus: Why and how does it disproportionately affect Latina/o students? In this chapter we highlight previous research related to in-state tuition, the DREAM Act (2001), and federal funding for HSIs. Policy analysis areas apt for examination include state, city, or campus sanctuary policies and the role of coalitions for and against such policies; state merit-based funding, its disproportionate affect on Latina/o students, and embedded assumptions on meritocracy as artic-ulated by policy actors and coalitions; and the past and present process of federal minority-serving institutions funding and how HSIs orga-nize, advocate, coalesce, and negotiate policy priorities. Third, identify methods that align with the area of interest. We introduced two frame-works with different theoretical assumptions. Policy analysis requires an understanding and knowledge of policymaking levels, actors, and history of the specific or related policy issues. State and federal legis-lative tracking resources, such as GovTrac, facilitate data gathering on policies. The sites often include a historical overview of bills, meeting minutes, videos, and testimony. They are valuable resources to anyone interested in policy but unfamiliar with the policymaking process, bill history, or primary actors and coalitions.

Latinos are the fastest-growing demographic in the nation. It is expected that they will be the majority-minority by 2050 (Freeman & Martinez, 2015). These two important facts, coupled with the low rates of higher education achievement among Latinos, warrant an understanding of how actors shape and contribute to higher education policy. Of particular import is the role that national Latina/o-focused organizations, associations, and research communities play in shaping policy problems, solutions, and outcomes.

REFERENCES

Abrar, S., Lovenduski, J., & Margetts, H. (2000). Feminist ideas and domestic violence policy change. *Political Studies, 48*, 239–262.

Calderón Galdeano, E., Flores, A. R., & Moder, J. (2012). The Hispanic Association of Colleges and Universities and Hispanic-serving institutions: Partners in the advancement of Hispanic higher education. *Journal of Latinos and Education, 11*(3), 157–162.

Coleman, J. S. (1988). Social capital in the creation of human capital. *American Journal of Sociology, 94*, S95–S120.

Cook, C. E. (1998). *Lobbying for higher education: How colleges and universities influence federal policy.* Nashville, TN: Vanderbilt University Press.

Developing Hispanic-Serving Institutions Program, Title V, Part A of the Higher Education Act, 20 U.S.C. § 1101 *et seq.* (1999).

Dewey, J. (1954). *The public and its problems.* Athens, OH: Swallow Press.

Dougherty, K. J., Nienhusser, H. K., & Vega, B. E. (2010). Undocumented immigrants and state higher education policy: The politics of in-state tuition eligibility in Texas and Arizona. *The Review of Higher Education, 34*(1), 123–173.

DREAM Act of 2001, S. 1291, 107th Cong. (2001).

Fischer, F. (2003). *Reframing public policy: Discursive politics and deliberative practices.* Oxford, NY: Oxford University Press.

Fischer, F., & Forester, J. (Eds.). (1993). *The argumentative turn in policy analysis and planning.* Durham, NC: Duke University Press.

Fischer, F., & Gottweis, H. (Eds.). (2012). *The argumentative turn revisited: Public policy as communicative practice.* Durham, NC: Duke University Press.

Freeman, M. L., & Martinez, M. (Eds.). (2015). *College completion for Latino/a students: Institutional and system approaches* (New Directions for Higher Education, No. 172). San Francisco, CA: Jossey-Bass.

Gaitan, C. D. (2012). *Creating a college culture for Latino students: Successful programs, practices, and strategies.* Thousand Oaks, CA: Corwin Press.

Gasman, M., Baez, B., & Turner, C. S. V. (Eds.). (2008). *Understanding minority-serving institutions.* Albany, NY: SUNY Press.

Habermas, J. (1985). *The theory of communicative action.* Boston, MA: Beacon Press.

Hajer, M. A. (1993). Discourse coalitions and institutionalization of practice: The case of acid rain in Great Britain. In F. Fischer & J. Forester (Eds.), *The argumentative turn in policy analysis* (pp. 43–76). Durham, NC: Duke University Press.

Hajer, M. A. (1995). Acid rain in Great Britain: Environmental discourse and the hidden politics of institutional practice. In F. Fischer & M. Black (Eds.), *Greening environmental policy: The politics of a sustainable future* (pp. 145–164). New York, NY: Palgrave Macmillan.

Herron, K. G., & Jenkins-Smith, H. C. (2002). U.S. perceptions of nuclear security in the wake of the cold ware: Comparing public and elite belief systems. *International Studies Quarterly, 46*, 451–479.

Hojnacki, M. (1997). Interest group's decisions to join alliances or work alone. *American Journal of Political Science, 41*, 61–87.

Hula, K. (1999). *Lobbying together: Interest group coalitions in legislative politics.* Washington, DC: Georgetown University Press.

Kingdon, J. W. (1994). Agendas, ideas, and policy change. In L. Dodd & C. Jillson (Eds.), *New perspectives on American politics* (pp. 215–229). Washington, DC: Congressional Quarterly Press.

Kübler, D. (2001). Understanding policy change with the Advocacy Coalition Framework: An application to Swiss drug policy. *Journal of European Public Policy, 8*(4), 623–641.

MacDonald, V., Botti, J. M., & Clark, L. H. (2007). From visibility to autonomy: Latinos and higher education in the U.S., 1965–2005. *Harvard Educational Review, 77*(4), 474.

MacRae, D., & Wilde, J. (1979). *Policy analysis for public decisions.* Pacific Grove, CA: Duxbury Press.

Maramba, D. C., Sulè, V. T., & Winkle-Wagner, R. (2015). What discourse on the Texas Top Ten Percent Plan says about accountability for diversity. *The Journal of Higher Education, 86*(5), 751–776.

Martinez, D. (2008). Coalition formation among minority-serving institutions. In M. Gasman, B. Baez, & C. Turner (Eds.), *Understanding minority-serving institutions* (pp. 269–291). Albany, NY: State University of New York Press.

Martinez, M., & Fernández, E. (2004). Latinos at community colleges. In A. M. Ortiz (Ed.), *Special issue: Addressing the unique needs of Latino American students* (New Directions for Student Services, No.105, pp. 51–62). San Francisco, CA: Jossey-Bass.

McLendon, M. K. (2003). Setting the governmental agenda for state decentralization of higher education. *The Journal of Higher Education, 74*(5), 479-515. doi:10.1353/jhe.2003.0038

Merisotis, J. P., & O'Brien, C. T. (Eds.). (1998). *Minority-serving institutions: Distinct purposes, common goals.* New Directions for Higher Education, No. 102. San Francisco, CA: Jossey-Bass.

Miller, H. T., & Demir, T. (2006). Policy communities. In F. Fischer, G. Miller, & M. Sidney (Eds.), *Handbook of public policy analysis: Theory, politics, and methods* (pp. 137–149). London, United Kingdom: Taylor and Francis.

Ness, E. C., Tandberg, D. A., & McLendon, M. K. (2015). Interest groups and state policy for higher education: New conceptual understandings and future research directions. In M. B. Paulsen (Ed.), *Higher education: Handbook of theory and research* (Vol. 30, pp. 151–186). New York, NY: Springer International Publishing.

Nicholls, W. J. (2003). Forging a "new" organizational infrastructure for Los Angeles' progressive community. *International Journal of Urban and Regional Research, 27*(4), 881–896.

Nienhusser, H. (2015). Undocumented immigrants and higher education policy: The policymaking environment of New York state. *Review of Higher Education, 38*(2), 271–303.

Núñez, A. M., Hoover, R. R., Pickett, K., Stuart-Carruthers, C., & Vázquez, M. (2013). *Latinos in higher education: Creating conditions for student success* (ASHE Higher Education Report, Vol. 39, No. 1). San Francisco, CA: Jossey-Bass.

Nuñez, A., Hurtado, S., & Galdeano, E. C. (Eds.). (2015). *Hispanic-serving institutions: Advancing research and transformative practice.* New York, NY: Routledge.

Ortega, N. (2011). The role of higher education associations in shaping policy that connects immigration to educational opportunity: A social capital framework. *Journal of Hispanic Higher Education, 10*(1), 41–65.

Parsons, M. D. (2004). Lobbying in higher education. In E. P. St. John & M. D. Parsons (Eds.), *Public funding of higher education: Changing contexts and new rationales* (pp. 215–230). Baltimore, MD: Johns Hopkins University Press.

Perez, P., & Ceja, M. (Eds.). (2015). *Higher education access and choice for Latino students: Critical findings and theoretical perspectives.* New York, NY: Routledge.

Pérez, W., & Cortés, R. D. (2011). *Undocumented Latino college students: Their socioemotional and academic experiences.* El Paso, TX: LFB Scholarly Pub. LLC.

Sabatier, P. A., & Jenkins-Smith, H. (1988). An advocacy coalition model of policy change and the role of policy oriented learning therein. *Policy Sciences, 21*, 129–168.

Sabatier, P. A., & Jenkins-Smith, H. (1993). *Policy change and learning: An advocacy coalition approach.* Boulder, CO: Westview Press.

Sabatier, P. A., & Jenkins-Smith, H. (1999). The advocacy coalition framework: An assessment. In P. A. Sabatier (Ed.), *Theories of the policy process* (pp. 117–166). Boulder, CO: Westview Press.

Sáenz, V. B., Ponjuán, L., & Figueroa, J. L. (2016). *Ensuring the success of Latino males in higher education: A national imperative.* Sterling, VA: Stylus.

Schmidt, V. A. (2012). Scope, dynamics, and philosophical underpinnings. In F. Fischer & H. Gottweis (Eds.), *The argumentative turn revisited: Public policy as communicative practice* (pp. 85–113). Durham, NC: Duke University Press.

Shaw, K. M. (2004). Using feminist critical policy analysis in the realm of higher education: The case of welfare reform as gendered educational policy. *The Journal of Higher Education, 75*(1), 56–79.

Simon, H. A. (1957). *Models of man: Social and rational.* New York, NY: John Wiley and Sons.

Tandberg, D. A. (2010). Politics, interest groups and state funding of public higher education. *Research in Higher Education, 51*(5), 416–450.

True, J. L., Jones, B. D., & Baumgartner, F. R. (1999). Punctuated-equilibrium theory: Explaining stability and change in American policymaking. In P. A. Sabatier (Ed.), *Theories of the policy process* (pp. 97–115). Boulder, CO: Westview Press.

Weible, C. M., & Sabatier, P. A. (2007). A guide to the advocacy coalition framework. In F. Fischer, G. Miller, & M. Sidney (Eds.), *Handbook of public policy analysis: Theory, politics, and methods* (pp. 123–136). Philadelphia, PA: Taylor & Francis.

Yanow, D. (2000). *Conducting interpretive analysis.* Newbury Park, CA: Sage.

Zafonte, M., & Sabatier, P. A. (2004). Short-term versus long-term coalitions in the policy process. *Policy Studies Journal, 32*(1), 75–107.

CHAPTER 3

PURSUING THE DREAM

Policy, Practice, and Broken Promises
for Undocumented Students

Joel Pérez and Gerardo Ochoa

I n the United States, immigration continues to be a pressing social issue that has led to a shift in enrollment on many college campuses. The number of Latinos living in the United States increased from 35.7 million in 2000 to 55.4 million in 2014 (Krogstad & Lopez, 2015). Despite their population numbers being recently outpaced by those of Asians, Latinos still represented 54% of the population growth between 2000 and 2014 (Stepler & Lopez, 2016). Latino population growth can be attributed to both an increase in birth rates and an uptick in international migration. However since 2000, 40% of the population growth can be attributed solely to international migration (Pew Hispanic Center, 2008). This surge in international migration has subsequently increased the number of undocumented youth. The authors of this chapter will draw from their 33 years of combined higher education experience working in and consulting with private colleges to serve Latino students. This chapter will provide a historical context on immigration issues and an overview of legislative policies, and it will outline institutional practices to serve undocumented students on college campuses.

Among the 40 million immigrants currently residing in the United States, 11.5 million are unauthorized immigrants, and approximately 1 million are presumed to be undocumented children of immigrants (Pew Hispanic Center, 2013). These undocumented students—not born in the United States and residing without legal immigration status—received much of their K–12 education in the United States (Gonzales, 2009). While 65,000 undocumented high school students graduate every year, the majority come from Latin American countries and most emigrate from Mexico (Gonzales, 2009). Because of these demographic trends, this chapter will focus on undocumented students of Mexican origin who, due to immigration policy, are living a life in limbo (Gonzales, 2016).

In the absence of comprehensive federal immigration reform, states have had to address the needs of undocumented students. Washington (Expanding Higher Education Opportunities for Certain Students, 2014), Oregon (Relating to Cost of Attending Public Universities, 2015), and California (California Dream Act II, 2011; California Nonresident Tuition Exemption, 2001) have responded with policies to address educational access and mitigate financial barriers of undocumented students by allowing them to qualify for state grants. In contrast, South Carolina (South Carolina Illegal Immigration Reform Act, 2008), Alabama (Beason-Hammon Alabama Taxpayer and Citizen

Protection Act, 2011), and Georgia (Georgia Board of Regents' Policy 4.1.6 and 4.3.4) have passed legislation that explicitly denies undocumented students admission to state colleges (Vasilogambros, 2016).

IMMIGRATION BACKGROUND

The United States has a long and complicated immigration history. Since the 1600s, the country has experienced multiple waves of immigration that have resulted in an increased number of Western European, Eastern European, and Latin American immigrants (Vatz, 2013). After 1965, both authorized and unauthorized immigration from Latin America, fueled by employment opportunities in the United States and economic and political instability in Latin American countries, gradually increased in the United States (Pedraza & Rumbaut, 1996). From 1990 to 2000, the Hispanic population increased from 22.4 million to 35.3 million, based on emigration form Central America, the Caribbean, and Mexico (Shirey, 2012). Within this immigration increase was what Shirey (2012) deemed the world's largest movement of workers between two countries, from Mexico to the United States.

By the 1980s, the U.S. Census estimated the number of undocumented immigrants in the United States to be between 2.5 and 3.5 million (Pedraza & Rumbaut, 1996). To curb this undocumented immigration, the United States responded with the passage of the 1986 Immigration Reform and Control Act (IRCA; 1986). Considered to be the last comprehensive immigration reform the United States has seen, the IRCA dramatically reduced the number of undocumented laborers by 3 million by implementing the legalization process (Pedraza & Rumbaut, 1996).

Although critics have questioned the IRCA's effectiveness in halting unauthorized immigration (Taylor & Thilmany, 1993), by the mid-1990s, unauthorized entrances into the United States were fueled by the implementation of the North American Free Trade Agreement (NAFTA) (Portes, 2006). NAFTA had an impact on both Mexico and the United States: While Mexico experienced displacement in rural communities, the United States experienced an increase in Mexican migration. According to Portes (2006), states that had a small number of Hispanics in 1990 now have sizable Hispanic populations. Since 1990, the number of undocumented immigrants has increased three-fold (U.S. Department of Homeland Security, 2012). It is estimated that 11.5 million undocumented immigrants reside in the United States, of which an estimated 1.3 million are under the age of 18 (12%), and 1.6 million are between the ages of 18 and 24 (U.S. Department of Homeland Security, 2012). Hence, 12% of the undocumented population is potentially traditional-age college students; the majority will receive their primary and secondary education in U.S. schools and will have lived in the United States for at least five years (Kim & Diaz, 2013).

FEDERAL LEGISLATION

The Higher Education Act (HEA) of 1965 was enacted to support and encourage low-income students to attend college. This policy allowed students to access federal financial assistance and support programs like TRIO (HEA 1965, Title IV, Part A). The HEA mandates that in order to receive financial aid to attend a two- or four-year postsecondary institution, students must be U.S. citizens, permanent residents, or eligible noncitizens (U.S. Department of Education, 2016). While the HEA provided access to federal aid to support college students, undocumented students are ineligible for federal assistance because of the citizenship requirement.

Undocumented college students were also excluded from the 1982 U.S. Supreme Court decision in *Plyler v. Doe*, which stipulates that undocumented children must be provided access to a public education. According to Contreras (2009), this much-needed law afforded equal safeguard for undocumented children under the 14th Amendment of the U.S. Constitution; however, this ruling provides access to public education and protection from discrimination only in primary and secondary schools. Undocumented students who graduate from high school and aspire to attend college are not eligible for financial support to realize their college dreams and contribute positively to the U.S. economy. The economic benefits of graduating from college are substantial: College graduates earn 60% more than their high school graduate counterparts over their working life (Gonzales, 2009). Additionally, it is estimated that undocumented immigrants contribute $11.6 billion in taxes annually and if granted legal status would contribute an additional $2.1 billion per year (Gee, Gardner, & Wiehe, 2016). In a time when state support for higher education has been stagnant, these additional tax revenues could make an impact on public education.

Public education is a state-provided benefit. However, it was not until the Personal Responsibility and Work Opportunity Reconciliation Act (PRWORA, 1996) was passed that *state public benefit* was defined as any grant, contract, loan, professional license, and postsecondary education (Manuel, 2014). According to Manuel's (2014) legal analysis, the PRWORA also "bars states from providing [state] benefits to unlawfully present aliens unless they enact legislation that 'affirmatively provides' for unlawfully present aliens' eligibility" (p. 7). In other words, states have authority to enact legislation to provide state benefits to undocumented college students as long as they enact legislation defining their eligibility. Additionally, the Illegal Immigration Reform and Immigrant Responsibility Act (IIRIRA, 1996) barred states from providing higher education benefits to unlawfully present aliens, based on their state residency, unless U.S. citizens are also eligible for such benefits (Manuel, 2014). These two acts paved the way for states to independently determine whether they would support undocumented students in pursuit of higher education (Olivas, 2004). A state could provide undocumented students benefits for higher education as long as the state affirmatively enacted legislation that allowed them to qualify for state aid and as long as other U.S. citizens in the state were also eligible for such benefits (Olivas, 2004).

The absence of comprehensive immigration reform has presented challenges to states in instituting policies that are responsive to the needs of undocumented students. While the PRWORA (1996) denied undocumented students federal aid, the IIRIRA provided states the discretionary authority to provide undocumented students with the same benefits as in-state residents. States such as Texas (HB1403: The Texas DREAM Act, 2001), Oregon (SB932: Extends Eligibility for Receiving Oregon Financial Aid, 2015), California (AB540: California Nonresident Tuition Exemption, 2001), and Washington (SB6523: Expanding Higher Education Opportunities, 2014) enacted policies that go beyond charging undocumented students in-state tuition. For example, Oregon's SB932 exempted undocumented students from paying nonresident tuition and made them eligible for the Oregon Opportunity Grant. This policy is consistent with California and Washington, which allocates state grants to undocumented students. Although these state policies partly address barriers of access, they fall short in addressing barriers of persistence and providing social, emotional, and mental health support.

UNDOCUMENTED STUDENTS

Undocumented students face many tests, including emotional challenges that affect their daily lives. Dozier (1993) identified three emotional concerns—deportation, loneliness, and depression—for undocumented college students. Their undocumented status leaves many of these students feeling hopeless and seeking answers. These feelings increase in high school and—if these students are able to persevere—affect them in college (Gonzales, 2016). Particularly, these concerns hindered students from seeking out assistance from teachers and counselors as well as developing close relationships, as they fear that they may be reported to Immigration and Customs Enforcement. According to Pérez and Cortés (2011), other challenges that undocumented students, particularly those in college, face include losing close relationships, a sense of isolation, obtaining legal documentation, going through the acculturation process, negotiating their ethnic identity, changing their family roles, and adjusting to their experience in school. In addition, Pérez and Cortés (2011) found that high school students who want to pursue higher education had many challenges that they would need to overcome in order to achieve their dreams—in particular, high poverty, which leads to an environment unconducive to academic preparation. If not for teachers and counselors, many of these students would have abandoned their pursuit of higher education, making these students "early exiters" (Gonzales, 2016). The teachers and counselors provided needed mentoring, resources, and support.

Development, Relief, and Education for Alien Minors Act (DREAM Act)

For many undocumented students, the DREAM Act (2001) was legislation that provided them with a sense of hope that they could pursue their dreams of attending an institution of higher learning and establish a path to citizenship. The DREAM Act was first introduced in 2001 as bipartisan legislation to clarify the rights of states to provide in-state tuition and offer a path to citizenship for undocumented students. Many revisions to the original piece of legislation have been made since 2001 (Gildersleeve, Rumann, & Mondragón, 2010). The DREAM Act would have allowed high school graduates to apply for legal conditional status. During this conditional period, undocumented students would be required to attend college and graduate, or serve in the U.S. military for at least two years. If they met these requirements, then undocumented students would be given permanent residency at the end of the conditional period (Gildersleeve et al., 2010). After 10 years of trying to move this legislation forward, the DREAM Act fell short in the U.S. Senate (Pérez & Cortés, 2011).

Deferred Action for Childhood Arrivals

In response to the failure of the DREAM Act to move forward, in 2012 President Barack Obama directed Secretary of Homeland Security Janet Napolitano (2012) to issue a memorandum to U.S. Customs and Border Protection, U.S. Citizenship and Immigration Services, and U.S. Immigration and Customs Enforcement aimed at providing some relief to undocumented youth to receive temporary status. The policy was referred to as Deferred Action for Childhood Arrival (DACA) and was intended to assist undocumented students with obtaining work permits and to defer deportation (Muñoz, 2015). An estimated 1.2 million immigrants were eligible, because they arrived in the United States prior to age 16, resided in the country continuously for five years, and were under age 31 prior to the executive order (Gonzales, 2016).

In 2015 an estimated 573,704 people applied for DACA (Muñoz, 2015). DACA was not limited to college students, but it did provide them with the ability to work nonfederal work-study positions on their respective campuses or off-campus. More important, it allowed DACA students to pursue careers in the United States after graduation. This order was seen as a relief for many, but there was still concern about whether future presidential administrations would support this public policy. More than 600 college and university presidents have signed a letter to the current president in support of maintaining DACA. In addition, institutional leaders have begun to designate their campuses as sanctuary campuses as a result of pressure from students, staff, and faculty. The term *sanctuary campus* does not have a national agreed-upon definition. Some campuses have resisted applying this designation because there is no universal agreement as to what constitutes a sanctuary campus. The one characteristic that all sanctuary campuses share is that they will not provide federal agencies with any information about students without a court order. Sanctuary campuses will look for ways to continue the employment of their undocumented students in absence of a DACA number, provide legal immigration services, and continue to provide institutional financial aid support. With so much uncertainty as it relates to DACA and the possibility of comprehensive immigration reform, institutions must determine how to support prospective and current undocumented students on college campuses. Some campuses have created Dream Centers. These centers have provided support groups, advising, counseling, legal clinics, and mentoring for undocumented students to assist them in persisting and graduating from their institutions.

The gains made by the DACA program (Napolitano, 2012) are presently in flux as the future of DACA remains uncertain under the policies of President Donald Trump's administration. In the fall of 2017, the administration issued a DACA rescission that terminated the program effective March 5, 2018. Uncertainty about the future of DACA has challenged students, faculty, and administrators to continue campus efforts to support and retain DACA students.

RECOMMENDATIONS

Given the current political and social climate, with the future of DACA (Napolitano, 2012) uncertain, higher education administrators will need to revisit strategies intended to support undocumented students. We have outlined several strategies to guide administrators, faculty, and staff, but it is not our intent to provide an exhaustive list; rather, this is a list that can start conversations on campuses that want to continue to provide support for their students. The strategies that administrators ultimately decide to implement will be influenced by a range of factors, such as state laws, social context, campus climate, and institutional setting.

Evaluate existing mission and values. If institutions are going to sustain these efforts, then they should make sure their initiatives align with their mission and values; this is particularly the case for private institutions. We believe that if creating an inclusive community is part of a campus's mission and values, then these institutions can make a case as to why their efforts are important, as undocumented and DACA students are a part of our country. Institutions need to conduct a self-examination process or institutional audit that starts with mission and values. They need to ensure that their endeavors match their espoused values before they begin to look for ways to create communities that are inclusive of undocumented students. Such introspection should include having high-level conversations with governing boards, senior-level administrators, and key faculty. In addition, student affairs departments should have those same conversations to identify how they can also be supportive of the undocumented student population. These conversations are important, as they ensure that members of the community understand why supporting DACA (Napolitano, 2012) and undocumented students is important to the institution. Not taking these steps will undermine institutions' commitment to supporting their undocumented students and conveying to their constituents the importance of this endeavor, particularly in a charged political climate. Once an institution determines that an initiative is in line with its mission, then it can begin to look for ways to support its undocumented student population. This could take the form of creating centers such as those that exist at institutions within the California State University System—Dreamer Resource Centers. These centers provide academic resources, emotional support, and information to students about financial assistance. The centers' mission is to provide support for undocumented students with academic and emotional support to assist them in their academic endeavors.

Evaluate and update policies. Admissions, financial aid, housing, campus safety, registrar, and all other campus departments should undertake a policy audit to ensure that policies and procedures are inclusive and responsive to the needs of undocumented students. Special emphasis should be made to ensure that student information is protected to the highest standards as outlined by the Family Educational Rights and Privacy Act of 1974 (FERPA). Students should be made explicitly aware about their right to be removed from the student directory if they so choose.

Financial aid officers need to establish trust by conducting outreach and building relationships with current and prospective undocumented students as well as community organizations. In establishing relationships, financial aid offices build credibility and can decrease fear and barriers experienced by undocumented students; at the same time, financial aid staff members become central personnel for providing students accurate and timely financial information. While both public and private colleges and universities are bound by federal and state financial aid policies, private colleges have the most flexibility with their own privately funded scholarships. Eligibility requirements for privately funded financial aid are determined by the institution and/or the individual donor; in most cases, the true intent of such scholarships is to provide students financial assistance based on need and/or merit and not citizenship status. The top five eligibility criteria among the nation's top private scholarship providers are academic achievement, extracurricular activities, financial need, athletic participation, and service (Institute for Higher Education Policy, 2005). Thus, when it comes to providing privately funded scholarships to students, colleges should ensure that their institutional policies do not have unnecessary citizenship requirements, are in alignment with their mission, and are inclusive of undocumented students. The institutional challenge lies in updating policies and procedures, having campuswide values-based discussions, and moving proposed policies forward through the appropriate on-campus channels in order to open up funding that was previously unavailable to undocumented students.

Although merit for scholarship eligibility can be determined from a student's transcript, measuring financial need of undocumented students is more challenging for financial aid officers, as such students are ineligible to complete a Free Application for Federal Student Aid (FAFSA). Because many scholarships are awarded on a combination of both merit and financial need, states like California, Oregon, and Washington that enacted legislation to provide state grants to undocumented students also developed online tools similar to the FAFSA to determine a student's financial need by accounting for assets, household size, and number of family members in college, among other factors. Students from these states benefited because they were provided a vehicle for proving their financial need, and if they met their state's need requirements, they also received a state grant for attending an in-state college. For example, Washington's 2015 Real

Hope Act allocated $5 million annually to support approximately 1,100 students (Long, 2014).

Students who attend colleges in states that have not enacted legislation in support of undocumented students are caught in a bind, as they may have to pay out-of-state tuition. This is where many private colleges are better equipped to support undocumented students; many already have institutional alternative methods for determining financial need. Federal and institutional methodologies for determining financial need can be problematic: They cannot fully reflect a student's financial circumstance because they do not account for personal expenses beyond cost-of-living allowances. We know from anecdotal evidence that many undocumented students pay hefty sums of money for legal representation or filing fees for themselves and/or their families; this is discretionary money that could be used to pay for their education, but prioritizing the potential to legalize their immigration status often prohibits students from putting this money toward tuition.

The *Federal Student Aid Handbook* allows for financial aid administrators to make financial adjustments on a case-by-case basis, through a process called professional judgment, in order to more accurately determine the student's financial need (U.S. Department of Education, 2016). In situations where an eligible student has undue financial hardships, the money paid to cover such expenses can be excluded from federal financial aid calculations and could allow a student to qualify for a Pell Grant or an increase in institutional scholarships or state grants. Professional judgment could be extended beyond federal student aid and exercised for undocumented students' privately funded aid. Considering the financial limitations and pressures faced by undocumented students, the professional judgment policy could be a useful tool to alleviate financial burden;

it could allow undocumented students to qualify for scholarships or grants for which they may not otherwise be eligible. Prior to DACA (Napolitano, 2012), colleges and universities established scholarships tied to student leadership positions so that undocumented students who met certain criteria could have access to funds. The criteria included GPA, a student's geographic area, letters of recommendation, and prior leadership involvement. In addition, schools encouraged students to seek dual enrollment programs prior to graduating from high school so that they would be able to transfer earned credits; this way, the time to degree was shortened and students would not have to pay as much for their education.

Provide on-campus support. All college employees should be equipped with knowledge, awareness, and tools to work with undocumented students. Regular training and updates on immigration policies should be part of professional development programs on campus. Special emphasis should be made on building relationships. Gonzales (2016) found that a strong network and relationships led to academic success among undocumented students. Additionally, colleges should identify an individual or department to spearhead support for undocumented students. Institutions could also look for ways to educate administrators, faculty, staff, and students about how to support undocumented students both socially and emotionally on campus. This has taken the form of undocumented ally training that addresses such topics as what to do if a student discloses that they are undocumented, how to react to that disclosure, things one should not say, and ways that people can help. Institutions could also look for ways to integrate components of this training to new staff and faculty orientation programs. This will help in communicating to new staff that creating an inclusive community for DACA and undocumented students is a value of the institution. If an institution does not believe that a desire to support undocumented students is in line with its mission, then it is our belief that the institution should refrain from making false promises, as doing so can send mixed messages to students. For example, stakeholders will not be able to connect why this endeavor is important or central to an institution's mission.

Create a rapid response team. Students are impacted both directly and indirectly by immigration policy in general and enforcement in particular. Colleges should be prepared to use their institutional mission and influence to protect and support undocumented students. By having a response team, the college will be positioned to respond quickly and effectively—particularly if students are detained. Leverage points exist among media relations staff, legal counsel, boards of trustees, faculty experts, and campus housing and counseling departments, among others.

Partner with community-based organizations. Many of the undocumented students who decide to attend institutions of higher learning receive support from community-based organizations. Institutions should look for ways to partner with these organizations in order to create a system of support that may include financial aid as well as legal counsel. One such organization is Educators for Fair Consideration, located in Oakland, California. It provides information about financial aid, legal advice, tax and self-employment webinars, and other resources.

Assist in advocating for comprehensive immigration reform. Institutions can play an active role in meeting with legislators to advocate for comprehensive immigration reform. Consider reaching out to alumni who are legislators to lobby for legislative relief for undocumented students in the form of financial aid as well as a path to legal residency.

CONCLUSION

Undocumented students are gaining access to higher education in larger numbers. They have overcome barriers, harbor a fear of deportation, feel a sense of isolation, have obtained legal documentation, have learned English, and must adjust to their experience in school. Yet, in many ways, undocumented students are vulnerable to policies and rhetoric outside of the campus community. Each college is uniquely positioned to support undocumented students to get them through graduation. Short of comprehensive immigration reform, DACA and undocumented students will continue to live in uncertainty and will need the support of their institutions. It will be extremely important for colleges and universities to continue to monitor the political climate and provide the support necessary for undocumented students to succeed. The success of all students is an important value that all of those involved in higher education should hold. Therefore it is imperative that professionals in this field look for ways to support, mentor, and assist these students in pursuing their dreams of obtaining a college degree.

REFERENCES

Beason-Hammon Alabama Taxpayer and Citizen Protection Act, Assem. 56 (Ala. 2001). Retrieved from http://arc-sos.state.al.us/PAC/SOSACPDF.001/A0008649.PDF

California Dream Act II, Assem. 131, 2011–2012 Leg., Reg. Sess. (Cal. 2011) (codified at Cal. Educ. Code § 66021.6).

California Nonresident Tuition Exemption, Assem. 540, 2001–2002 Leg., Reg. Sess. (Cal. 2001) (codified at Cal. Educ. Code § 68130.5).

Contreras, F. (2009). Sin papeles y rompiendo barreras: Latino students and the challenges of persisting in college. *Harvard Educational Review, 79*(4), 610–631.

Dozier, S. B. (1993). Emotional concerns of undocumented and out-of-status foreign students. *Community Review, 13,* 29–33.

DREAM Act, S. 1291, 107th Cong. (2001).

Expanding Higher Education Opportunities for Certain Students, S. 6523, 63rd Leg., Reg. Sess. (Wash., 2014). Retrieved from http://lawfilesext.leg.wa.gov/biennium/2013-14/Pdf/Bills/Senate%20Passed%20Legislature/6523.PL.pdf

Family Educational Rights and Privacy Act of 1974, 20 U.S.C. § 1232g (1974).

Gee, L. C., Gardner, M., & Wiehe, M. (2016). *Undocumented immigrants' state & local tax contributions.* Washington, DC: Institute on Taxation and Economic Policy.

Georgia Board of Regents' Policy 4.1.6 and 4.3.4. (2017). Retrieved from http://www.usg.edu/policymanual/section4/C327

Gildersleeve, R. E., Rumann, C., & Mondragón, R. (2010). Servicing undocumented students: Current law and policy. In J. Price (Ed.), *Special issue: Understanding and supporting undocumented students* (New Directions for Student Services, No. 131, pp. 5–18). San Francisco, CA: Jossey-Bass.

Gonzales, R. G. (2009). *Young lives on hold: The college dreams of undocumented students.* Retrieved from College Board Advocacy & Policy Center website: https://secure-media.collegeboard.org/digitalServices/pdf/professionals/young-lives-on-hold-undocumented-students.pdf

Gonzales, R. G. (2016). *Lives in limbo: Undocumented and coming of age in America.* Oakland, CA: University of California Press.

Higher Education Act of 1965, 20 U.S.C. § 402A (2013).

Immigration Reform and Control Act of 1986, 8 U.S.C. § 1101 (1986).

Illegal Immigration Reform and Immigrant Responsibility Act of 1996, 5 U.S.C. §§ 500–511 (1996).

Institute for Higher Education Policy. (2005). *Private scholarships count: Access to higher education and the critical role of the private sector.* Retrieved from http://www.ihep.org/sites/default/files/uploads/docs/pubs/privatescholarshipcount.pdf

Kim, E., & Diaz, J. (2013). *Immigrant students and higher education* (ASHE Higher Education Report, Vol. 38, No. 6). Hoboken, NJ: Wiley.

Krogstad, J. M., & Lopez, M. H. (2015). *Hispanic population reaches record 55 million, but growth has cooled.* Washington, DC: Pew Research Center.

Long, K. (2014, March 1). Immigrant students see "Real Hope" for financial aid now. *The Seattle Times.* Retrieved from https://www.seattletimes.com/seattle-news/immigrant-students-see-lsquoreal-hopersquo-for-financial-aid-now

Manuel, K. M. (2014). *Unlawfully present aliens, higher education, in-state tuition, and financial aid: Legal analysis.* Washington, DC: Congressional Research Service.

Muñoz, M. S. (2015). *Identity, social activism, and the pursuit of higher education: The journey stories of undocumented and unafraid community activists.* New York, NY: Peter Lang.

Napolitano, J. (2012). Exercising prosecutorial discretion with respect to individuals who came to the Unites States as children. Retrieved from https://www.dhs.gov/xlibrary/assets/s1-exercising-prosecutorial-discretion-individuals-who-came-to-us-as-children.pdf

Olivas, M. (2004). IIRIRA, the Dream Act, and undocumented college student residency. *Journal of College and University Law, 30*(2), 435–464.

Pedraza, S., & Rumbaut, R. G. (1996). *Origins and destinies: Immigration, race, and ethnicity in America*. Belmont, CA: Wadsworth.

Pérez, W., & Cortés, R. D. (2011). *Undocumented Latino college students: Their socioemotional and academic experiences*. El Paso, TX: LFB Scholarly Publishing.

Personal Responsibility and Work Opportunity Reconciliation Act of 1996, Pub. L. No. 104-193, § 411, 110 Stat. 2268 (1996).

Pew Hispanic Center. (2008). *Latino settlement in the new century*. Retrieved from http://www.pewhispanic.org/2008/10/22/latinos-account-for-half-of-us-population-growth-since-2000/#about-this-report

Pew Hispanic Center. (2013). *A nation of immigrants: A portrait of the 40 million, including 11 million unauthorized*. Retrieved from http://www.pewhispanic.org/files/2013/01/statistical_portrait_final_jan_29.pdf

Plyler v. Doe, 457 U.S. 202, 230 (1982).

Portes, A. (2006). NAFTA and Mexican immigration. *Border battles: The U.S. immigration debates*. Retrieved from http://borderbattles.ssrc.org/Portes

Relating to Cost of Attending Public Universities; and Declaring an Emergency, S. 932, 78th Leg., Reg. Sess. (Or., 2015). Retrieved from https://olis.leg.state.or.us/liz/2015R1/Downloads/MeasureDocument/SB932

Shirey, W. (2012). Immigration waves. *Immigration in America*. Retrieved from http://immigrationtounitedstates.org/603-immigration-waves.html

South Carolina Illegal Immigration Reform Act, H.R. 4400, Assem., S. C. G. 117th Leg. Sess. (S.C. 2008). Retrieved from http://www.scstatehouse.gov/sess117_2007-2008/bills/4400.htm

Stepler, R., & Lopez, M. H. (2016). *U.S. Latino population growth and dispersion has slowed since onset of the great recession*. Washington, DC: Pew Research Center.

Taylor, J. E., & Thilmany, D. (1993). Worker turnover, farm labor contractors, and IRCA's impact on the California farm labor market. *American Journal of Agricultural Economics, 75*(2), 350.

U.S. Department of Education. (2016). *Federal student aid handbook*. Washington DC: Author.

U.S. Department of Homeland Security. (2012). *Estimates of the unauthorized immigrant population residing in the United States: January 2011*. Retrieved from https://www.dhs.gov/sites/default/files/publications/Unauthorized%20Immigrant%20Population%20Estimates%20in%20the%20US%20January%202011_0.pdf

Vasilogambros, M. (2016, March 16). The folly of under-educating the undocumented. *The Atlantic*. Retrieved from http:// https://www.theatlantic.com/politics/archive/2016/03/the-folly-of-under-educating-the-undocumented/473877

Vatz, S. (2013, May 5). Interactive timeline: History of immigration in America. *KQED News*. Retrieved from http://blogs.kqed.org/lowdown/2013/05/05/u-s-immigration-policy-timeline-a-long-history-of-dealing-with-newcomers

PART II

UNDERSTANDING LATINX/A/O IDENTITY IN THE UNITED STATES

BETWEEN TWO WORLDS

A Chicana Coming of Age in Higher Education

Anesat León-Guerrero

I t can be said that socialization begins as soon as one is born into the world. In the Latinx/a/o community, many believe that the vision of what a child will become is prescribed—what accomplishments they should pursue, what their character will be. It is all formulated in the minds of the guardians and the family. The life that the family hopes for themselves may be projected onto the future of the baby. My parents and extended family had predicted that I would be born male, and preparations had been made months before. However, to everyone's surprise, I was born female and would bring challenges for my parents who had recently immigrated from Mexico to the United States. It is easier to live as a man; this is a fact worldwide. But rather than being disappointed with the false hope of having a boy—an important accomplishment in a Mexican family—my parents accepted me completely and simply chose to use all of the gendered clothing and toys that had been gifted to me as an expected male. From the beginning, my parents demonstrated that they valued and understood that as a woman of color in the United States, I should be raised with a mindset of gender equality, and they continued to use elements of both binary genders in their parenting throughout my early childhood.

FAMILY AND EARLY EDUCATION

My parent's approach to parenting me around gender identity can be described as unique within Mexican culture. Before arriving in the United States, my father worked the land in Mexico, but when the North American Free Trade Agreement was enacted in 1994, it became difficult for him to provide for my mother, who was pregnant with me. After leaving Mexico, my family settled in eastern Oregon, where my father had extended family, and I was born in the United States in late 1994. Culture shock and nostalgia influenced my parents' decision to return to Mexico in 1997, in an attempt to raise my siblings and me in a Mexican community. But my father struggled to find steady work because of his lack of education, and in 2001 we returned to the United States permanently. Unlike my father, who was born in a humble village, my mother came from an industrialized town and from a family of educators. She had earned a degree in accounting and displayed her diploma in our living room, even though her degree was basically worthless in the United States. As a child, I remember staring at that document with ornate script text and an oval-shaped portrait of her. I didn't understand its meaning then, but I knew that it was very official and that my mom was very proud of it. I also knew that to my parents, education was the most important aspect of our lives. For my siblings and me, everything revolved around earning good grades, impressing our teachers, and pleasing our parents.

Luckily, my siblings and I were fairly accomplished students and did well in school. The first years of our education were in Mexico, and we were brought up to respect our teachers and learned that through discipline anything could be accomplished. Once in Oregon, because we were Mexican immigrants, we were sent to English as a Second Language classes in elementary school even though we had knowledge that surpassed that of the average student in our grades. I felt frustrated, transitioning from an all-Mexican environment to a predominantly White state. Despite my ethnic background, the White students seemed willing to approach me because of my lighter complexion; however, I began to observe that their treatment toward other students of color, especially those with darker skin, was different. Also, they were open to including me in group activities within the classrooms, but their attitudes shifted outside of class, and I was not invited to play or sit with them at lunch. I felt confused but was left with the impression that if I acted like and tried to look like the White kids, I would be accepted and gain more access and privileges.

PATHWAY TO COLLEGE AND FINDING A CAREER PATH

However, I was not the only one being challenged in our new life in the United States. My mother felt frustrated that she could not practice her skills as an accountant, and she focused all her energy in raising my siblings and me and finding college-preparation opportunities for us. She first sought out programs that would prepare us to live and study in our new country and registered us with the Oregon Migrant Program.

This state program offered many services but focused primarily on providing educational opportunities for children of Latinx/a/o migrant families as well as resources for student success and cultural preservation. During the summer of my sophomore year in high school, my counselor suggested that I apply to the Oregon Migrant Leadership Program (OMLP), a two-week summer leadership program at Oregon State University (OSU). I gladly accepted and visited OSU for the first time. There, we were welcomed by the College Assistance Migrant Program (CAMP) staff who facilitated OMLP, and I was introduced to my first mentor, Oscar Montemayor, who would become my advisor for the next five years. During the two weeks of the program, I expanded my knowledge of Chicano history and started to learn that I could become a leader. The last workshop before the program's graduation was about how to apply to CAMP and helping us to understand that we were good enough to attend OSU. Montemayor played a key role in my transition into my senior year in high school, when I turned my attention to college and scholarship applications. He encouraged me and highlighted my intellectual worth when at times I felt that I had little support back in eastern Oregon, especially since my family did not know how to navigate the college process in the United States.

As I entered my senior year in high school at age 16, I felt unsure of my future. My parents urged me to attend the local community college so I could live at home while working to save up money to transfer to a state school. I wasn't happy with my parents' opinion that I should attend a community college, but I decided to apply to less costly state universities and take advanced placement classes to earn some college credits while in high school. However, when the time finally came to plan my leaving for college, my parents became concerned about my ability to succeed academically and urged me to stay at home with them. It wasn't that they wanted me to get married and have children; they simply feared that I would struggle and fail at the university. In the end, I applied to only one university, which was the only campus I had visited: OSU.

Once accepted at OSU, I began to focus on my future career choice. My parents had always told me that I could choose any career I wanted, but it had to be something that I was good at—and my choice had to be realistic. I thought about working in education, but I didn't want to teach in public schools. This left me unsure of what I would ultimately major in, but I knew that with my experience through CAMP, I would have more clarity as the year progressed. I also understood that having a college degree would help me to secure entry not only into a professional job but also into a new world of learning and esteemed peers and role models. Being successful was important to me because I did not want anyone to doubt that I was intelligent and that I feel intrinsically driven to succeed. I have been deeply motivated by the image of my grandmother about whom my mother would tell me stories as a child. She was a highly respected and elegant woman in her district, and she was about to receive her master's degree in adult education when she was tragically killed in a car accident—only one semester before graduation. I aspired to be like her: a leader in her community and an advocate for education and social justice. Eventually, through my learning and many experiences in college, it became clear that I wanted to work in higher education and pursue a career in student affairs.

CULTURE AND IDENTITY

Although I have been inspired by strong women in my family and their intense focus on education, it has not been easy to navigate a new cultural experience at school and to overcome obstacles faced by my parents as immigrants to the United States. As a result of all those experiences, however, I have learned to hold onto and to honor my culture and identity as a form of self-care; often it has felt like the only thing that I knew was certain. For example, I learned about the Mexican revolution and culture when I was in elementary school in Mexico, and this knowledge strengthened the bond I felt to my cultural roots. Unlike many of my Mexican school peers in the United States, my connection to Mexico felt unique because I had lived and attended school there. But despite my experiences, my Mexican identity has been questioned by others because I did not fit into the stereotype of a Mexican, with my lighter skin, tall and slender body shape, and my high aspirations to excel in academics. Even with other Mexicans, I was considered an assimilated Mexican. Thus, the concept of authenticity and measuring my brownness came into my mind early in high school, and my connection to Chicana feminism solidified as I continued to learn and become aware of my indigeneity, on both sides of my family, while also recognizing my Spanish heritage. This new knowledge has led to new questions and reflections about why as a child and young adult I separated my sense of self from such a fundamental part of who I was, why I initially refused to expand my knowledge about my family history and identity in the past. Reclaiming my past is reclaiming my body and mind; it is imperative for my process of self-preservation. Chicana feminism revealed to me that Mexican female strength did not have to be "traditional" in the way Alma Garcia (1989) described it: "the glorified Chicanas as strong, long-suffering women who had endured and kept Chicano culture and family intact" (p. 222). I should not feel shame to have a vast vocabulary, wit, and confidence, or feel shame over my desire to embrace my curves one day and wear androgynous clothes the next. Through Chicana feminism, I have learned about other social movements and intersectional feminism. I also learned to acknowledge the necessity to build community with other women of color so we may work collaboratively toward further justice and empowerment.

PRESENT DAY

I have discovered that my sense of identity as a Latinx/a/o, first-generation student of color is always changing and expanding. To be successful, I have needed to make the most of my life experiences, forgo the conventional paths, and seek new challenges intentionally. Although my mother's family had access to education, my parents and most of my family had humble beginnings and were forced to move north, work hard, find opportunities, and succeed in unfamiliar terrain. As is the case for many immigrants, my parents' experience in the United States included struggles, but they managed to establish themselves and to successfully raise their family in the United States. Thus, I feel that I have no choice but to challenge myself to achieve more than the expected. I have also found my passion and purpose, and I am currently pursuing a master's degree in student affairs at Indiana University in Bloomington.

In December 2016, my family and I traveled to Mexico City together, my first time visiting the capital. During the trip, I climbed the 2,000-year-old pyramids of Teotihuacan and explored old and modern streets downtown. One of the last places we visited before our departure was the Zocalo, the main square in central Mexico City, boasting an enormous Mexican flag that flew high above all. Being there felt like a blessing and was a reminder that despite all of it, *el pueblo Mexicano* (the Mexican community) has always been one that persevered through hardships and never forgot its history. My family and my community needed neither boots nor laces; my ancestors built countries with their *bare feet*. I am grateful for all I have learned so far but even more excited about my future as a successful educator and the opportunity to help other students, like me, to transform their lives, just as I have.

REFERENCE

Garcia, A. M. (1989). The development of Chicana feminist discourse, 1970–1980. *Gender & Society, 3*(2), 217–238.

CHAPTER 4

EXPLORING LATINX/A/O IDENTITY, CULTURAL VALUES, AND SUCCESS IN HIGHER EDUCATION

Sofia B. Pertuz

> *The diversity and historical/social context of Latinos in the United States greatly impacts how an individual Latino student may see himself or herself in the college environment. As a result, an educator needs to understand nuances among cultures, historical issues within the cultures, and conditions that may impact individual Latino students.* (Torres, Howard-Hamilton, & Cooper, 2003, p. 59)

The Latinx/a/o identity is complex and consists of a variety of characteristics that move the conversation about identity beyond the Black and White dichotomy that has historically informed the national dialogue around racial and ethnic identities in the United States. Latinx/a/os are one of the fastest-growing identity groups and will have the highest number of high school graduates with potential for college enrollment in the near future (Ennis, Ríos-Vargas, & Albert, 2011). Despite increasing enrollment, Latinx/a/o undergraduates lag behind their peers in college completion (Fry, 2011). Thus, Latinx/a/o students need supportive Latinx/a/o staff and faculty who can provide them with mentorship and role modeling as they navigate their college experiences.

Unfortunately, Latinx/a/o faculty and staff face their own challenges with representation and promotion. In the faculty ranks, Latinx/a/os are underrepresented, comprising only 4% of total faculty in higher education in the United States (Kena et al., 2016). As administrators, Latinx/a/os are bottlenecked in entry-level and mid-level positions, with very few moving up to senior leadership jobs (Leon & Nevarez, 2007). As plans for recruiting students and professionals from this growing population are developed, it is important that policy and decision makers in higher education who do not identify as Latinx/a/o understand how Latinx/a/o identity and cultural values influence the retention and persistence of Latinx/a/o students and professionals.

Although participation in higher education seems to be challenging for Latinx/a/o individuals in all areas, this chapter will focus specifically on undergraduates and administrators. It provides a brief overview of the evolution of labels that attempt to capture the Latinx/a/o identity and explores how cultural values influence Latinx/a/o student and professional engagement and success at institutions of higher education. The chapter begins with a brief discussion about how terminology and naming conventions influence cultural connections to the language used to describe Latinx/a/os. It then describes several selected Latinx/a/o cultural values and the challenges that arise when values and identity clash with institutional culture, especially at places with low representation of non-White individuals, which will be referred to as *historically White institutions* (HWIs) for the purpose of this chapter instead of the term *predominantly White institutions*. Along with challenges, ideas are discussed for how colleges and universities can work with cultural values to create opportunities for inclusion and belonging for Latinx/a/o students and professionals. The chapter concludes with a summary of strategies and best practices for the consideration of higher education leadership.

BACKGROUND

Most college and university mission statements foster welcoming environments where all community members, including students and professionals, can thrive and achieve their academic and career goals (Morphew & Hartley, 2006). However, the literature demonstrates that higher education has not been an idealized environment for Latinx/a/o students and professionals; rather, members of this population have had to struggle and develop strategies to survive hostile and unwelcoming environments, especially at HWIs (Aldaco, 2010; Arredondo & Castellanos, 2003; Castellanos & Jones, 2003; Haro & Lara, 2003).

The ideal setting for Latinx/a/os would be a pluralist or diverse institution, which Smith, Yosso, and Solórzano (2007) defined as "one that admits, enrolls, retains, and graduates underrepresented racial and ethnic groups by extending equal opportunities to guidance, support, and resources for academic success" (p. 560). The experiences of Latinx/a/os on college campuses can be influenced by how they describe themselves versus how they are perceived and labeled by others, especially depending on outward appearances, individual views on race, language, nationalities, immigration status, and gender and sexual identity (Canul, 2003; Comas-Diaz, 2001; Torres,

2004; Torres, Howard-Hamilton, & Cooper, 2003). The next section discusses the evolution of terminology and labels for Latinx/a/os in higher education.

UNDERSTANDING LABELS AND THE COMPLEXITY OF THE LATINX/A/O IDENTITY

Latinx/a/os represent diverse groups of people with a variety of nationalities, cultures, familial backgrounds, and perspectives on self-identification. How Latinx/a/os self-identify depends heavily on region, upbringing, skin color, and many other factors. Inconsistencies and possible mislabeling of the Latinx/a/o populations do not allow a clear understanding of when Latinx/a/os were first integrated into higher education.

Although several terms exist for people in the United States who descend from Spanish-speaking countries, one of the earliest was the word *Hispanic*. Comas-Diaz (2001) described the use of the word *Hispanic* as a way "to refer collectively to all Spanish speakers" and "connotes a lineage or cultural heritage related to Spain" (p. 116). However, there are many who loathe this term because of its connection to colonialism and the negative regard in which this group was held by White politicians who worked to create this group label in the 1960s, providing the first opportunity for individuals to select this choice on the 1970 U.S. Census (Comas-Diaz, 2001; Rodriguez, 2002). The term *Latino* has been preferred over *Hispanic* because "[the former] excludes Europeans such as Spaniards from being identified as ethnic minorities in the United States" (Comas-Diaz, 2001, p. 117). Latinx/a/os in higher education could not have been categorized as *Hispanic* or *Latino* any sooner than 1970 and 1990, respectively, because that was when the U.S. Census first used those labels as self-identifying demographic descriptors. Before these censuses, each person of Latin American descent would have had to self-identify as "Other" or by "National Origin" (see, e.g., U.S. Census Bureau, 1961).

While the term *Latino* has been used to refer to individuals from all genders, the term *Latina* has been used to refer only to female-identifying women, thus illustrating a gendered language that focuses on maintaining traditional views of gender as strictly binary. For example, a group of only Latinas would be labeled as *Latinas,* but when only one Latino male joins the group, the collective group would now be referred to as *Latinos*. More recently, to address this language inequity, there has been an evolution of a new term, *Latinx*, which has not come without some controversy among members of the Hispanic community (Johnston-Guerrero, 2016). The author of this chapter has chosen to adopt the term *Latinx* and expand it to *Latinx/a/o*, as has been done elsewhere in this book, as a way to embrace the idea of looking to the future, where gendered language is recognized for the bias that it brings, with its old-fashioned customs that created a hierarchy within the genders that favored a patriarchal society and ignored the contributions of women. The other reason to use *Latinx/a/o* is to be inclusive of individuals who do not identify within the gender binary and to embrace the evolving nature of self-identification of all Latinx/a/os. While this chapter will use *Latinx/a/o* as an identifier, the author here recognizes that some individuals also identify with their country of origin and might use the term referring to a person's ethnicity or country of origin—for example, Mexican, Dominican, or Cuban. The use of a hyphen in addition to *American* is also common, such as Dominican-American, Mexican-American, or Cuban-American.

Although the label *Latinx/a/o* is used to refer to ethnicity, neither this term, *Latino*, nor *Hispanic* are considered racial labels according to the way that the U.S. Census collects information. The census asks: "Is Person 1 of Hispanic, Latino, or Spanish origin?" and offers the choices of "No, not of Hispanic, Latino, or Spanish origin," or "Yes," followed by more specific nationalities from which to choose, including Mexican, Mexican-American, Chicano or Puerto Rican, or Cuban; then a box allows for a write-in answer. Meanwhile, Suro (2005) in a report by the Pew Hispanic Center described Hispanic/Latino identity as:

> not a racial group, nor does it share a common language or culture. The single overarching trait that all Hispanics share in common is a connection by ancestry to Latin America. This population, in fact, traces its origins to many countries with varied cultures, and while some Latinos have family histories in the United States that date back centuries, others are recent arrivals. Some speak only English, others only Spanish, and many are bilingual. (p. 3)

This definition adds to the inconsistencies between and among the different nationalities that fall under the label of *Latino* or *Hispanic* because it ignores race and the racism that exists within the Latino culture (Hernández, 2003; Torres-Saillant, 2003). This was a point emphasized by Trucios-Haynes (2001), who spoke of Latina/os experiencing "their daily lives as Non-White people in terms of their race, color, national origin, language, culture, and/or citizenship status," making Latinx/a/os in the United States feel like "foreigners" (p. 3).

All factors involved with labeling further complicate things for Latinx/a/os in higher education, because—depending on how they are socialized, the regions where they live, or how they choose to self-identify—any one of these identity factors can become more relevant or salient than others at any given time and occasion. Also, elements of the Latinx/a/o identity that include nationality, immigration status, language, culture, gender, socioeconomic class, and sexual identity impact the experiences of Latinx/a/o students and professionals in higher education, both positively and negatively—positively when they first arrive at their respective institutions with excitement about this achievement and hope for a good experience, and then negatively as they begin to realize that they must navigate hostile and unwelcoming campus environments because of their cultural difference (Aldaco, 2010; Cammarota, 2006; Castellanos & Jones, 2003; Fry, 2002; Gloria & Castellanos, 2003; Haro & Lara, 2003; Leon & Nevarez, 2007; Montelongo & Ortiz, 2001; Pertuz, 2017).

LATINX/A/O IDENTITY IN HIGHER EDUCATION

The complexity of the Latinx/a/o identity within the institutional structure of higher education can be examined by applying the well-established theoretical framework of intersectionality, which accounts for "multiple grounds of identity when considering how the social world is constructed" (Crenshaw, 1991, p. 1245). The concept of intersectionality is useful because it "acknowledges an individual's multiple social identities, thus creating a more complete portrayal of the whole person" (Wijeyesinghe & Jones, 2014, p. 10). Intersectionality is also instrumental when examining challenges Latinx/a/os face while straddling multiple worlds, which means that they must contend with navigating cultural values and expectations at home and opportunities in higher education environments, sometimes experiencing a clash in this regard (Huber, 2010; MacDonald & Garcia, 2003; Martin, 2010).

Gender differences, hypermasculinity and femininity, nationality, and skin color also influence how Latinx/a/os relate to each other and to their non-Latinx/a/o peers on college campuses (Rudolph, Chavez, Quintana, & Salinas, 2011; Sáenz & Ponjuán, 2009). In her seminal book *Why Are All the Black Kids Sitting Together in the Cafeteria?*, Tatum (1997) recognized that Latinos are not a racial group; rather, they are a group bound by shared cultural values that help them identify as a collective ethnic group, regardless of skin color or appearance. Therefore, the focus of the next section will be on selected shared cultural values and how they affect Latinx/a/o participation in higher education.

LATINX/A/O CULTURAL VALUES AND PARTICIPATION IN HIGHER EDUCATION

Latinx/a/os in higher education experience challenges that are compounded by the interchange between gender, race, and ethnic identity and the cultural values that these individuals bring as part of their identities. Although Latinx/a/os are heavily recruited and can bring unique gifts to college campuses, they face many challenges, depending on the type of institution they attend. Latinx/a/os are accustomed to navigating their identities in different settings and straddling multiple worlds as they consider their cultural values and the mainstream, predominantly White, environments they may encounter (Torres & Baxter Magolda, 2004). Latinx/a/os can also be negatively affected when their identities become a focus as they navigate their campuses, preventing them from fulfilling their potential for success and their desire to fully participate and reach their academic or professional goals, unless those cultural values are perceived as providing a benefit to the campus environment (Pertuz, 2017). It is possible that the same cultural values causing clashes with mainstream society and HWIs can also provide opportunities for Latinx/a/os to thrive—if they are provided with the right opportunities for engagement.

Borrowing from the field of medicine and mental health care, where health care providers seek to learn ways to more effectively serve the unique needs of Latinx/a/os, scholars have reviewed Latinx/a/o cultural values and provided strategies that higher education practitioners can use to be responsive and to better engage Latinx/a/o students and professionals (Antshel, 2002; Bean, Perry & Bedell, 2001; Flores, 2000). Antshel (2002) discussed how medical professionals can encourage higher levels of treatment adherence in patients and acknowledged how being familiar with Latino cultural values "will be an important facet of medical training and clinical service, particularly as it pertains to treatment adherence" (p. 437). For example, with regard to pediatric care, Antshel (2002) recognized how strongly Latinos value family and respect for elders in their decision making. Thus, allowing family members to be part of the conversations regarding treatment plans may increase the chances that treatment recommendations will be followed by the pediatric patient.

Leaders in higher education can learn to be sensitive to the cultural influences that inform the way that Latinx/a/o students and professionals navigate campuses where they may be underrepresented. The following sections highlight some selected Latinx/a/o cultural values, challenges, and opportunities for students and professionals in higher education. While there are many commonly shared values in Latinx culture, the following will be discussed: collectivism and *familismo,* hierarchy and *respeto,* and traditional gender roles.

Cultural Value: Collectivism and *Familismo*

Collectivism in Latinx/a/o culture is when individuals favor the goals of the cultural group with whom they feel a strong connection over their own personal goals (Triandis, Bontempo, Villareal, Asai, & Lucca, 1988). Sáenz & Ponjuán (2009) described *familismo* as "the strong identification and attachment to immediate and extended family" (p. 62). The value of *familismo* among Latinx/a/o families serves to define gender roles and expectations for family members, and it is the idea of sacrificing the needs of the individual for the needs of the family (Sáenz & Ponjuán, 2009). *Familismo* means that loyalty to the family is expected, which influences how Latinx/a/os involve their families in their decision making, how they are emotionally tied to their families, and how they support their families physically (e.g., by assisting with household chores) and financially (e.g., by working jobs to contribute to household expenses) (Lendof, 2013; Sáenz & Ponjuán, 2009). *Family* is considered to include the nuclear family, extended family, and nonfamily members such as godparents, and members typically rely on one another for emotional, financial, and practical support (Sáenz & Ponjuán, 2009).

Decision making happens as a family; individualism, a basic value in higher education and in American society, is a foreign concept. Along with regard and value of family, *familismo* also symbolizes a familiarity with others and a closeness that is expected from colleagues and friends who are studying and working together in a higher education setting. Therefore, Latinx/a/o students and professionals may focus on relationships rather than the task orientation that is valued in higher education. Together, these traits form a preference for positive and friendly interactions, even among strangers. Therefore, it can be off-putting for Latinx/a/os who attend college for the first time, as they may find that the environment is colder and less friendly than what they are accustomed to in their familiar environments.

Opportunities for students. Latinx/a/o students who are accustomed to the cultural values of *familismo* and collectivism may work harder with regard to their college transitions because they are habituated to being nice to strangers and reaching out to others—something they may have been taught to do their whole lives. However, this outreach may not always be reciprocated unless they are in smaller settings with opportunities for more personal, one-on-one connections. Therefore, Latinx/a/o students would thrive in cohort-based programs in which they are making connections with other students, providing support for one another, and relying on each other to be successful. Cohort-based programs such as the Posse Program, Higher Education

Opportunity Programs, and other TRIO programs provide the *family feel* for students as they enter higher education; they bring groups of undergraduate students together to bond and build community as a group before the academic year begins.

In addition, programs that emphasize the involvement of families would greatly benefit Latinx/a/o students and would let them know that not only are they welcome at their institutions but so are their families. They would also work well in groups with goals centered on a strong organizational mission and the good of the collective (fraternity and sorority life, cultural and affinity clubs, etc.). Finally, cultural centers on campus can serve as places where Latinx/a/os can gather and support each other and where they can contribute and share their culture with other stakeholders.

Opportunities for professionals. Latinx/a/o professionals who embrace the cultural value of *familismo* become great coworkers who value their relationships with students and their colleagues. Latinx/a/o professionals thrive in student affairs, where collective thinking is appreciated. Joining professional associations would come naturally, so support for professional development should be provided. Family programs offices would be a great place for Latinx/a/o professionals to work because they already feel a deep connection to the importance of families. Latinx/a/o professionals don't consider involved parents "helicopter" parents—a perception that can sometimes negatively affect interactions with families and the well-being of college students' mental health (Schiffrin et al., 2014). Rather, Latinx/a/o professionals would value family partnerships and contributions to campus life and to the success of students. Latinx/a/o professionals also serve as natural mentors to Latinx/a/o students by virtue of their value to reach out and build community with fellow Latinx/a/os, including students and other Latinx/a/o professionals.

Cultural Value: Hierarchy and *Respeto*

Hierarchy and *respeto* (respect) is the aspect of Latinx/a/o culture that includes a deference to authority figures and an appreciation for older generations that demands respect for elders. For example, the ideas of authority and status are built into the Spanish language with variations of the pronoun *you* that changes according to the level of respect being shown: *Usted* is used to address elders or someone in a position of authority, and *Tú* is used to address someone who is considered an equal or peer. Another example of showing *respeto* is the custom of asking for a *bendición* (blessing) when encountering an elder (Smokowski, Rose, & Bacallao, 2008). Latinx/a/os are often raised in households where they must be conscious of age and seniority in order to know what language to use and the kind of deference they need to demonstrate.

Opportunities for students. Mentoring programs would work well for Latinx/a/o students, as they respect the experience of elders and would appreciate having a peer who is at a more advanced level of education who can offer advice on navigating the campus and course-work successfully. Loyalty is an asset to be explored as students become alumni; they may tend to stay connected to their alma maters years after they graduate. Finally, Latinx/a/o students would work well in student government structures where seniority and earning respect can be of great value in order to maintain order and civility.

Opportunities for professionals. Latinx/a/o professionals who value *respeto* are loyal to teams and organizations and thrive in areas of compliance or conduct where they need to hold others account-able. Respect for authority is also helpful for professionals who work with state and federal legislatures and other governing agencies where positional hierarchies are the norm. Latinx/a/o professionals would also thrive in union environments, as their understanding of hierarchy and seniority would help them value the connection to benefits and regular operations.

Cultural Value: Traditional Gender Roles

The concepts of hypermasculinity and hyperfemininity play out heavily in the Latinx/a/o community due to gender roles that have been passed down from generation to generation; however, gender roles have evolved, and they are influenced by immigration to the United States. Perspectives and roles often need to shift with the change in settings and family dynamics (Gil & Vazquez, 1996; Lendof, 2013; Liou, Antrop-Gonzalez, & Cooper, 2009). Ideas about traditional roles that are strictly male and strictly female can influence views about sexual identity and gender expression. The two terms often connected with the gendered roles of men and women are *machismo* and *marianismo*, respectively.

Machismo. *Machismo* is the respect, pride, honor, and sense of responsibility men have as the providers and protectors of the family (Garrison, Roy, & Azar, 1999; Guzmán & Carrasco, 2011). And though it is noble in its basic description, there is a negative connection to the idea of being *machista* (a male chauvinist). The term *machista* is often mistaken for *machismo*, and being labeled as *machista* comes with a cultural belief that endorses the negative treatment of women, often in the form of verbal and physical abuse (Comas-Diaz, 2001; Guzmán & Carrasco, 2011). The prescribed masculinity that is connected with the role of the male in Latinx/a/o families can present challenges in terms of accepting and understanding lesbian, gay, bisexual, and transgender individuals.

Marianismo. *Marianismo* is a way of framing the gendered expectations of Latinas to be the subordinate to men and to be virtuous and chaste while serving as the spiritual and subdued pillar in the family

(Nuñez, et al., 2016; Piña-Watson, Lorenzo-Blanco, Dornhecker, Martinez, & Nagoshi, 2016). Women in the United States have been fighting for equality since the suffrage movement, when women demanded the right to vote. The 1960s and 1970s were another major time when women sought additional access, including to higher education. Latinas were caught up in this bicultural inner and outer struggle with identities and continue to struggle with these issues. This is when concepts of femininity and masculinity clash. As a result, Latinas can have markedly distinct experiences in higher education than their Latino peers (Bonilla-Rodriguez, 2011).

In addition to dealing with perceptions from others, Latinas must also grapple with their self-concept and evolving identity—and the relevant cultural implications. To date, however, identity development specific to Latinas has surfaced in literature mostly related to undergraduate student experiences. An opportunity exists to explore gender identity and Latina experience in higher education more deeply. Ferdman and Gallegos (2001) explained that gender, ethnicity, and racial identity for Latinas is complex. Often, Latinas have a difficult time distinguishing which parts of their identity are being targeted in a negative experience. For example, the authors also found that "within the family structure and in society at large, Latinas are seen as representing both women and Latinos rather than one or the other" (Ferdman & Gallegos, 2001, p. 36). The confusion and uncertainty augment self-doubt in Latinas in a variety of situations and can make them sensitive to the perceptions and expectations of others (Ferdman & Gallegos, 2001).

Opportunities for students. Because Latinx/a/os often live in households where gender roles were emphasized, Latinx/a/o students can share nuanced understandings of gender roles and can provide examples of critical thinking with regard to shifting norms. Title IX (1972) legislation regulating gender equity can liberate Latinas and provide them with new perspectives on gender roles that can be instrumental in their campus participation. Latinx/a/o students, therefore, would contribute sophisticated views on gender when they are participating in student organizations and classroom discussions and as they take on leadership positions on campus.

Opportunities for professionals. Latinx/a/o professionals may be challenged by traditional gender roles, but with Title IX (1972) legislation regulating gender equity in higher education, Latinas can place their own successes and leadership in perspective and can serve as role models who affirm that gender roles do not need to be conformed to and that patriarchy does not have to be perpetuated. The perspective of Latinx/a/o professionals may be particularly helpful around Title IX work, as they may have a deeper understanding and empathy for the experiences of survivors of relationship violence, resulting from their exposure to complex gender dynamics, power, and control within their Latinx/a/o communities.

CONCLUSION

It is administrators who determine how the mission of the institution is carried out and thus influence how inclusive the environment can feel for many groups of people. (Torres, Howard-Hamilton, & Cooper, 2003, p. 82)

Although the Latinx/a/o identity may be complex and varied, there are ways to promote a shared understanding by engaging common Latinx/a/o cultural values as a way to create more inclusive campus environments in which Latinx/a/o students and professionals can thrive. This chapter provides a snapshot of a few cultural values that are common in some Latinx/a/o cultures and discusses how these values can provide opportunities for students and professionals. An understanding of Latinx/a/o cultural values will assist leadership in higher education; such insight about the challenges that Latinx/a/os may encounter in higher education environments can help leaders to minimize these challenges and to create environments where Latinx/a/os can succeed.

REFERENCES

Aldaco, R. (2010). *Latinas attainment of higher education: What factors contribute to their success?* Retrieved from ProQuest database. (Order No. 1486395)

Antshel, K. M. (2002). Integrating culture as a means of improving treatment adherence in the Latino population. *Psychology, Health and Medicine, 7*(4), 435–449.

Arredondo, P, & Castellanos, J. (2003). Latinas and the professoriate. In J. Castellanos & L. Jones (Eds.), *The majority in the minority: Expanding the representation of Latina/o faculty, administrators and students in higher education* (pp. 167–175). Sterling, VA: Stylus.

Bean, R. A., Perry, B. J., & Bedell, T. M. (2001). Developing culturally competent marriage and family therapists: Guidelines for working with Hispanic families. *Journal of Marital and Family Therapy, 27*(1), 43–54. doi:10.1111/j.1752-0606.2001.tb01138.x

Bonilla-Rodriguez, D. M. (2011). *A profile of Latina leadership in the United States: Characteristics, positive influences, and barriers* (Doctoral dissertation). Retrieved from ProQuest database. (Accession No. 3619372)

Cammarota, J. (2006). Disappearing in the Houdini education: The experience of race and invisibility among Latina/o students. *Multicultural Education, 14*(1), 2–10.

Canul, K. (2003). Latina/o cultural values and the academy: Latinas navigating through the administrative role. In J. Castellanos & L. Jones (Eds.), *The majority in the minority: Expanding the representation of Latina/o faculty, administrators and students in higher education* (pp. 167–175). Sterling, VA: Stylus.

Castellanos, J., & Jones, L. (2003). *The majority in the minority: Expanding representation of Latina/o faculty, administrators and students in higher education.* Sterling, VA: Stylus.

Comas-Diaz, L. (2001). Hispanics, Latinos, or Americanos: The evolution of identity. *Cultural Diversity and Ethnic Minority Psychology, 7*(2), 115.

Crenshaw, K. (1991). Mapping the margins: Intersectionality, identity politics, and the violence against women of color. *Stanford Law Review, 43*, 1241–1299.

Ennis, S. R., Ríos-Vargas, M., & Albert, N. G. (2011). The U.S. Hispanic population: 2010. Retrieved from https://www.census.gov/prod/cen2010/briefs/c2010br-04.pdf

Ferdman, B. M., & Gallegos, P. I. (2001). Racial identity development and Latinos in the United States. In C. L. Wijeyesinghe & B. W. Jackson, III (Eds.), *New perspectives on racial identity development: A theoretical and practical anthology* (pp. 32–66). New York, NY: NYU Press.

Flores, G. (2000). Culture and the patient-physician relationship: achieving cultural competency in health care. *The Journal of Pediatrics, 136*(1), 14–23.

Fry, R. (2002). *Latinos in higher education: Many enroll, too few graduate.* Washington, DC: Pew Hispanic Center.

Fry, R. (2011). Hispanic college enrollment spikes, narrowing gaps with other groups. Retrieved from http://www.pewhispanic.org/files/2011/08/146.pdf

Garrison, E. G., Roy, I. S., & Azar, V. (1999). Responding to the mental health needs of Latino children and families through school-based services. *Clinical psychology review, 19*(2), 199–219.

Gil, R. M., & Vazquez C. I. (1996) *The Maria paradox: How Latinas can merge old world traditions with new world self-esteem.* New York, NY: G. P. Putnam's Sons.

Gloria, A. M., & Castellanos, J. (2003). Latino/a and African American students at predominantly white institutions: A psychosociocultural perspective of cultural congruity, campus climate, and academic persistence. In J. Castellanos & L. Jones (Eds.), *The majority in the minority: Expanding the representation of Latina/o faculty, administrators and students in higher education* (pp. 71–94). Sterling, VA: Stylus

Guzmán, M. R., & Carrasco, N. (2011). Counseling and diversity: Counseling Latino/a Americans. Belmont, CA: Brooks/Cole

Haro, R., & Lara, J. F. (2003). Latinos and administrative positions in American higher education. In J. Castellanos & L. Jones (Eds.), *The majority in the minority: Expanding the representation of Latina/o faculty, administrators and students in higher education,* (pp. 153–165). Sterling, VA: Stylus.

Hernández, T. K. (2003). 'Too black to be Latino/a:' Blackness and blacks as foreigners in Latino studies. *Latino Studies, 1*(1), 152–159.

Huber, L. P. (2010). Using Latina/o critical race theory (LatCrit) and racist nativism to explore intersectionality in the educational experiences of undocumented Chicana college students. *The Journal of Educational Foundations, 24*(1/2), 77.

Johnston-Guerrero, M. P. (2016). Embracing the messiness: Critical and diverse perspectives on racial and ethnic identity development. In E. S. Abes (Ed.), *Special issue: Critical perspectives on student development theory* (New Directions for Student Services, No. 154 pp. 43–55). San Francisco, CA: Jossey-Bass.

Kena, G., Hussar W., McFarland J., de Brey C., Musu-Gillette, L., Wang, X., Zhang, J., Rathbun, A., Wilkinson-Flicker, S., Diliberti, M., Barmer, A., Bullock Mann, F., & Dunlop Velez, E. (2016). The condition of education 2016 (NCES 2016-144). Washington, DC: U.S. Department of Education, National Center for Education Statistics.

Lendof, D. M. (2013). *University administrators, Latina/o students and Latina/o parents: Perceptions of parental involvement in higher education and the impact on the student college experience* (Doctoral dissertation). Retrieved from ProQuest database. (Accession No. 3557569)

Leon, D. J., & Nevarez, C. (2007). Models of leadership institutes for increasing the number of top Latino administrators in higher education. *Journal of Hispanic Higher Education, 6*(4), 356–377.

Liou, D. D., Antrop-Gonzalez, R., & Cooper, R. (2009). Unveiling the promise of community cultural wealth to sustaining Latina/o students' college-going information networks. *Educational Studies, 45*(6), 534–555.

MacDonald, V. M., & Garcia, T. (2003). Historical perspectives on Latino access to higher education: 1848–1990. In J. Castellanos & L. Jones (Eds.), *The majority in the minority: Expanding the representation of Latina/o faculty, administrators and students in higher education* (pp. 15–46). Sterling, VA: Stylus.

Martin, I. R. (2010). *Insights into the complexities of identity in persisting Latina college students* (Doctoral dissertation). Retrieved from ProQuest database. (Accession No. 250907514)

Montelongo, R., & Ortiz, D. (2001). Comprehending cultural factors that impact success: Emerging views of the Latina/o experience at predominantly white institutions. Paper presented at the meeting of People of Color in Predominantly White Institutions, Lincoln, NE.

Morphew, C. C., & Hartley, M. (2006). Mission statements: A thematic analysis of rhetoric across international type. *The Journal of Higher Education, 77*(3), 456–471. doi:10.1353/jhe.2006.0018

Nuñez, A., González, P., Talavera, G. A., Sanchez-Johnsen, L., Roesch, S. C., Davis, S. M., & Penedo, F. J. (2016). Machismo, marianismo, and negative cognitive-emotional factors: Findings from the Hispanic Community Health Study/Study of Latinos Sociocultural Ancillary Study. *Journal of Latina/o Psychology, 4*(4), 202.

Pertuz, S. B. (2017). *The chosen tokens: Exploring the work experiences and career aspirations of Latina midlevel student affairs administrators in higher education* (Doctoral dissertation). Retrieved from http://scholarship.shu.edu/dissertations/2276

Piña-Watson, B., Lorenzo-Blanco, E. I., Dornhecker, M., Martinez, A. J., & Nagoshi, J. L. (2016). Moving away from a cultural deficit to a holistic perspective: Traditional gender role values, academic attitudes, and educational goals for Mexican descent adolescents. *Journal of Counseling Psychology, 63*(3), 307–318. doi:10.1037/cou0000133

Rudolph, B., Chavez, M., Quintana, F., & Salinas, G. (2011). Filial responsibility expectations among Mexican American undergraduates: Gender and biculturalism. *Journal of Hispanic Higher Education, 10*(3), 168–182.

Rodriguez, R. (2002). *Brown: The last discovery of America.* New York, NY: Viking.

Sáenz, V. B., & Ponjuán, L. (2009). The vanishing Latino male in higher education. *Journal of Hispanic Higher Education, 8*(1), 54–89.

Schiffrin, H. H., Liss, M., Miles-McLean, H., Geary, K. A., Erchull, M. J., & Tashner, T. (2014). Helping or hovering? The effects of helicopter parenting on college students' well-being. *Journal of Child and Family Studies, 23*(3), 548–557.

Smith, W. A., Yosso, T. J., & Solorzano, D. G. (2007). Racial primes and black misandry on historically white campuses: Toward critical race accountability in educational administration. *Educational Administration Quarterly, 43*(5), 559–585.

Smokowski, P. R., Rose, R., & Bacallao, M. L. (2008). Acculturation and Latino family processes: How cultural involvement, biculturalism, and acculturation gaps influence family dynamics. *Family Relations, 57*(3), 295–308.

Suro, R. (2005). *Hispanics: A people in motion.* Washington, DC: Pew Research Center.

Tatum, B. (1997). *Why are all the Black kids sitting together in the cafeteria? And other conversation about race.* New York, NY: Basic Books.

Title IX of the Education Amendments of 1972, 20 U.S.C. §§ 1681–1688 (1972).

Torres, V. (2004). The diversity among us: Puerto Ricans, Cuban Americans, Caribbean Americans, and Central and South Americans. In A. M. Ortiz (Ed.), *Special issue: Addressing the unique needs of Latino American Students* (New Directions for Student Services, No. 105, pp. 5–16). San Francisco, CA: Jossey-Bass.

Torres, V., & Baxter Magolda, M. B. (2004). Reconstructing Latino identity: The influence of cognitive development on the ethnic identity process of Latino students. *Journal of College Student Development, 45*(3), 333–347.

Torres, V., Howard-Hamilton, M. F., & Cooper, D. L. (2003). *Identity development of diverse populations: Implications for teaching and administration in higher education* (ASHE Higher Education Report, Vol. 29, No. 6). San Francisco, CA: Jossey-Bass.

Torres-Saillant, S. (2003). Inventing the race: Latinos and the ethnoracial pentagon. *Latino Studies, 1*(1), 123–151.

Triandis, H. C., Bontempo, R., Villareal, M. J., Asai, M., & Lucca, N. (1988). Individualism and collectivism: Cross-cultural perspectives on self-ingroup relationships. *Journal of Personality and Social Psychology, 54*(2), 323–338. doi:10.1037/0022-3514.54.2.323

Trucios-Haynes, E. (2001). Why "race matters": LatCrit theory and Latina/o racial identity. *La Raza Law Journal, 12*(1), 1–42.

U.S. Census Bureau. (1961). *Census of population: 1960.* Washington, DC: U.S. Government Printing Office.

Wijeyesinghe, C. L., & Jones, S. R. (2014). Intersectionality, identity, and systems of power and inequity. In D. Mitchell, Jr. (Ed.), *Intersectionality and higher education: Theory, research, and praxis* (pp. 9–19). New York, NY: Peter Lang.

CHAPTER 5

GENDER AND SEXUAL IDENTITY IN THE LATINX/A/O COMMUNITY

Brianna Carmen Sérráno

I
t is estimated that more than 1.4 million people in the United States identify as transgender and more than 8 million identify as lesbian, gay, bisexual, transgender, queer, intersex, and asexual (LGBTQIA; Flores, Herman, Gates, & Brown, 2016; Gates, 2011). Of the more than 1.4 million Latinx/a/o adults in the United States who identify as LGBTQIA, 29% have children (Kastanis & Gates, 2013).

Although the exploration of gender expression, gender identity, and sexual identity has been limited within the Latinx/a/o community in higher education, student affairs professionals are serving more LGBTQIA students within communities of color every day, and their challenges are heightened in the current national and global climate.

The research about Latinx/a/o LGBTQIA students in higher education is limited mostly to a deficit model—in other words, there exists research that is intersectional, but much of the research on Latinx/a/os does not include intersectional identities. This chapter will address why higher education professionals and students should be aware of the issues facing LGBTQIA Latinx/a/os in higher education, which is a population that will continue to grow.

The chapter will also examine social constructs of masculinity, femininity, the term *Latinx*, and challenges facing LGBTQIA Latinx/a/os in higher education, and will offer recommendations on how to support this population of students. While some may believe that the campus climate is becoming more positive for LGBTQIA people, new research shows disparities within the LGBTQIA community, which will also be discussed. The chapter will discuss masculinity and femininity's influence of gender expression to campus climate, and it will explore the meanings of and effects of masculinity and femininity—especially on the impact of an individual's gender expression—including the popularity and concept of the term *Latinx*. Additionally, studies on campus climate in higher education provide insight about the discrimination LGBTQIA people and specifically Latinx individuals, face on a consistent basis (Harrison-Quintana, Pérez, & Grant, 2011; Rankin, Weber, Blumenfeld, & Frazer, 2010). In response, this chapter will present future considerations and provide recommendations to support LGBTQIA Latinx/a/os students and professionals, including advocating for new legislation.

As a Latinx, nonbinary, queer person who is neurodiverse and a first-generation student in higher education, I found that I lacked resources in navigating higher education and discovering my own identity. During my time at California State University, Fullerton, from 2007 to 2011, the university did not have an LGBTQIA resource center and/or staff professional. Knowing the vocabulary within the LGBTQIA community and being aware of multiple identities could have helped me to come out, manage, and understand my own identities more positively. I did not come out publicly until graduate school, at 23 years old, once I had fully understood what my identities were. Campus resources are necessary for students to be able to develop and manage their lives.

To better serve Latinx students, higher education professionals and faculty should better understand the experiences and challenges for LGBTQIA Latinx/a/os, especially as so-called Generation Z will be entering higher education within the next decade. According to one survey, more than half of Generation Z in the United States does not identify as exclusively straight (Greene, 2015). Generation Z represents youth who are 13 to 20 years old in 2017; that is, the generation after the millennials. The survey also showed that more than 56% of people in Generation Z know someone who uses the pronouns *they*, *them*, and *theirs* in the singular sense. According to the Pew Research Center (Krogstad, 2016), Latino college enrollment increased from 22% in 1993 to 35% in 2014. The high school dropout rate of Latinos has decreased, with the rate in 1993 at 33% and only 12% in 2014. With the combination of LGBTQIA Generation Z students entering higher education and the amount of Latinx/a/os already there, there is an added need for competent higher education professionals who understand their experiences. It is important to be aware of trends in generations—in terms of both identity and cultural implications—as Latinx/a/os enter higher education.

LATINX

One way to begin to increase awareness is by exploring the complexities surrounding the recently popular term *Latinx*. The word has gained popularity over the past few years and continues to be increasingly used throughout higher education; some institutions, such as Princeton, have written guides on how to use and understand the term *Latinx* (Cuervo, 2016). *Latinx* has been used most often to describe someone who does not identify within the social norms and/or binary of the descriptors *Latino/Latina* offered by the Spanish language (Cuervo, 2016). *Latinx* is a more inclusive term for people who do not identify within the binary and/or who are LGBTQIA and of Latin descent; however, there has been some pushback to using the term and complaints of "imperializing language," a sentiment related to the colonization of indigenous cultures by the Spanish. Further, more and more members of the community are opting to use the term more generally, as a way to replace the label of *Latino/a*. These factors have led to the use of the term becoming a topic of much discussion within and outside of the Latinx/a/o community, even gaining online and national attention (Google Trends, 2017).

In January 2016, National Public Radio featured a special to explore the word and its origin (Padilla, 2016). The special described how in 2006, the then-new and popular term *Latin@* was created in a first attempt to expand inclusivity when referring to multiple genders within the Latinx/a/o community. At the time, the use of *Latin@* also stirred debate, as some felt that the term was contaminating the language's preference to assign feminine or masculine forms and that it was challenging for people to pronounce.

The current argument was outlined in an op-ed from Swarthmore College's *The Phoenix* titled "The Argument Against the Use of the Term 'Latinx'" (Guerra & Orbea, 2015). The authors expressed the opinion that *Latinx* is a buzzword that may not stick permanently. They described the evolution of the Spanish language that millions of people use today as a result of linguistic imperialism. They argue that the term *Latinx* is a result of the United States' attempt to make the

Spanish language more "American" because the language does not match the hegemonic culture in the United States. Guerra and Orbea (2015) shared that the term is popular only in the United States and that using it is reverse appropriation. They discussed challenges in making the Spanish language gender-inclusive, such as pronunciation (Latinx, amigx, etc.). They further argued that these gender-inclusive terms may not be accessible to people who are not experienced in higher education in the United States and that the *Latinx* term may not apply outside of the United States, which can cause erasure of the Spanish language by degendering the language.

The debate over *Latinx* has also reached affinity membership organizations in higher education. In 2016, the NASPA–Student Affairs Administrators in Higher Education Latino/a Knowledge Community (LKC) conducted a survey of LKC members and non-members to explore potentially revising the group's name to include the new *Latinx* term. The LKC officially changed its name to the Latinx/a/o Knowledge Community in March 2017. However, results from the survey revealed that within the LKC, there was a lack of clarity and even discontent about changing the name of the group. The survey results showed that 56% of the 313 respondents strongly supported the term *Latinx* (Rodriguez, Cabello, Mata, & Naphan, 2016). Members who were between 18 and 25 years old expressed significantly higher levels of support, compared with members from other age groups. Respondents who were 41 to 50 years old were significantly less supportive of the change. These results seem to suggest that there are generational differences among members and perhaps a lack of familiarity with or understanding of the term. Participants who had not supported the term made such comments as, "Terms are always changing" and "The word *Latino* is already gender-neutral." They also touched on the idea that it is "'Anglo-cizing' the Spanish language because [*Latinx*] originated in the U.S." Supporters said that *Latinx* "removes the risk of mis-gendering others." They felt that "the term is pronounceable," and "it's [their] chance as student affairs professionals to be more inclusive for students and professionals." The differences in answers to the LKC survey illustrate an ongoing debate and the differences within the Latinx/a/o community itself. These differences extend to institutions of higher education, as demographics and political changes in our society continue to evolve. However, as long as Spanish continues to be a gendered language, the binary assignation of masculinity and femininity will also continue to be pervasive.

FEMININITY AND MASCULINITY

In my *Chicanx* (gender-inclusive term for Chicano/a) culture, I struggled with the concept of femininity and masculinity as an adolescent—and I still do as a nonbinary adult. Because I was assigned a female gender at birth, I was socialized to wear dresses, have long hair, sit with my legs crossed, play with certain toys, and communicate differently than my peers who were assigned male at birth. I can now recognize how I internalized my socialization; occasionally, I still experience internalized femme-phobia (*femme* meaning feminine expression) and must manage the way I have privilege and/or take up space in social contexts with masculine-of-center—that is, presenting more masculine (versus feminine) in my gender expression—especially when around those who present as femme.

The concept of gender identity is, therefore, a social construct, and our society often defines the ways in which we communicate with each other through physical appearance. My early socialization and the inherent gendering within the Spanish language also influenced my struggle to express my sense of masculinity and femininity. According to Bradley (2013), as a social construct, the application of the term *gender expression* as an identifier can inherently result in a gendered hierarchy that applies to those who present as more masculine, androgynous, or feminine. Regardless of gender identity, gender expression (makeup, clothing, mannerisms) can be attributed to all people and has specific implications for women of color (Pyke & Johnson, 2003). The gendered hierarchy results from assigned expectations around what binary people should look like or how they should express themselves, and these expectations are culturally tied to gender expression. As a result of how people are culturally gendered within the Latinx/a/os community in the United States, they often learn to change their gender expression depending on the social context, generational identity, and level of acculturation.

LATINX/A/O SEXUAL AND GENDER IDENTITY

While there are many common experiences for Latinx/a/os as a cultural group, research shows that the experiences of LGBTQIA Latinx/a/os in higher education are different, especially when compared to those of their White counterparts. As Garcia (1998) noted, LGBTQIA Latinx/a/os face challenges stemming from racism, heteronormativity of looking straight, cisnormativity of conforming to expectations as a cisgender person, and homophobia within the larger society, and they must manage these challenges on a daily basis. As a result of feeling disconnected, in terms of LGBTQIA and other intersecting identities, Garcia further argued, some students feel the need to choose between the LGBTQIA center, the Latinx/a/o center, and other clubs altogether; for many students, this choice is made more difficult by the limitations of what is offered in programming that is inclusive of intersectionality. Boehmer (2002) found that 85% of research on LGBTQIA issues had not explored the intersectionality of race for study participants, showing that the research has not supported LGBTQ+ people of color.

Nevertheless, it is also true that many LGBTQIA Latinx/a/os do not feel a sense of inclusion in terms of the LGBTQIA movement in the United States. According to Anzaldúa & Keating (2009) and Kumashiro (2001), people of color view the gay movement as something that's "White" and that gayness is a "White disease" and does not belong in their communities. Gay Latino men, for example, are often seen as conforming or giving into Whiteness, according to Sánchez (2015). The author further noted that the use of the word *gay* is commonly used to describe White, upper-middle-class gay men and does not embody the identity of gay Latino men. In response, for example, when writing about Chicano LGBTQIA people, Anzaldúa (2009) argued for a reclamation of words in the Spanish language in an effort to be more inclusive, because common words like *lesbian*, *gay*, *bisexual*, and *queer* are not generally affiliated with the history of Chicano people.

Identity Development

In response to Latinx LGBTQIA individuals not feeling included, Morales (1983, 1989) developed an identity model for gay Latino men that describes gay Latino men who live in Latino and predominantly White communities. This model outlines the following stages for gay and bisexual Latino men: (a) denial of conflict, (b) bisexual versus gay or lesbian, (c) conflicts in allegiances, (d) establishing priorities in allegiance, and (e) integration of communities. The model shows that gay Latino men initially may not pay attention to their queer identity because of the racial identity discrimination they experience in the denial-of-conflicts stage, where they have not reconciled their multiple identities. The second stage is arguably where gay Latino men figure out if they are gay or bisexual. The third stage, conflicts in allegiances, is where individuals experience anxiety around their perceived oppressed intersecting identities of being both gay and Latino, resulting in a potential internal conflict. During the next two stages, the individuals can experience racism within the gay community as they accept their identity as a gay Latino. However, Morales (1983, 1989) argued that due to internalized homophobia, many Latino men may not fully accept or be aware of their gay identity, and many never fully come out throughout their entire lives, especially to their families. Because the family is so incredibly important in the Latinx/a/o community, coming out as gay may be seen as a lack of loyalty and respect (Smith & Montilla, 2006). Furthermore, inherent cultural values and beliefs relating to religion, family, and differences about communal versus individual beliefs can cause Latinx/a/o gay individuals, or LGBTQIA in general, to feel unwelcome in their own families.

Coming Out in Latinx/a/o Families

Thus, as a result of these cultural factors, many Latinx/a/os may experience challenges coming out to their families and often look for support from other sources. As a queer Latinx person, I felt supported in my coming-out process through my graduate assistantship experience. There were no LGBTQIA coming-out support resources offered by my undergraduate institution, and I struggled to figure out how to safely come out to my family. Although my parents were generally supportive, they were raised Catholic, and I grew up in a traditional household. As a child, I consistently heard stereotypical and negative discourse about LGBTQIA people in society and knew that my parents regarded them as unacceptable, which made it difficult for me to share my gender identity with them. However, after acquiring new-found confidence and understanding of LGBTQIA identities in my graduate program, gaining financial independence from my parents, and finding a supportive LGBTQIA community, I decided to come out to my family. Luckily, they have been accepting and affirming of who I am; although they may not agree with someone identifying as LGBTQIA, as a *familia* they unconditionally love me.

Despite my positive experience with my own family, I have observed, both personally and professionally, how difficult it can be for many LGBTQIA individuals to come out. Ocampo's (2014) research on the experiences of Filipino and Latino gay men discussed the context in which gay Latino men consider when to come out. The respondents in his study talked about their families being ruled by *machismo,* or an exaggerated sense of masculinity, and strong Catholic beliefs, which often did not allow these gay Latino men to be fully themselves within their families. The researchers found that families see gay men as cross-dressers and/or people who act very effeminate in their mannerisms. Some of the respondents also felt that it is challenging to come out since they themselves identified as Catholic; this resulted in internal conflict in terms of their own sexual and religious identity. One of the gay men shared that his grandmother would say, "Don't talk like that— you're going to sound like a gay!" This led him to believe that there would be negative repercussions if he displayed a certain behavior that could be deemed as "gay." Some of the men also developed a network outside their families and connected with local LGBTQIA individuals but constantly feared being outed. Other respondents decided to disassociate from family altogether, as they did not have a supportive family environment.

All of the participants in Ocampo's (2014) study shared that they were out and/or were in the process of coming out to their families, but they "eased" their families into understanding LGBTQIA people through media and/or by introducing their LGBTQIA peers to their families in order to challenge stereotypes. For example, one person discussed inviting a friend over to meet his family particularly because he identified as gay and presented a more masculine gender expression. Before coming out, some participants indicated that they had read about LGBTQIA people in literature or research, consulted with other LGBTQIA people to understand different processes of coming out, or decided to come out when they were autonomous and no longer financially dependent on their family.

But even after coming out to their families, some participants continued to experience challenges with family members. Some family members did not want to share with their own children that their sibling was gay or said that they would prefer if their child were not gay but still loved them unconditionally. Other families chose to have their child share about their sexual identity but did not want to talk about it again.

Women in Latinx/a/o Culture

But while gay Latinx/o men face many challenges in the coming-out process, LGBTQIA Latinx/a women have different experiences and unique challenges, especially transgender women. For example, Acosta (2008) described how lesbian migrant women managed their sexual identity and attempted to create balance between their family, work, and personal lives by creating and joining queer Latina community networks. According to Acosta (2008), immigrant women can become a minority when immigrating to the United States since they need to assimilate to the more commonly used term of *Latino/a* rather than their specific ethnic identity (e.g., Puerto Rican, Dominican, Mexican). Acosta (2008) found that Latina LGBTQIA women preferred their own Latina LGBTQIA groups, as they felt largely excluded in predominantly White LGBTQIA groups. Many of the women reported that their families were not accepting of their identity as lesbians, and others had not disclosed their sexual identity to their families because they did not want to disrespect or disappoint them. However, Acosta (2008) also acknowledged that the study sample included only women who were active within the LGBTQIA community. In the sample group some women were less involved on campus and did not access resources because they feared disclosing their undocumented status.

Transgender Issues and the Latinx Community

While Latinx/a/os must overcome many challenges, the reality is even direr for transgender individuals. The National Center for Transgender Equality has published studies on the experiences of transgender people in the United States, specifically Latinx/a/os. According to the center's findings, non-U.S. citizen Latinx/a/o transgender individuals experienced the highest rates of abuse and violence, and 28% of Latinx/a/os who are transgender lived on $10,000 or less per year (Harrison-Quintana et al., 2011). The rate of suicide attempts is 47% for transgender Latinx/a/os, 77% of those who are students have experienced harassment, and 21% reported leaving school due to the severity of the harassment (Harrison-Quintana et al., 2011).

A study of Latinx/a/os in Southern California completed by Caraves & Salcedo (2016) included 129 self-identified transgender Latinx/a/os and was conducted through a community-based participatory research project. Among the major findings were that 18.8% of participants reported being homeless or living in short-term housing and that 80.0% did not have full-time employment. The state of health for the participants was concerning in that 49.5% of participants were dependent on government-issued insurance, such as Medi-Cal, to cover their health care needs; at the time of the study, 50.5% were experiencing consistent anxiety, with 26.4% of the participants experiencing depression as well. The study found that 57.4% of participants earned an income of less than $10,000 per year, and 20.9% earned between $10,000 and

$19,999 per year. Additionally, 25.6% of survey respondents were unemployed and looking for work, and 12.8% were receiving disability benefits from the government (Caraves & Salcedo, 2016). In higher education settings, challenges for transgender students are particularly unique and include an intersection of such concerns as racism, navigating use of preferred names and gender-inclusive facilities, and seeking health-related support.

FUTURE IMPLICATIONS AND CONSIDERATIONS FOR HIGHER EDUCATION

Higher education staff, faculty, and students in leadership roles are expected to support all students—regardless of whether they identify similarly or differently than themselves. It is critical that they recognize that as the demographics continue to shift, Latinx/a/o students are coming into higher education in greater numbers. Supporting transgender students—Latinx/a/o or not—in terms of facilities access, offering hormone replacement therapy on campus, gender-inclusive housing, preferred name policies, and gendered activities is also important. The challenges faced by transgender Latinx/a/os illustrate the need for and importance of student affairs professionals to ensure their own competency in order to best serve these students.

It is also important for educators to acknowledge the gendered language that is used in higher education and its potential impact on a student's identity development. A recent NPR special discussed how people consistently refer to gender in educational settings, such as using the terms *boys* and *girls* or *men* and *women* (Padilla, 2016). One article on child development by Leaper and Bigler (2004) explained that when gendered language is used, the imagery that is evoked is to a specific gender as it is prescribed socially. For example, the use of the word *man* to describe all people can fundamentally generate gender-biased thinking, because it ignores other gender identities (Henley, 1989; Hyde, 1984). Therefore, it is important for higher education professionals to increase awareness of this issue and be mindful to use inclusive language, including noting the gendering of words and the potential impact on the development of students.

Accordingly, it is critical for higher education to recognize its responsibility and influence in terms of setting national policy and legislation. These efforts are an important component of supporting Latinx/a/o students' success in higher education. Some ways to be well informed include reviewing the May 2016 recommendations of the U.S. Department of Education and the U.S. Department of Justice (Lhamon & Gupta, 2016). This report includes suggestions for addressing the different types of discrimination that violate Title IX (1972), increasing education and awareness about the challenges faced by students, and understanding the impact of new legislation. Now more than ever this is crucial, given both the campus and the national climate for LGBTQIA Latinx/a/o individuals and groups.

As previously noted, Latinx/a/o people in higher education face unique challenges. It can be difficult for Latinx/a/o people to come out to their families because of religious and family issues that can lead to conflicts. The experiences of undocumented transgender and queer Latinx/a/os further complicate matters for many in the community who face poverty, lack of health care, homelessness, and lack of access to resources. It is essential that college staff, faculty, and students be inclusive of varying gender and sexual identities within the Latinx/a/o community by developing new policies, providing gender-inclusive facilities, offering transgender inclusive health care, and supporting students who may not have support from their families.

REFERENCES

Acosta, K. L. (2008). Lesbianas in the borderlands: Shifting identities and imagined communities. *Gender & Society, 22*(5), 639–659. doi:10.1177/0891243208321169

Anzaldúa, G., & Keating, A. (2009). *The Gloria Anzaldúa reader.* Durham, NC: Duke University Press.

Boehmer, U. (2002). Twenty years of public health research: Inclusion of lesbian, gay, bisexual, and transgender populations. *American Journal of Public Health, 92*(7), 1125–1130.

Bradley, Kym. (2013). *Queer! Narratives of gendered sexuality: A journey in identity* (Master's thesis). Retrieved from http://pdxscholar.library.pdx.edu/cgi/viewcontent.cgi?article=2068&context=open_access_etds

Caraves, J., & Salcedo, B. (2016). *The state of trans health: Trans Latin@s and their healthcare needs.* Los Angeles, CA: TransLatin@ Coalition.

Cuervo, A. B. (2016). *Latinx: A brief handbook.* Retrieved from https://www.academia.edu/29657615/Latinx_A_Brief_Guidebook

Flores, A. R., Herman, J. L., Gates, G. J., & Brown, T. N. T. (2016). *How many adults identify as transgender in the united states?* Los Angeles, CA: The Williams Institute.

Garcia, B. (1998). *The development of a Latino gay identity.* New York, NY: Garland.

Gates, G. J. (2011). *How many people are lesbian, gay, bisexual, and transgender?* Los Angeles, CA: The Williams Institute.

Google Trends. (2017). Retrieved from https://www.google.com/trends/explore?q=latinx

Greene, L. (2015). Generation Z [PowerPoint slides]. Retrieved from http://www.slideshare.net/jwtintelligence/jwt-generation-z-48070734

Guerra, G., & Orbea, G. (2015, November 19). *The argument against the use of the term "Latinx."* Retrieved from http://swarthmorephoenix.com/2015/11/19/the-argument-against-the-use-of-the-term-latinx

Harrison-Quintana, J., Pérez, D., & Grant, J. (2011). *Injustice at every turn: A look at the Latino/a respondents in the National Transgender Discrimination Survey.* Retrieved from http://www.transequality.org/sites/default/files/docs/resources/ntds_black_respondents_2.pdf

Henley, N. M. (1989). Molehill or mountain? What we know and don't know about sex bias in language. In M. Crawford & M. Gentry (Eds.), *Gender and thought: Psychological perspectives* (pp. 59–78). New York, NY: Springer-Verlag.

Hyde, J. S. (1984). Children's understanding of sexist language. *Developmental Psychology, 20,* 697–706.

Kastanis, A., & Gates, G. J. (2013). *LGBT Latino/a individuals and Latino/a same-sex couples.* Retrieved from the Williams Institute website: http://williamsinstitute.law.ucla.edu/wp-content/uploads/Census-2010-Latino-Final.pdf

Kumashiro, K. K. (2001). *Troubling intersections of race and sexuality: Queer students of color and anti-oppressive education.* Lanham, MD: Rowman & Littlefield.

Krogstad, J. M. (2016, July 28). 5 facts about Latinos and education. *Pew Research Center Fact Tank.* Retrieved from http://www.pewresearch.org/fact-tank/2016/07/28/5-facts-about-latinos-and-education

Leaper, C., & Bigler, R. S. (2004). Gendered language and sexist thought. *Monographs of the Society for Research in Child Development, 69*(1), 128–142. doi:10.1111/j.0037-976X.2004.00283.x

Lhamon, C. E., & Gupta, V. (2016). *Dear colleague letter on transgender students.* Retrieved from https://www2.ed.gov/about/offices/list/ocr/letters/colleague-201605-title-ix-transgender.pdf

Morales, E. S. (1983). Third world gays and lesbians: A process of multiple identities. Paper presented at the 91st Convention of the American Psychological Association, Anaheim, California.

Morales, E. S. (1989). Ethnic minority families and minority gays and lesbians. *Marriage and Family Review, 14*(3–4), 217–239.

Ocampo, A. C. (2014). The gay second generation: Sexual identity and family relations of Filipino and Latino gay men. *Journal of Ethnic and Migration Studies, 40*(1), 155–173. doi: 10.1080/1369183X.2013.849567

Padilla, Y. (2016). *What does "Latinx" mean? A look at the term that's challenging gender norms.* Retrieved from http://www.complex.com/life/2016/04/latinx/

Pyke, K. D., & Johnson, D. L. (2003). Asian American women and racialized femininities: "Doing" gender across cultural worlds. *Gender and Society, 17*(1), 33–53.

Rankin, S., Weber, G., Blumenfeld, W., & Frazer, S. (2010). *2010 state of higher education for lesbian, gay, bisexual, & transgender people.* Retrieved from https://www.campuspride.org/wp-content/uploads/campuspride2010lgbtreportssummary.pdf

Rodriguez, S., Cabello, C., Mata, S., & Naphan, D. (2016). [NASPA and the Latino/a Knowledge Community's inclusion of diverse identities and expressions]. Unpublished raw data.

Sánchez, V. A. (2015). "Latino gay men and their relationship to the gay movement, Latino communities, and higher education," *The Vermont Connection, 35,* 106–112. Retrieved from http://scholarworks.uvm.edu/tvc/vol35/iss1/13

Smith, R. L., & Montilla, R. E. (2006). *Counseling and family therapy with Latino populations: Strategies at work.* New York, NY: Routledge.

Title IX of the Education Amendments of 1972, 20 U.S.C. §§ 1681–1688 (1972).

PART III

Developing Pathways to Latinx/a/o Student Success

A LATINA GRADUATE STUDENT'S REFLECTION ON THE IMPORTANCE OF BEING GUIDED IN HER EDUCATIONAL JOURNEY

Lorena Michelle Jirón

My mother immigrated to the United States from Nicaragua during the civil war that resulted from a 30-year-long U.S.-backed dictatorship. She met my father in Miami, married him, and then got divorced shortly after I was born. She raised me alone and is the strongest woman I have known. She did what she could to provide me with the best opportunities, but because she was new to the United States, her capacity to help me succeed was limited. However hard my mother tried, she could not guide me through my education because she did not know where to find the best schools for me nor did she have the means to help me financially. As a result, however hard I tried, I did not have the resources to fulfill my potential as a student. Although my mother's support for me was unwavering, it could only go so far. She provided the foundation for me to launch into my education but—like most recent immigrants—she did not have the know-how to show me the way.

Nevertheless, my mother did her best to provide me with opportunities from the very beginning, enrolling me in the Catholic pre-K–8 school in our neighborhood because she believed that it was the best school in town. Corpus Christi educated me well, but it was definitely not a feeder school into the Ivy League. Due to a clerical error, the principal realized I was too young to start only after my mother had bought all of my supplies. She allowed me to stay but told my mother that I would probably fail that grade. Not only did I excel, but I was the best student in my class throughout my time there—and valedictorian at graduation.

MY LIFE AT CORPUS CHRISTI

But my path through Corpus Christi was not easy. Allapattah, my Miami neighborhood, was marked by high crime rates and low-performing schools. Thus, my first educational experience also brought me closer to the culture of the neighborhood, resulting in critical challenges. As a young student at the school, I was bored and misbehaved. I fought with other kids every day, and my teachers wrote comments such as, "talks too much and distracts other students" after awarding me 10 straight A's on my report cards. As an adult, I realize that the work was too easy for me and that after finishing assignments quickly, I would find something to distract me. It is hard to understand why no one flagged this. However, my mother noticed, and during summers she enrolled me in the local public school at one grade above the one I had just finished. It was all she could do to keep me challenged and growing.

Besides dealing with boredom, I also had to figure out how to keep my smarts under wraps because I did not want to be ostracized all the time. I would hide my grades from my friends and sometimes blatantly lied about how well I had done on an exam or assignment. In our neighborhood, it was—and probably still is—not "cool" to be smart. This *needs* to change, especially for girls. Our school systems have to address this issue earlier, and educators should work with non-educators, psychologists, counselors, and young women to teach girls at a younger age about confidence and self-esteem. This is a much longer debate, another book, but it certainly affects educational outcomes for women to a great extent. For me, it was incredibly confusing to balance my social life and the need to be accepted by my peers with doing well in school—the only thing that my mother ever asked of me.

TRANSITION AND MY NEW LIFE AT CURLEY HIGH SCHOOL

Nevertheless, I continued to earn good grades and, following my time at Corpus Christi, I went to a Catholic high school in Little Haiti. The public high school in my neighborhood, Jackson High, was an "F"-rated school, and my mother refused to allow me to attend such a bad institution. Instead, she worked to pay for the tuition at nearby Archbishop Curley Notre Dame High School, despite the added financial pressure on our small family of two.

At Curley, I was the only person from my middle school who tested into all honors classes. Not only was that incredibly isolating, but the classes were also void of Latinx/a/o students; indeed, there were only White and Asian American students in my classes. I still felt a deep desire to be "cool" and to represent my middle school, so I began to act like I didn't care and to misbehave. As a result, I was sent to detention almost every day. Looking back, I think my behavior was a statement of rebellion because I was angry with the school for separating me from my peers and making me start all over socially. But I snapped out of it my sophomore year and adapted, despite still feeling like I did not belong, which had serious effects on my learning outcomes. Little did I know that this theme would mark my entire student career, even into the future.

MY CHOICE TO ATTEND THE HONORS COLLEGE AT MIAMI DADE COLLEGE

When I was about to graduate from high school, the Honors College at Miami Dade College was still a new concept, and I was part of its second or third recruitment group. When I first heard about the program, it seemed like a great deal, especially because on graduation, the school guaranteed 50% payment of tuition at the University of Miami. I considered myself a "city girl" and thought I never wanted to leave, so this seemed right. However, admitted students got their tuition paid in full, and that was the biggest attraction to the program because it meant I could earn an associate's degree at no cost to my mom. Options were very limited, and no good schools came to our college fair, which mostly was attended by only local schools and the U.S. Army. I certainly was not aware of—or discussed with anyone— the idea of attending an Ivy League school. Besides, even if I could get into the Ivy League, who would pay for it? No one had ever told me about the scholarships that might be available.

Despite my confusion and questions, I did well at the Honors College and graduated with a 3.95 GPA. Students in the program attended special honors college classes and then regular classes along with other students from the whopping 165,000 enrollees who attended Miami Dade College, the largest institution in the Florida college system. As members of the honors college, we were each assigned our own advisor; mine was Virginia Fuillerat, my first real educational mentor. Looking back, it seems Virginia and others at the Honors College intentionally worked to help the primarily Latinx/a/o student population understand the higher education system in the United States and find our place in it.

Like me, many of my peers at the honors college were children of immigrants or immigrants themselves; did really well in high school; and wanted to stay in Miami because they felt they wanted to be near family, were expected to stay, or simply were unaware of how "normal" it is to go away to college. But Virginia always encouraged me to step out of my comfort zone and to take advantage of travel scholarships that took me to France (which I did with a scholarship) and to Austria (with another scholarship), as well as to apply to schools outside of Miami. She eased me into it with the idea of looking at women's colleges because my family might be less skeptical about them, encouraging me to apply to Smith and Wellesley and then finally to Middlebury College in Vermont.

I followed Virginia's advice and was accepted by all of these schools, but my family did not react well to the news. They questioned my motivations for wanting to leave. Was it so that I could have a boyfriend? These schools were so far away. Were there no schools that I could apply to in Miami? In order to convince my family to let me go, I did research to show them how women and people of color who graduated from these schools had increased earning potential. I even made a graph to show them. Although I aimed to make my family proud for most of my life, I was also convinced at this point that going to one of these schools would be better for my educational trajectory. I still felt that boredom I had experienced as a young child at Corpus Christi, and I was not being challenged enough in Miami—a fact I felt was proven by my 3.95 GPA.

CULTURE SHOCK IN MIDDLEBURY, VERMONT

I chose Middlebury College, but my mother was not happy with the location, which made leaving home more difficult. I will always regret the way my drop-off at Middlebury panned out: she made her discontent with my choice clear, and we had an argument about it. Now that she is gone, it's one of my worst memories, and I wish I had known how to handle it better. Basically, she thought I would disappear into the darkness that was Vermont—so much nature, not enough people. She feared that I would be kidnapped and taken into the woods, missing for days, and no one would know. It was a different world to her than the urban areas of Managua and Miami that she was accustomed to. I didn't know how to defend my decision because I didn't quite know what I had done wrong.

Because my grandmother had experienced the drop-off and also lived with my mother, she knew how much my mom did not like that I was away. Years later, in 2009, my grandmother blamed me after my mother died, saying that she couldn't take the loneliness and heartache of my being away. That was a horrible thing to tell a 22-year-old, and yet I understood. I am the only grandchild who has ever left Miami—the only one out of her seven grandchildren and four children. My family has tried to understand and has been supportive, but it's also easy to see how they felt offended by my departure, even if they don't realize that it shows. Now, as an adult, I resent that I had to feel guilty for getting into one of the best schools in the country. Unfortunately, I think this is a common reality for first-generation students, this clash of cultures and lack of understanding. We want to make our families proud, but many times the way to do this goes against what our families think is right.

Regardless of all of these changes, I remained close to my family, and I was still able to find myself at Middlebury. I was finally challenged and engaged the way I wish I would have been all my life, but it was a rough transition. After my first two months there, I almost called Wellesley to implore them to take me. But then I found Shirley Collado, the current president of Ithaca College, who was Middlebury's dean of diversity at the time. Shirley became my beacon of light in the sea of homogeneity that was Middlebury. As a Latina, Shirley understood me and was able to help me talk to my mom. She counseled me out of my frustrations so often that I don't even remember the extent of all our conversations anymore. But I do remember that she was a person in a position of authority who looked like me and who understood me. She was a comfort anchor of sorts, giving me the strength to push past my limits while feeling uncomfortable at Middlebury. I—and other students—needed her as a role model and an advocate. This is an illustration of how important it is for colleges to provide such mentors to their students: Because I saw that Shirley was successful despite her background, I began to believe that I could be, too. And although I almost quit Middlebury, I now often think that I am the school's biggest fan.

After Middlebury, I taught English in the Middle East for a while, then landed back in school, this time to study law in New York City. Although I was in what many would argue is the most diverse city in the world, there is still only one Latina professor, that I know of, in the entire school and very few Latinx/a/o students. Law school was a whole new beast to tackle and brought another kind of culture shock that I wish someone could have helped me navigate better. As a recent law school graduate, I fear that until there are more Latinx/a/os reaching high professional levels, Latinx/a/o students like me are going to continue to swim upstream to achieve their educational goals, feeling frustrated—sometimes unchallenged—and insecure the whole way there. I hope that sharing my story helps to increase awareness about how important and impactful it is to nurture and support these students in order for them to succeed.

Chapter 6

Advancing an Anti-Deficit Achievement Framework for Latinx/a/o College Students

David Pérez II, Claudia García-Louis,

Tracy Arámbula Ballysingh, and Eligio Martinez Jr.

Despite the proliferation of research on the academic success of Latinx/a/o college students (Cerna, Pérez, & Sáenz, 2008; Gloria, Castellanos, & Orozco, 2005; Hurtado & Sinha, 2016), scholars continue to perpetuate deficit-based narratives that focus on these students' lack of success throughout the P–16 pipeline. Identifying attainment gaps between Latinx/a/o students and other racial/ethnic groups can be beneficial (Gándara & Contreras, 2009), but this often reinforces deficit-based narratives rather than yields solutions. Educational inequities are rooted in sociohistorical factors (Noguera, Hurtado, & Fergus, 2012; Sáenz

117

& Ponjuán, 2009) and are perpetuated by fictitious claims of racial/ ethnic differences (García-Louis, 2016; Núñez, 2014; Solórzano, Villalpando, & Oseguera, 2005). Rather than viewing Latinx/a/o students as a monolithic community, scholars need to explore how gender, race, and other socially constructed identities converge into distinct educational pathways. In this chapter, we focus on the unique cultural strengths Latinx/a/o students possess, by extending Harper's (2010) anti-deficit achievement framework (ADAF).

Consistent with Project MALES's Faculty and Research Affiliates Program goals,[1] the authors of this chapter advance anti-deficit scholarship on Latinx/a/o students to inform research, policies, and practices. As faculty affiliates, we focus our research agendas on myriad factors that are relevant to increasing Latinx/a/o students' success in K–12 settings and postsecondary institutions. Eligio Martinez and his colleagues explored how race, class, and gender intersect and influence Chicano and Latino males' educational trajectories after middle school (Martinez, Fernandez, Perez, & Montes, 2016). Tracy Arámbula Ballysingh (2016) examined Latina/o students' social capital, college access, and first-year transition experiences. David Pérez (2017) integrated anti-deficit theories to understand and duplicate conditions that increase Latino undergraduate men's success at selective public and private universities. Claudia García-Louis's (2016) critical research on AfroLatinx college students advanced scholarship on Latinx/a/o heterogeneity, race, and ethnicity. In this chapter, we will use our collective expertise to challenge deficit thinking among student affairs educators and to foster the professional competencies needed to increase Latinx/a/o college students' success.

---

[1] MALES stands for Mentoring to Achieve Latino Educational Success.

CHALLENGING DEFICIT THINKING
IN STUDENT AFFAIRS

ACPA–College Student Educators International and NASPA–Student Affairs Administrators in Higher Education (2015) advanced a common set of professional competencies intended to inform the work of student affairs educators. Efforts to support minoritized college students often center on social justice and inclusion (SJI). The SJI competency is defined as "both a process and a goal that includes the knowledge, skills, and dispositions needed to create learning environments that foster equitable participation of all groups and seeks to address issues of oppression, privilege, and power" (p. 30). Although addressing systemic and historical oppression is a starting point, scholars and practitioners must recognize Latinx/a/o students as unique and distinct from other student populations. For example, Latinx/a/o students continue to experience racial microaggressions based on language, perceived immigration status, and age (González, 2009; Portes & Zhoe, 2005). Nonetheless, few scholars have concentrated on the ways in which Latina/o students use their unique cultural assets to overcome these challenges (Yosso, 2005; Yosso, Smith, Ceja, & Solórzano, 2009).

Disrupting deficit thinking, which manifests in blaming victims of systemic oppression for their own victimization, cannot be achieved by offering courses, workshops, and other professional development opportunities that solely focus on social justice and inclusion (Pérez, Ashlee, Do, Karikari, & Sim, 2017). Scholars and practitioners need to integrate empirically grounded, anti-deficit scholarship that advances research, policies, and practices intended to increase Latinx/a/o college student success. Anti-deficit approaches cited by Pérez et al. (2017) are widely used to prepare educators who serve diverse student populations in K–12 schools (Valencia, 2010), but these practices are not widely used in higher education (Tange & Jensen, 2012).

ADVANCING AN ANTI-DEFICIT ACHIEVEMENT FRAMEWORK

The adapted ADAF helps scholars and practitioners understand myriad factors that contribute to Latinx/a/o student success in higher education (see Figure 6.1). Although the ADAF was designed to advance anti-deficit perspectives of Black undergraduate men, this framework has been utilized to study Latino men who have successfully transitioned from high school to college (Harper, 2014). Hence, the ADAF can help scholars and practitioners "better understand how [Latinx/a/o students] persist and successfully navigate their ways to and through [higher education]" (Harper, 2010, p. 67). Building on Harper's (2010) framework, the authors of this chapter incorporate four dynamic and interrelated contexts—social, institutional, community, and familial—that influence Latinx/a/o students' pathways in higher education.

Figure 6.1. Anti-Deficit Achievement Framework

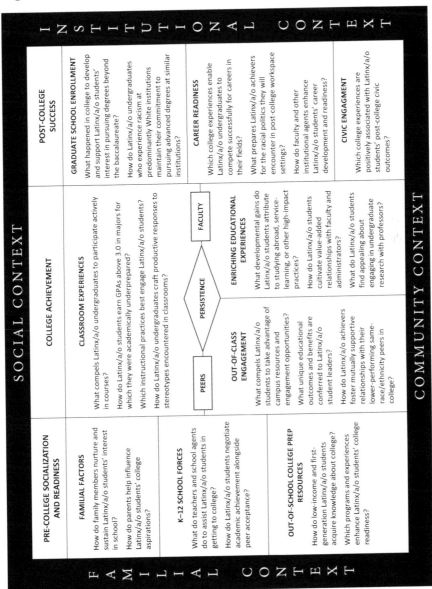

Social context encompasses AfroLatina/o and Latino heterogeneity (García-Louis, 2016; Torres & Solberg, 2001), intragroup differences (Torres & Solberg, 2001; Valenzuela, 1999), and the importance of considering sociocultural factors when serving Latina/o students (Crisp, Taggart, & Nora, 2015). Although the ADAF accounts for students' in- and out-of-class engagement, the addition of *institutional context* centers on the role that campus climate plays in Latinx/a/o student success (Harper & Hurtado, 2007; Yosso et al., 2009). *Community context* includes experiences such as engaging peers with similar cultural backgrounds, which plays an important role in fostering students' sense of belonging (Maldonado, Rhoads, & Buenavista, 2005; Villalpando, 2003). Whereas Harper (2010) contended familial factors shape students' collegiate aspirations, we argue that *familial context* directly influences Chicano and Latino students' academic outcomes before, during, and after college (Ceja, 2004; Jimenez-Silva, Jimenez Hernandez, Luevanos, Jimenez, & Jimenez, 2009; Kiyama et al., 2015). Familial, community, institutional, and social contexts are all relevant throughout Latinx/a/o college students' educational pathways. At times, one or more of these contextual factors may influence students' experiences.

LITERATURE REVIEW

This section summarizes the existing literature relevant to advancing anti-deficit perspectives on Latinx/a/o student success that account for social, institutional, community, and familial contexts. While Harper's (2010) framework centers on three higher-education pipeline points (i.e., pre-college socialization and readiness, college achievement, and post-college success), our adapted ADAF expands on contextual factors that influence Latinx/a/o college students' educational pathways. Although these contexts influence a student's experiences throughout college, the contexts may converge at different points, depending on the student's background.

Social Context

Latinx/a/o students have traditionally been described as a homogenous population, which has led to overgeneralizations about their educational pathways and campus experiences (García-Louis, 2016). In considering how to support this burgeoning student population, scholars and practitioners should look at the intersection of personal stories and sociocultural factors such as race, ethnicity, socioeconomic status, and cultural identity in order to gain a better understanding of student needs. Numerous scholars have called for an interdisciplinary approach to higher education research that shifts away from "a single dimension of identity . . . preventing scholars from understanding and responding to the changing educational landscape" (Taylor, Miller, & García-Louis, 2014, p. 230). Moreover, practitioners must move beyond the tendency of treating race and ethnicity as mutually exclusive categories and incorporate social factors (e.g., education, location, family, religion, nation of origin) into research and practice.

Social factors such as upbringing, beliefs, traditions, customs, environment, and so on directly inform all students' academic experiences and decisions. Crisp et al. (2015) conducted a systematic review of literature on Latina/o undergraduates and found gender, parental education, and socioeconomic status were related to Latina/o students' grades, persistence decisions, and odds of degree completion. Torres and Solberg (2001) found that family support directly affected the level of academic self-efficacy for Latino students, but these authors suggest that educators consider how the sociocultural history of specific ethnic groups (e.g., Mexican Americans, Dominican Americans) in the United States could affect students' academic self-efficacy and overall educational experience.

Valenzuela (1999) highlighted the pervasiveness of microaggressions in education and their negative impact on the educational experiences of Mexican students. She found that, due to negative stereotypes, teachers provided Mexican American students with less guidance, support, and encouragement than their immigrant peers. However, teachers were not aware of their stereotypes and the detrimental impact they had on students' educational attainment. It is pertinent to understand that Latinx/a/o students' educational experiences could be complicated due to the "confluence of physical appearance, language, self-ascribed ethnic identity, cultural affinity, and other demographic factors" (García-Louis, 2016, p. 25). Cultural affinity has been associated with academic self-efficacy, sense of belonging, and successfully navigating hostile campus climates (Hurtado, Carter, & Spuler, 1996). Furthermore, racism and prejudice manifest into distinct experiences for students of color, but often a one-size-fits-all approach is adopted in an attempt to address these problems (Harper & Hurtado, 2007; Yosso et al., 2009).

Students of color tend to report hostility and differential treatment on campus, but intensity and situations vary by racial and ethnic group (Harper & Hurtado, 2007). Black students tend to report higher levels of racism and discrimination, while their Latinx/a/o counterparts are forced to navigate a campus climate where they are perceived to be beneficiaries of affirmative action and/or considered to be undocumented (Harper & Hurtado, 2007; Hurtado, 1994). Yet, the homogenous approach to Latinx/a/os has overlooked the fact they are multiracial and multiethnic, with transnational and pan-ethnic histories and cultures (Flores & Jiménez Román, 2009). Sociocultural factors (e.g., beliefs, traditions, values, attitudes) and racism could, in effect, complicate academic performance and scholarly engagement. Furthermore, numerous scholars have identified intragroup differences in academic achievement by gender (Ballysingh, 2016; Harper, 2010; Hurtado et al., 1996; Sáenz

& Ponjuán, 2009), which further validates the need for an interdisciplinary approach. Considering the degree to which sociocultural factors converge will aid in conceptualizing divergent Latinx/a/o experiences.

Institutional Context

Improving educational outcomes for Latinx/a/o students depends on fostering inclusive campus climates (Harper & Hurtado, 2007; Hurtado, Milem, Clayton-Pedersen, & Allen; 1999; Hurtado & Ponjuán, 2005; Milem, Chang, & Antonio, 2005). Whereas the previous section addressed how social context influences Latinx/a/o educational experiences, this section centers on three internal dimensions of climate—psychological (e.g., perceptions of discrimination, attitudes, prejudice reduction), behavioral (e.g., social interactions across race/ethnicity, degree of intra- or cross-racial involvement), and structural (e.g., curriculum, policies)—that shape the institutional context (Hurtado et al., 1999). Harper and Hurtado's (2007) synthesis of campus-climate research underscored how racial/ethnic minority college students perceived the climate as more hostile and experienced prejudicial treatment more often than did their White peers. These experiences can diminish Latinx/a/o students' psychological well-being and academic performance (Crisp et al., 2015), and even academically talented Latinx/a/o college students are susceptible to the negative effects of hostile campus climates (Hurtado, 1994; Pérez, 2014).

Context matters when exploring how Latinx/a/os experience campus climate. Latinx/a/o undergraduates are often subjected to microaggressions—characterized as "verbal, behavioral, and environmental indignities, whether intentional or unintentional, that communicate hostile, derogatory, or negative racial slights and insults" (Sue et al., 2007, p. 273)—that contribute to their negative perceptions of campus climate. Yosso et al. (2009) identified how Latinx/a/o undergraduates experienced interpersonal microaggressions, racial jokes, and institutional microaggressions at three selective predominantly White institutions (PWIs). The authors conceptualized *institutional microaggressions* as "racially marginalizing actions and inertia of the university evidenced in structures, practices, and discourses that endorse a campus racial climate hostile to People of Color" (p. 673). With the exception of McCabe (2009), studies published on Latinx/a/o undergraduates have not used disaggregated data to explain how gender, ethnicity, and/or class factors affect students' perceptions and experiences of the campus climate (Franklin, Smith, & Hung, 2014; Kim, Rennick, & Franco, 2014; Yosso et al., 2009). McCabe's (2009) analysis of racial and gender microaggressions among Black, Latina/o, and White undergraduates at a PWI revealed that Latinas were viewed as sexually exotic and subjected to men's advances. In contrast, Pérez (2014) reported that Latino men were perceived as intellectually incompetent by their White peers. The nature of these microaggressions may explain why Latinx/a/os use different strategies to cope with hostile campus climates (Barajas & Pierce, 2001; Gloria et al., 2005; Gloria, Castellanos, Scull, & Villegas, 2009; Pérez & Sáenz, 2017).

Hurtado and Ponjuán (2005) outlined how efforts to integrate diversity into the curriculum, cocurricular initiatives (e.g., intergroup dialogue), and service-learning programs can improve students' educational outcomes and the campus climate. Yet, Latinx/a/o students often assume sole responsibility for navigating institutions that are unresponsive to their needs (Gloria et al., 2009; Yosso et al., 2009). Whereas Latinas derive support from their peers—typically, other women of color (Barajas & Pierce, 2001)—Latino men tend to cope with adversity on their own (Gloria et al., 2009; Pérez, 2014). Qualitative studies that focused exclusively on Latino undergraduate men indicate that in some instances, peers and faculty played an integral role in fostering their success at PWIs (Huerta & Fishman, 2014; Perez & Taylor,

2015). Although Latinx/a/os rely primarily on peer networks to navigate PWIs, Sáenz, Ponjuán, Segovia, and Del Real Viramontes (2015) noted how peer mentoring helped Latino students identify strategies to succeed in college, forge meaningful connections with faculty, and maintain connections to Latino communities through service-learning.

Community Context

Some scholars contend that students of color experience cultural incongruence between their home communities and the campus environment (Braxton, Sullivan, & Johnson, 1997; Gloria, 2005; Museus & Quaye, 2009). As Latinx/a/o students enter college, they may find it difficult to negotiate differences between the campus culture and their own ethnic, gendered, and class identities (Gloria & Rodriguez, 2000; Huerta & Fishman, 2014). These differences can result in students feeling isolated and searching for a sense of belonging on campus (Crisp et al., 2015). Latinx/a/o students must also contend with family and cultural obligations, such as contributing to the household income and helping run the home (Abrica & Martinez, 2016; Sy & Romero, 2008).

Researchers have found that Latinx/a/o faculty and staff—through the creation of spaces that reaffirm students' ability to be successful—can play a critical role in helping students transition to college and in bridging the gap between campus and home communities (Rendón, 1994; Rendón & Muñoz, 2011). Validation allows students to learn from faculty and staff who come from similar backgrounds; students see how to be a college student but also maintain the important relationship to home.

In addition to academic validation, engaging in cultural empowerment programs and projects allows Latinx/a/o and other students of color to develop a sense of belonging and empowerment on campus, permitting them to challenge institutional norms and practices while also reaffirming their commitment to their communities (Maldonado et al., 2005; Yeh, 2010). Kiyama and Luca (2014) found that peer mentoring programs provide a mutually beneficial relationship for students; peer mentors are trained to become advocates, role models, and "human bridges" to students while also benefiting from those same forms of institutional support. Peer mentoring promotes student success by allowing students to share their experiences and knowledge with younger students while also actively reshaping their college environment for themselves and others (Cutright & Evans, 2016; Kiyama & Luca, 2014).

Villalpando (2003) found that participation in service for their home community allows Latino students to reaffirm their cultural identity and improve their sense of belonging on campus. Community service can also help to counteract some of the campus hostility that students feel, ultimately leading them to feel more included on campus (Nuñez, 2009). Participating in programs that engage parents and community members allows students to give back and creates a bridge between the university and home communities (Alemán, Pérez-Torres, & Oliva, 2013).

Familial Context

Chief among deficit narratives related to family is the myth that Latinx/a/o student achievement lags because parents do not value education—thus shifting the explanation for underachievement to students and their families (Valencia, 2010). In stark contrast, asset-based perspectives regarding family suggest that *familismo*, or the emphasis placed on maintaining strong familial ties, plays a prominent role in Latinx/a/o student success (Grant & Ray, 2010; Williams & Dawson, 2011). *Familismo* extends beyond mere encouragement and economic or academic scaffolding to encompass supportive gestures such as listening, understanding, goal-setting, and motivation (Ballysingh, 2016; Perez & Rodriguez, 2011; Yosso, 2005). Family is an essential network that shapes college-going processes, college experiences, persistence, and postcollege outcomes (Jimenez-Silva et al., 2009; Kiyama, 2010).

Some studies indicate that Latinx/a/o students obtain mentorship, support, and guidance from siblings and extended family members (Gloria & Segura-Herrera, 2004). However, Latino parents play a key role in nurturing their children's educational aspirations and transmitting values such as *respeto* (respect), *caballerismo* (chivalry), and *verguenza* (humility; Calzada, Fernandez, & Cortes, 2010; Ceja, 2004). Academic achievement increases when parental support is harnessed through family–school partnerships and embraced as a form of capital (De Gaetano, 2007). For example, Larrotta and Yamamura (2011) found that parental participation in a family literacy program promoted long-term educational successes.

Asset-based discourses that more fully recognize Latinx/a/o parental values and aspirations for children are needed, including a focus on parental support, or *apoyo,* from the perspectives of parents themselves (Auerbach, 2007). To fully catalyze familial assets, researchers and practitioners must recognize that Latinx/a/o families provide essential contexts that hold considerable social, cultural, and intellectual capital (Rios-Aguilar, Kiyama, Gravitt, & Moll, 2011) and potential to forge meaningful partnerships with academic institutions (Moll, Amanti, Neff, & Gonzalez, 2005).

IMPLICATIONS FOR RESEARCH AND PRACTICE

Using the ADAF, this section draws connections between theory and practice to inform student affairs praxis and offers implications for research and practice.

Implications for Research

Far too often, research findings are used to perpetuate deficit-based narratives about Latinx/a/o college students (Pérez et al., 2017;

Solórzano et al., 2005; Valencia, 2010). When scholars fail to acknowledge the cultural assets that Latinx/a/o students bring with them to campus, faculty and staff tend to adopt practices based on deficit-based narratives (Lederman, 2013), which result in inequitable educational outcomes (Sólorzano et al., 2005). To counter this practice, we extended Harper's (2010) ADAF by integrating culturally specific assets that Latinx/a/os bring to campus.

Disaggregating data to examine the unique experiences of Latinx/a/o subgroups is essential to advancing anti-deficit perspectives (Harper, 2013; Pérez et al., 2017). Moreover, scholars must devote greater attention to intersectional identities (e.g., ethnicity, gender, class, nation of origin) and contextual factors outlined in this chapter as well as the roles they play in determining Latinx/a/os' academic outcomes. Addressing these complexities in educational research would provide a more holistic understanding of Latinx/a/o student experience in U.S. higher education; the expansion of methodological approaches should also be considered. For example, scholars using quantitative methods must expand the use of large-scale longitudinal data sets to account for Latinx/a/o subgroup differences (Crisp et al., 2015). Scholars using qualitative methods should consider exploring intersections between the ADAF and contextual factors outlined in this chapter to advance anti-deficit perspectives on Latinx/a/o undergraduates.

Implications for Practice

Student affairs educators can play an important role in supporting Latinx/a/o students as they transition to campus and in encouraging these students to maintain connections to their families and communities (Gloria & Rodriguez, 2000). Initiatives such as Project MALES are purposefully designed to maintain partnerships among faculty, practitioners, family, and community members in order to augment

Latinx/a/o success (Sáenz et al., 2015). In addition to increasing academic preparedness and access to college information, strong partnerships between community leaders, families, and schools make college a viable path (Alemán et al., 2013; Allen, Sáenz, Ballysingh, & Yamamura, 2016).

Rather than viewing students and their families as beneficiaries of college services, practitioners should treat them as partners and engage them in making decisions. Moreover, practitioners need to recognize that Latinx/a/o students do not represent a monolithic community. Accordingly, practitioners should approach student affairs in a way that accounts for differences of ethnicity, national origin, gender, gender expression, sexuality, language, legal status, and other salient social identities that shape Latinx/a/o students' experiences. Finally, higher education and student affairs graduate preparation programs should make deliberate efforts to prepare practitioners, using anti-deficit perspectives that empower them to recognize and harness the cultural strengths of diverse college students (Pérez et al., 2017).

CONCLUSION

Using Harper's (2010) framework, this chapter extended the ADAF by addressing the important role that familial, community, institutional, and social contexts play in Latinx/a/o students' educational pathways. The adapted ADAF underscores the importance of students maintaining close familial and community ties during college. Additionally, we challenge scholars and practitioners to assume greater responsibility for creating and sustaining inclusive campus environments. Critical perspectives such as the adapted ADAF can yield useful insights into Latinx/a/o students' assets and needs as well as the roles faculty and student affairs practitioners play in supporting their success during and after college.

Acknowledging how social forces undermine and contribute to student success is equally important in student affairs and higher education. Scholars and practitioners committed to fostering Latinx/a/o student success must remain vigilant about how they perpetuate deficit-based perspectives. Practitioners should also engage Latinx/a/o students as collaborators who bring expertise in designing, implementing, and assessing initiatives that are based on asset-based frameworks such as the ADAF. Furthermore, they should reconsider how the ADAF can be used to improve research, policies, and practices that are intended to foster the success of Latinx/a/o college students.

REFERENCES

ACPA–College Student Educators International & NASPA–Student Affairs Administrators in Higher Education. (2015). *Professional competency areas for student affairs educators.* Washington, DC: Author.

Abrica, E. J., & Martinez, E., Jr. (2016). Strategies for navigating financial challenges among Latino male community college students: Centralizing race, gender, and immigrant generation. *Journal of Applied Research in the Community College, 23*(2), 59–72.

Alemán, E., Jr., Pérez-Torres, J. C., & Oliva, N. (2013). Adelante en Utah: Dilemmas of leadership and college access in a university–school–community partnership. *Journal of Cases in Educational Leadership, 16*(3), 7–30.

Allen, T. O., Sáenz, V. B., Ballysingh, T. A., & Yamamura, E. K. (2016). Increasing Latina/o student success: Examining culturally responsive college-readiness in the Rio Grande Valley of South Texas. *Journal of School Leadership, 26*(1), 153–182.

Auerbach, S. (2007). From moral supporters to struggling advocates: Reconceptualizing parent roles in education through the experience of working-class families of color. *Urban Education, 42*(3), 250–283.

Ballysingh, T. A. (2016). Caballeros making capital gains in college: The role of social capital in first-year persistence at a predominantly white 4-year institution. In V. Sáenz, L. Ponjuán, & J. L. Figueroa (Eds.), *Ensuring the success of Latino males in higher education* (pp. 152–173). Sterling, VA: Stylus.

Barajas, H. L., & Pierce, J. L. (2001). The significance of race and gender in school success among Latinas and Latinos in college. *Gender and Society, 15*(6), 859–878.

Braxton, J. M., Sullivan, A. S., & Johnson, R. M. (1997). Appraising Tinto's theory of college student departure. In J. C. Smart (Ed.), *Higher education: A handbook of theory and research* (Vol. 12, pp. 107–164). New York, NY: Agathon.

Calzada, E., Fernandez, Y., & Cortes, D. E. (2010). Incorporating the cultural value of *respeto* into a framework of Latino parenting. *Cultural Diversity & Ethnic Minority Psychology, 16*(1), 77–86.

Ceja, M. (2004). Chicana college aspirations and the role of parents: Developing educational resiliency. *Journal of Hispanic Higher Education, 3*(4), 338–362.

Cerna, O. S., Perez, P. A., & Sáenz, V. B. (2008). Examining the precollege attributes and values of Latina/o bachelor's degree attainers. *Journal of Hispanic Higher Education, 8*(2), 130–157.

Crisp, G., Taggart, A., & Nora, A. (2015). Undergraduate Latina/o students: A systematic review of research identifying factors contributing to academic success outcomes. *Review of Educational Research, 84*(2), 249–274.

Cutright, T. J., & Evans, E. (2016). Year-long peer mentoring activity to enhance the retention of freshmen STEM students in a NSF scholarship program. *Mentoring & Tutoring: Partnership in Learning, 24*(3), 201–212.

De Gaetano, Y. (2007). The role of culture in engaging Latino parents' involvement in school. *Urban Education, 42*(2), 145–162.

Flores, J., & Jiménez Román, M. (2009). Triple-consciousness? Approaches to Afro-Latino culture in the United States. *Latin American and Caribbean Ethnic Studies, 4*(3), 319–328.

Franklin, J. D., Smith, W. A., & Hung, M. (2014). Racial battle fatigue for Latina/o students: A quantitative perspective. *Journal of Hispanic Higher Education, 13*(4), 303–322.

Gándara, P. C., & Contreras, F. (2009). *The Latino education crisis: The consequences of failed social policies.* Cambridge, MA: Harvard University Press.

García-Louis, C. (2016). Beyond multiracialism: Acknowledging AfroLatina/o students. *Journal of Student Affairs in Higher Education, 25*, 21–27.

Gloria, A. M. (2005). An examination of academic nonpersistence decisions of Latino undergraduates. *Hispanic Journal of Behavioral Sciences, 27*(2), 202–223.

Gloria, A. M., Castellanos, J., & Orozco, V. (2005). Perceived educational barriers, cultural congruity, coping responses, and psychological well-being of Latina undergraduates. *Hispanic Journal of Behavioral Sciences, 27*(2), 161–183.

Gloria, A. M., Castellanos, J., Scull, N. C., & Villegas, F. J. (2009). Psychological coping and well-being of male Latino undergraduates: Sobreviviendo la universidad. *Hispanic Journal of Behavioral Sciences, 31*(3), 317–339.

Gloria, A. M., & Rodriguez, E. R. (2000). Counseling Latino university students: Psychosociocultural issues for consideration. *Journal of Counseling & Development, 78*, 145–154.

Gloria, A. M., & Segura-Herrera, T. M. (2004). Ambrocia and Omar go to college: A psychosociocultural examination of Chicanos and Chicanas in higher education. In R. J. Velasquez, B. McNeill, & L. Arellano (Eds.), *Handbook of Chicana and Chicano psychology* (pp. 401–425). Mahwah, NJ: Lawrence Erlbaum.

González, J. C. (2009). Latinas in doctoral and professional programs: Similarities and differences in support systems and challenges. In M. F. Howard-Hamilton, C. L. Morelon-Quainoo, S. D. Johnson, R. Winkle-Wagner, & L. Santiague (Eds.), *Standing on the outside looking in: Underrepresented students' experiences in advanced degree programs*. Sterling, VA: Stylus.

Grant, K. B., & Ray, J. A. (2010). *Home, school, and community collaboration: Culturally responsive family involvement*. Thousand Oaks, CA: Sage.

Harper, S. R. (2010). An anti-deficit achievement framework for research on students of color in STEM. In S. R. Harper & C. B. Newman (Eds.), *Students of color in STEM: Engineering a new research agenda* (New Directions for Institutional Research, No. 148, pp. 63–74). San Francisco, CA: Jossey-Bass.

Harper, S. R. (2013). *Five things student affairs administrators can do to improve success among college men of color*. Washington, DC: NASPA–Student Affairs Administrators in Higher Education.

Harper, S. R. (Ed.). (2014). *Succeeding in the city: A report from the New York City Black and Latino male high school achievement study*. Philadelphia, PA: University of Pennsylvania, Center for the Study of Race and Equity in Education.

Harper, S. R., & Hurtado, S. (2007). Nine themes in campus racial climates and implications for institutional transformation. In S. R. Harper & L. D. Patton (Eds.), *Special issue: Responding to the realities of race on campus* (New Directions for Student Services, No. 120, pp. 7–24). San Francisco, CA: Jossey-Bass.

Huerta, A. H., & Fishman, S. M. (2014). Marginality and mattering: Urban Latino male undergraduates in higher education. *Journal of the First-Year Experience & Students in Transition, 26*(1), 85–100.

Hurtado, S. (1994). The institutional climate for talented Latino students. *Research in Higher Education, 35*(1), 21–41.

Hurtado, S., Carter, D. F., & Spuler, A. (1996). Latino student transition to college: Assessing difficulties and factors in successful college adjustment. *Research in Higher Education, 37*(2), 135–157.

Hurtado, S. H., Milem, J., Clayton-Pedersen, A., & Allen, W. (1999). *Enacting diverse learning environments: Improving the climate for racial/ethnic diversity in higher education*. ASHE-ERIC Reader Higher Education Report. Washington, DC: The George Washington University, Graduate School of Education and Human Development.

Hurtado, S. H., & Ponjuán, L. (2005). Latino educational outcomes and the campus climate. *Journal of Hispanic Higher Education, 4*(3), 235–251.

Hurtado, A., & Sinha, M. (2016). *Beyond machismo: Intersectional Latino masculinities*. Austin, TX: University of Texas Press.

Jimenez-Silva, M., Jimenez Hernandez, N., Luevanos, R., Jimenez, D., & Jimenez, A. Jr., (2009). Results not typical: One Latino family's experiences in higher education. *Harvard Educational Review, 79*(4), 730–745.

Kim, Y. K., Rennick, L. A., & Franco, M. A. (2014). Latino college students at highly selective institutions: A comparison of their college experiences and outcomes to other racial/ethnic groups. *Journal of Hispanic Higher Education, 13*(4), 245–268.

Kiyama, J. M. (2010). College aspirations and limitations: The role of educational ideologies and funds of knowledge in Mexican American families. *American Educational Research Journal, 47*(2), 330–356.

Kiyama, J. M., Harper, C. E., Ramos, D., Aguayo, D., Page, L. A., & Reister, K. A. (2015). *Parent and family engagement in higher education.* Hoboken, NJ: Wiley.

Kiyama, J. M., & Luca, S. G. (2014). Structured opportunities: Exploring the social and academic benefits for peer mentors in retention programs. *Journal of College Student Retention, 15*(4), 489–514.

Larrotta, C., & Yamamura, E. K. (2011). A community cultural wealth approach to Latina/Latino parent involvement: The promise of family literacy. *Adult Basic Education and Literacy Journal, 5*(2), 74–83.

Lederman, B. D. (2013). *Building students' "cultural capital."* Retrieved from http://www.insidehigher. com/news/2013/11/05/can-colleges-buildstudents-cultural-capital-and-should-they

Maldonado, D. E. Z., Rhoads, R., & Buenavista, T. L. (2005). The student-initiated retention project: Theoretical contributions and the role of self-empowerment. *American Educational Research Journal, 42*(4), 605–638.

Martinez, E., Jr., Fernandez, D., Perez, I., & Montes, G., (2016) Reclaiming the innocence of Latino males: A message from middle school Latino boys to their teachers. In T. E. J. Marsh & N. Croom (Eds.), *Envisioning critical race praxis in K–12 education through counter-storytelling* (pp. 25–48). Charlotte, NC: Information Age Publishing.

McCabe, J. (2009). Racial and gender microaggressions on a predominantly-white campus: Experiences of black, Latina/o and white undergraduates. *Race, Gender & Class, 16*(1/2), 133–151.

Milem, B. J. F., Chang, M. J., & Antonio, A. L. (2005). *Making diversity work on campus: A research-based perspective.* Washington, DC: Association of American Colleges and Universities.

Moll, L. C., Amanti, C., Neff, D., & Gonzalez, N. (2005). Funds of knowledge for teaching: Using a qualitative approach to connect homes and classrooms. In N. Gonzalez, L. C. Moll, & C. Amanti (Eds.), *Funds of knowledge: Theorizing practices in households, communities, and classrooms* (pp. 1–14). Mahwah, NJ: Lawrence Erlbaum Associates.

Museus, S. D., & Quaye, S. J. (2009). Toward an intercultural perspective of racial and ethnic minority college student persistence. *The Review of Higher Education, 33*(1), 67–94.

Noguera, P., Hurtado, A., & Fergus, E. (2012). *Invisible no more: Understanding the disenfranchisement of Latino men and boys.* New York, NY: Routledge.

Nuñez, A. M. (2009). Latino students' transitions to college: A social and intercultural capital perspective. *Harvard Educational Review, 79*(1), 22–48.

Núñez, A. M. (2014). Employing multilevel intersectionality in educational research: Latino identities, contexts, and college access. *Educational Researcher, 43*(2), 85–92.

Pérez, D., II. (2014). Exploring the nexus between community cultural wealth and the academic and social experiences of Latino male achievers at two predominantly white research universities. *International Journal of Qualitative Studies in Education, 27*(6), 747–767.

Pérez, D., II. (2017). In pursuit of success: Latino male college students exercising academic determination and community cultural wealth. *Journal of College Student Development, 58*(2), 123–140.

Pérez, D., II, Ashlee, K. C., Do, V. H., Karikari, S. N., & Sim, C. (2017). Re-conceptualizing student success in higher education: Reflections from graduate student affairs educators using anti-deficit achievement framework. *Journal of Excellence in College Teaching, 28*(3), 5–28.

Pérez, D., II, & Sáenz, V. B. (2017). Thriving Latino males in selective predominantly white institutions. *Journal of Hispanic Higher Education, 16*(2), 162–186.

Pérez, D., II, & Taylor, K. B. (2015). Cultivando logradores: Nurturing and sustaining Latino male success in higher education. *Journal of Diversity in Higher Education, 9*(1), 1–19.

Perez, P. A., & Rodriguez, J. L. (2011). Access and opportunity for Latina/o undocumented college students: Familial and institutional support factors. *Association of Mexican American Educators Journal, 5*(1), 14–21.

Portes, A., & Zhoe, M. (2005). The new second generation: Segmented assimilation and its variants. In M. M. Suárez-Orozco, C. Suárez-Orozco, & D. B. Qin (Eds.), *The new immigration: An interdisciplinary reader* (pp. 85–104). New York, NY: Routledge.

Rendón, L. I. (1994). Validating culturally diverse students: Toward a new model of learning and student development. *Innovative Higher Education, 19*(1), 33–51.

Rendón, L. I., & Muñoz, S. M. (2011). Revisiting validation theory: Theoretical foundations, applications, and extensions. *Enrollment Management Journal, 2*(1), 12–33.

Rios-Aguilar, C., Kiyama, J. M., Gravitt, M., & Moll, L. C. (2011). Funds of knowledge for the poor and forms of capital for the rich? A capital approach to examining funds of knowledge. *Theory and Research in Education, 92*(2), 163–184.

Sáenz, V. B., & Ponjuán, L. (2009). The vanishing Latino male in higher education. *Journal of Hispanic Higher Education, 8*(1), 54–89.

Sáenz, V. B., Ponjuán, L., Segovia, J., & Del Real Viramontes, J. (2015). Developing a Latino mentoring program: Project MALES (Mentoring to Achieve Latino Educational Success). In C. S. Turner (Ed.), *Mentoring as transformative practice: Supporting student and faculty diversity* (New Directions for Higher Education, No. 171, pp. 75–85). San Francisco, CA: Jossey-Bass.

Solórzano, D. G., Villalpando, O., & Oseguera, L. (2005). Educational inequities and Latina/o undergraduate students in the United States: A critical race analysis of their educational progress. *Journal of Hispanic Higher Education, 4*(3), 272–294.

Sue, D. W., Capodilupo, C. M., Torino, G. C., Bucceri, J. M., Holder, A. M. B., Nadal, K. L., & Esquilin, M. (2007). Racial microaggressions in everyday life: Implications for clinical practice. *American Psychologist, 62*(4), 271–86.

Sy, S. R., & Romero, J. (2008). Family responsibilities among Latina college students from immigrant families. *Journal of Hispanic Higher Education, 7*(3), 212–227.

Tange, H., & Jensen, I. (2012). Good teachers and deviant learners? The meeting of practices in university level international education. *Journal of Research in International Education, 11*(2), 181–193.

Taylor, B. J., Miller, R. A., & García-Louis, C. (2014). Utilizing intersectionality to engage dialogue in higher education. In D. Mitchell, Jr. (Ed.), *Intersectionality & higher education: Theory, research, & praxis* (pp. 229–239). New York, NY: Peter Lang.

Torres, J. B., & Solberg, S. (2001). Role of self-efficacy, stress, social integration, and family support in Latino college student persistence and health. *Journal of Vocational Behavior, 59*, 53–63.

Valencia, R. R. (2010). *Dismantling contemporary deficit thinking: Educational thought and practice.* New York, NY: Routledge.

Valenzuela, A. (1999). *Subtractive schooling: U.S. Mexican youth and the politics of caring.* Albany, NY: SUNY Press.

Villalpando, O. (2003). Self-segregation or self-preservation? A critical race theory and Latina/o critical theory analysis of a study of Chicana/o college students. *Qualitative Studies in Education, 16*(5), 619–646.

Williams, S., & Dawson, B. A. (2011). The effects of familial capital on the academic achievement of elementary Latino/a students. *Families in Society: The Journal of Contemporary Social Services, 92*(1), 91–98.

Yeh, T. L. (2010). Service-learning and persistence of low-income, first-generation college students: An exploratory study. *Michigan Journal of Community Service Learning, 16*(2) 50–65.

Yosso, T. J. (2005). Whose culture has capital? A critical race theory discussion of community cultural wealth. *Race Ethnicity and Education, 8*(1), 69–91.

Yosso, T. J., Smith, W. A., Ceja, M., & Solórzano, D. G. (2009). Critical race theory, racial microaggressions, and campus racial climate for Latina/o undergraduates. *Harvard Educational Review, 79*(4), 659–690.

Chapter 7

Latinx/a/o Students and Community Colleges

Edward F. Martinez and Ignacio Hernández

This chapter addresses the role community colleges play in developing access and success for Latinx/a/o students; we the authors also discuss our own journeys to working at community colleges. We use data from the National Center for Education Statistics (NCES) and the U.S. Census Bureau to make sense of enrollment and population trends. These publicly reported data sources often use the term *two-year colleges* to refer to the nation's more than 1,100 community colleges (American Association of Community Colleges, 2017). The reality is that the concept of *two-year colleges* is outdated, given that today's community college students enroll for as many as six years (Juszkiewicz, 2016).

Figure 7.1. Percentage of Hispanic Students Ages
18–24 Enrolled in Degree-Granting Postsecondary
Institutions: 1972–2015

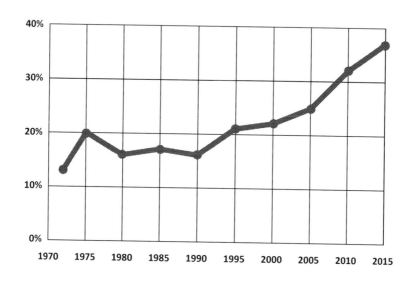

Note. Data from *Digest of Education Statistics, 2015a* (Table 302.6), by National Center for
Education Statistics. Public domain.

The number of Latinx/a/o students ages 18 to 24 enrolled in
degree-granting institutions of higher education has grown steadily
since 1972, as shown in Figure 7.1 (Fry & Lopez, 2012; Snyder, de
Brey, & Dillow, 2016). The 2015 *Digest of Education Statistics* estimates that 37% of Hispanic individuals in the United States are
enrolled in degree-granting institutions of higher education (Snyder
et al., 2016).

In terms of the percentage of Hispanic students enrolled in
degree-granting institutions of higher education, South Dakota leads
the states—including Washington, D.C.—with 49% enrolled, and
Mississippi lags at the end with 22% (see Table 7.1). Enrollment

increases over the past four decades are partly attributed to Hispanic population growth (Fry & Lopez, 2012), but on closer examination, there is more to these figures. Countless dedicated student affairs professionals working in a variety of outreach and educational opportunity programs have contributed to students' transition to higher education (Cowan Pitre & Pitre, 2009; Improving College Access and Completion, 2015).

Table 7.1. Percentage of Hispanic Students Ages 18–24 Enrolled in Degree-Granting Postsecondary Institutions, by Top Five and Bottom Five States: 2014

Top Five		Bottom Five	
South Dakota	48.8%	South Carolina	24.2%
District of Columbia	48.4%	Minnesota	23.7%
Montana	43.1%	Idaho	22.9%
Maryland	41.8%	Wyoming	22.4%
California	40.5%	Mississippi	21.9%

Note. Data from *Digest of Education Statistics, 2015b* (Table 302.65), by National Center for Education Statistics. Public domain.

The latest enrollment estimates indicate that community colleges enroll roughly 6.7 million students, of which 23% are Hispanic (Snyder et al., 2016). This enrollment figure is significant because of the 3.19 million Latinx/a/o individuals enrolled in all of higher education, 1.52 million (48%) attend community colleges (Snyder et al., 2016). As shown in Figure 7.2, this number has held relatively steady since 2009.

Figure 7.2. Percentage of Hispanic Students Ages 18–24 Enrolled in Community Colleges: 2009–2014

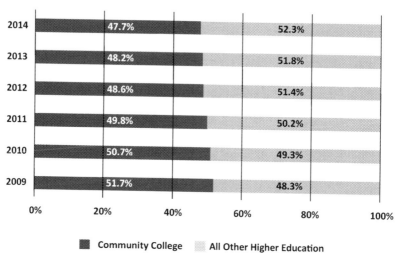

Note. Data from *Digest of Education Statistics, 2015c* (Table 306.20), by National Center for Education Statistics. Public domain.

Given these enrollment trends, when a Latinx/a/o student gains access to higher education, the student is more likely to do so through a community college than via any other institutional type (Gándara & Contreras, 2009; Krogstad & Fry, 2015; Kurlaender, 2006; Snyder et al., 2016). These enrollment trends make it clear that Latinx/a/o students and families continue to depend on community colleges as pathways to multiple educational outcomes. From vocational to career and technical education, to transfer coursework for bachelor's degrees, community colleges' multifaceted curricular offerings reflect the institutions' open-access missions (Cohen, Brawer, & Kisker, 2014; Juszkiewicz, 2016). We authors have our own journeys; just as students can take divergent roads toward their educational goals, so, too, can the professional educators who assume the responsibilities of guiding them.

PERSONAL NARRATIVES: EDWARD AND IGNACIO

Edward

When I first began working in higher education, I never considered working at a community college. However, my doctoral journey presented me with a personal, educational, and philosophical paradigm shift. Having been exposed to the synergy of being part of a doctoral cohort and different professors, a renewed sense of purpose developed. That journey led me to consider working in the community-college sector, where Latinx/a/o students are in abundance. I served as a student affairs professional for 17 years at four-year, predominantly White institutions when I began my doctoral work, and I was one of only two Latinos in my doctoral cohort. Doctoral study allowed for classroom discourse interspersed with private conversations about personal responsibilities and the importance for me to consider working with Latinx/a/o students once my terminal degree was obtained. Professors, friends, mentors, and colleagues encouraged me to explore institutions where I could make a difference for students of color, especially the Latinx/a/o community. And, at the completion of my doctoral degree in 2013, I began a new job search—and found that opportunity at Suffolk County Community College.

My aspiration to assist the Latinx/a/o community was validated in summer 2014, when I met David and his mother, Mrs. Maldonado. David was a first-generation college student who wished to work after completing high school, but his mother wanted him to attend college. When they entered my office, Mrs. Maldonado looked at my desk plate and asked, "Are you Dr. Martinez?" I replied, "Yes." She then asked if I was Latino, and I responded, "Yes, Puerto Rican . . . born and raised in the Bronx." She smiled. During our meeting, we discussed topics related to financial aid and navigating the college environment. I wanted David to know he could be successful at college.

After 45 minutes, Mrs. Maldonado began to tear up as I signed the form for David to register for classes. She gently put her hand on the side of my face and said, "*Dios te bendiga*" (God bless you). She hugged me and said, "I never expected a Puerto Rican would be the one to help my son today." My interactions with David and Mrs. Maldonado reaffirmed my commitment to working with Latinx/a/o students at community colleges and reminded me how lucky I am to have supportive parents who valued education when it was my turn to attend college.

Ignacio

My commitment to community college starts with my enrollment and maneuvering of the transfer function through graduate school and eventually the professoriate. In my household, access to higher education meant attending the local community college because it was close and more affordable than universities across the country. I knew Mt. San Antonio College (Mt. SAC) was located on the corner of Grand and Temple, and that the parking lots teemed with activity whenever I passed by. My two older brothers had attended Mt. SAC, so I really had no other choice to go to college anywhere else, if at all. When I graduated high school, I faced the realities of *a trabajar o a la escuela* (go to work or go to school), a saying often repeated as a direct verbal reminder from my parents. I also encountered this saying indirectly in the multiple part-time jobs I held before starting college as my coworkers lamented their lack of education. Two years after graduating high school, I decided to enroll at Mt. SAC. The busy-ness of the parking lots intimidated me. The large buildings with brick facades and winding staircases confused me. The constant din of thousands of students eager to get to their next class excited me, as the campus never felt silent.

Intimidated, confused, and excited I walked into the admissions office and did my best to follow instructions, taking placement tests and waiting in multiple lines. Along with the emotions swirling in my head, I went home that day with a parking permit, 12 units of coursework, and a student ID card. I was officially a college student! As a tenure-track assistant professor, I now advocate for community colleges not only through my research and service commitments but also in my teaching of students who aspire to work in community colleges. I offer my support of Latinx/a/o students by remaining current with emerging research trends and producing research that may impact professional practice in community colleges.

BACKGROUND

Supporting the community college success of Latinx/a/o students means supporting multiple pathways to certificate or degree completion as well as transfer to a baccalaureate-granting institution for students with varying levels of preparedness (Solórzano, Acevedo-Gil, & Santos, 2013). With a multitude of degree offerings and their open-access missions, community colleges must rely on a dedicated and skilled set of student affairs professionals (Hernández, Hernández, & de la Teja, 2017). Working at a community college means student affairs professionals have the opportunity to touch the lives of millions of students who may otherwise have no other pathways for accessing higher education (Zamani-Gallaher, 2007). As noted by ACPA–College Student Educators International and NASPA–Student Affairs Administrators in Higher Education (2015), the impact that student affairs professionals have as educators takes many forms and relies on multiple professional competency areas. ACPA and NASPA's (2015) *Professional Competency Areas for Student Affairs Educators* emphasizes 10 areas (we highlight Advising and Supporting, Leadership, Organizational and Human Resources, and Social Justice and Inclusion) for student affairs professionals to assess their growth and development—from foundational through intermediate to advanced. We focus on three challenges facing Latinx/a/o students in community colleges and recommend ACPA and NASPA (2015) competency areas as solutions.

Familial and Gender Roles

For many Latinx/a/o students, college attendance is not a rite of passage; it is trailblazing. Latinx/a/o students have ambitious college goals (Roorda & Brown, 2015). However, many Latinx/a/o students are the first in their families to attend college. Nuñez, Sparks, and Hernandez (2011) noted that Latinx/a/o students represent the highest percentage of first-generation college students. Similar to Mrs. Maldonado, the mother of the student Edward dealt with a few years ago, many parents may lack the experience to assist their children in the enrollment process (Perez & McDonough, 2008). Therefore, timely college decisions may be left unmade; thoughtful consideration of majors, courses, and cocurricular activities may be overlooked, and long-term consequences of decisions may not be understood. These challenges—among others—represent obstacles for Hispanic students at community colleges (Sáenz, 2002).

Pathways to success are riddled with family pressure to forgo college and pursue employment opportunities. This is especially true for many Latino males, as they are often less likely than other ethnic and gender groups to enroll and attain a college degree. In fact, Latina females outperform Latino males throughout the entire college pipeline (González, 2015). This phenomenon remains a conundrum. Part of the answer lies in Latinx/a/os' strong need to work. This is related to the concept of *familismo*, which often translates into males working right after high school or dropping out to contribute financially to their households. *Familismo* should not be viewed as exclusively negative, because it can also provide strong social connections and potentially a source of social capital that could assist these students in their educational success (Pérez & Taylor, 2015; Valenzuela, 1999).

Other challenges facing Latinx/a/o students include financial issues, a shortage of knowledge (Ortiz, 2004), and a diminished sense of belonging (Strayhorn, 2012). However, Brown, Santiago, and Lopez (2003) suggested that Latinx/a/o families have an information gap but not necessarily a values gap when trying to help students succeed in college. The role of family is strong within Latinx/a/o households, and a sense of responsibility to thrive in college is often tied to this strong connection. Moreover, many Latinx/a/o families view the accomplishments of children as a reflection of success for the whole family (Easley, Bianco, & Leech, 2012; Santiago, 2011).

Countless Latinx/a/o students attend community colleges in part because of the institutions' close proximity to their families (Cohen et al., 2014). Therefore, in response to these access and success issues, community college leaders need to be responsive to the challenges Latinx/a/o students experience, and develop supportive strategies. To begin with, community colleges should first understand how Latinx/a/o familial support varies and how family dynamics affect students differently. Some students feel guilty attending school because everyone else in the household is working. In fact, in a 2009 national survey of Hispanics by the Pew Research Center, 74% of all 16- to 25-year-old respondents indicated they could not pursue their education or had to cut it short after high school because they had to support their family financially (Lopez, 2009).

On the other hand, 86% of Hispanic parents said it is essential that their children earn a college degree; by comparison, only about two-thirds (67%) of White parents shared the view that college is a significant contributor to future success (Stepler, 2016). These data debunk stereotypes about Latinx/a/o family educational aspirations. For us, both of our parents were very supportive, and educational expectations were real. Nevertheless, it is apparent many Latinx/a/o college students experience family conflict about their higher education pursuits. Thus, college personnel (especially those charged with counseling and advising) within community colleges can play an important role in increasing Latinx/a/o student access, retention, and completion rates in higher education (Marquez Kiyama & Luca, 2014; Pérez & Sáenz, 2017; Rendón, 1994; Torres, Reiser, LePeau, Davis, & Ruder, 2006). Therefore, utilizing ACPA and NASPA's (2015) Social Justice and Inclusion, and Advising and Supporting professional competency areas will be helpful when working to understand the familial and gender roles of Latinx/a/o families.

Institutional Leadership: Role and Responsibility

The choice by Latinx/a/o students to attend community college and invest in education is grounded in the intersection of ability and resources (Kurlaender, 2006). Once a student has been admitted, community college leaders have a responsibility to address all issues influencing the success of Latinx/a/o students. This responsibility requires institutional commitment and individual leadership. One promising way to demonstrate a commitment to Latinx/a/o community college students is by supporting Latinx/a/os for leadership positions in their colleges (Hernández et al., 2017). Gutierrez, Castaneda, and Katsinas (2002) suggested that Latinx/a/os may find greater advancement opportunities within community colleges than within four-year colleges. Ideally, as the Latinx/a/o population increases, so should their representation among leadership positions in community colleges (Gutierrez et al., 2002). However, there remains an underrepresentation of Latinx/a/o professionals in decision-making roles within community colleges, and it is noteworthy and troubling (de los Santos & Vega, 2008; Hernandez, 2013; Valverde, 2003).

The data make it clear that Latinx/a/os attend community college in record numbers, and to provide specific support for this population, institutional policy specifically attuned to Latinx/a/o needs must be developed (Martinez & Fernandez, 2004). Institutional leadership—in particular, the college president—must address issues that not only lead the discourse of equality, equity, and inclusion but also address why these things matter (Rodriguez, 2015). While high enrollment numbers are important to the fiscal stability for community colleges, leaders must balance this pressure with policy and practice to support Latinx/a/o students. As an example, community colleges may consider becoming an Achieving the Dream (ATD) institution, which was initiated in 2004 by the Lumina Foundation for Education. ATD leads an all-inclusive nongovernmental reform network for community college student success focused on serving marginalized populations such as Latinx/a/o students (http://achievingthedream.org).

In addition to institutional initiatives, students need role models. Senior leadership within community colleges is mostly male and Caucasian (Ross & Green, 2000). College campuses should increase Latinx/a/o faculty and staff to help with the real and perceived discrimination by Whites and other dominant groups (Harper & Hurtado, 2007). This increase of Latinx/a/o personnel is essential to avoid unwelcoming environments that could lead to misunderstandings, which result in a decreased retention rate among minority faculty (Gutierrez et al., 2002). Rodriguez (2015) asserted that hiring minority faculty and staff is not only beneficial to students of color but also to the entire campus community. Institutional leadership must focus on developing and implementing diversity polices (Williams, 2013).

Although policies to serve Latinx/a/o students need to be addressed, leadership programs are increasing. As an example, the National Community College Hispanic Council (NCCHC) has produced more than 250 NCCHC Leadership Program Fellows, and alumni now serve in community college executive leadership positions (Martinez & Herney, 2017). The NCCHC leadership program offers, among other opportunities, the development of a national coalition of 11 community college districts to offer financial capital to sustain the program until 2019 (Martinez & Herney, 2017). Although this program highlights an example of opportunities, as of 2017, only 5% of Hispanics serve as community college CEOs (Martinez & Herney, 2017).

Community college institutional leadership should employ ACPA and NASPA's (2015) Leadership and Organizational and Human Resources professional competency areas to further the needed expansion of Latinx/a/o faculty and staff at community colleges.

Educational Pathways

When Latinx/a/o students consider college attendance, they call on their social networks to assist in the enrollment process (Carolan-Silva & Reyes, 2013; Nunez, 2009; Pérez & McDonough, 2008; Person & Rosenbaum, 2006; Stanton-Salazar, 2011). However, financial constraints are often barriers to college. Any financial assistance for Latinx/a/os is positively associated with degree completion; yet, over time, the positive effects of financial aid decline (Gross, Zerquera, Inge, & Berry, 2014). Interestingly, since Hispanic students are more likely than others to attend community colleges and not follow with a four-year degree, they generally have lower student debt (Krogstad, 2016).

Nevertheless, in 2016 members of NASPA's Community Colleges Division Latinx/a/o Task Force indicated three strategies to improve Latinx/a/o financial assistance for community college students: (a) increase efforts to help Latinx/a/os apply for financial aid, (b) create an emergency fund for students who encounter financial roadblocks, and (c) create performance-based scholarships that can be used as incentives to keep students on track and attending full time.

To better support educational pathways for Latinx/a/o students, institutions must find the best people to deliver information. McDonough and Calderone (2006) suggested that counselors are the primary sources for best communicating how to pay for college. This is important because research demonstrates that Latinx/a/o students' college aspirations are challenged by a lack of information communicated about college costs (Perna, 2000). Institutions can address financial constraints and create pathways to college by increasing budgetary funds dedicated to underrepresented populations (Rodriguez, 2015). As an example, community colleges can partner with local high schools to offer dual credit for courses taken at the high school. This way, students begin receiving college credits while enrolled in high school, which can lower costs, assist with college retention, and increase graduation rates (Perez & McDonough, 2008).

Community college administrators are held accountable for enrollment, so data collection matters (Gonzalez, 2015). Sarita Brown, president of Excelencia in Education, asserted that community colleges play an essential role for Latinx/a/o students' academic success and that institutions must assess decidedly what they are doing to assist these students (West, 2016). One way to intentionally address and formalize Latinx/a/o strategies is for community colleges to consider utilizing Latinx/a/o critical race theory (LatCrit) when working with this population. This theory emerged from critical race theory; however,

LatCrit examines experiences unique to the Latinx/a/o community, such as immigration status, language, ethnicity, and culture (Solórzano & Delgado Bernal, 2001). Therefore, when working with students to alleviate deficit-based perspectives on Latinx/a/o academic potential, LatCrit may help understand educational pathways for these students.

As scholar-practitioners, we have come to know the ACPA and NASPA (2015) professional competency areas through our personal experiences along the postsecondary education pathways of New York and California. These unique epistemological perspectives are grounded in our shared identities as Latinx/a/os in the United States. To help improve Latinx/a/o student success in community colleges, each of us brings these ways of knowing to multiple commitments within the student affairs profession. Practitioners should consider developing the aforementioned ACPA and NASPA (2015) competency areas robustly to advance community college Latinx/a/o educational pathways.

RECOMMENDATIONS

Martinez and Fernandez (2004) argued that institutional assistance is necessary in order to create environments that support diverse students. Therefore, to address effective access and success in community colleges, it seems appropriate to categorize and enumerate a few recommendations.

First, student affairs professionals are encouraged when working with Latinx/a/o students to utilize the ACPA and NASPA (2015) professional competency areas, which delineate the comprehensive professional knowledge, skills, and attitudes expected of all student affairs professionals. In particular, the Advising and Supporting competency area should be employed when working with Latinx/a/o students in community colleges. One example of this is when Edward was advising his student David a few years back, in order to ensure appropriate course selection, Edward worked in partnership with the academic chair of Arts and Sciences to best assist David. By collaborating with others, Edward ensured David's schedule was the best it could be. Martin and Seifert (2011) suggested the influence of student affairs professionals is real—especially in the cognitive domain. However, Tovar (2014) cautioned counselors, when advising students, not to use a single-pronged approach. He suggested that counselors approach advising and supporting students via multiple lenses and to utilize a variety of skill sets when working to enhance Latinx/a/o student success in community colleges. Additionally, Tovar (2014) asserted that administrators should ensure better advising and supporting programs for Latinx/a/o students at community colleges. By doing so, he contended, community colleges will better assist Latinx/a/o students' psychosocial needs and ultimately help them to complete their degrees.

Second, community college leadership should foster a systemic and collegewide paradigm shift to fully realize the inclusion of Latinx/a/o students, faculty, staff, and administrators. As Hernandez et al. (2017) suggested, recruiting and retaining Latinx/a/o professionals helps community colleges to recognize the value of a diverse staff. Once these individuals are hired, as a way to retain them, community colleges should encourage and create distinct professional development to support diversity and inclusion for Latinx/a/o faculty and staff members. Another important result of increasing the diversity of all administrators, faculty, and staff is that it creates academic role models for Latinx/a/o students.

Third, community colleges need to regularly disaggregate data on Latinx/a/o students (Harper, 2013). Only then can a true understanding of the distinct characteristics and experiences of the Latinx/a/o population be understood. Disaggregated data may better assist leadership to offer programs specifically geared to Latinx/a/o students.

Specific data collection may also help improve financial assistance to Latinx/a/o students, better allocating institutional funds for their recruitment, retention, and completion.

Fourth, develop and promote organized mentorship programs to foster Latinx/a/o students' sense of belonging. Perhaps at the heart of all obstacles is a student's sense of belonging or lack thereof. A sense of belonging includes feeling safe, secure, and recognized. But most important, a sense of belonging adds meaning to students' feeling of inclusion on campus. Latinx/a/o community college students are constantly navigating this sense of belonging because they need to balance, masterfully at times, their families, work, and school obligations. In fact, Strayhorn (2012) asserted that *sentido de pertenencia* (a sense of belonging) is a critical component for Latinx/a/o success. Students also need role models and mentors to create the space for open, safe, consistent, and courageous conversations about threats and microaggressions. Stone (2004) as well as Marquez Kiyama and Luca (2014) highlighted the reciprocal benefits of mentorship: It fosters development and growth for both the mentor and mentee.

CONCLUSION

Latinx/a/o student affairs professionals should have a solid theoretical foundation to facilitate student access and success; it will help in supporting colleagues outside of the profession to understand the importance of the work. Carolan-Silva and Reyes (2013) indicated that Latinx/a/o students draw on a combination of social networks to access the support needed to succeed. And, in many cases, student affairs professionals are one of the few supports in community colleges who can notably address Latinx/a/o student concerns and obstacles.

The opportunity to engage students where they spend most of their time (outside the classroom) provides a noteworthy teaching opportunity. One can argue that based on the amount of time student affairs professionals interact with students, their role is equally important as that of faculty to successful college attendance and completion.

Our journeys into higher education, while different, have similarities. Both of us had supportive families, but neither of us thought we would become educational leaders. Our stories are not uncommon; to add breadth and depth to the existing body of literature, we encourage all professionals, when possible, to use qualitative methodologies when conducting research because Latinx/a/o stories need and deserve to be heard.

REFERENCES

ACPA—College Student Educators International & NASPA–Student Affairs Administrators in Higher Education. (2015). *Professional competency areas for student affairs educators.* Washington, DC: Authors.

American Association of Community Colleges. (2017). *Fact sheet.* Retrieved from http://www.aacc.nche.edu/ABOUTCC/Pages/fastfactsfactsheet.aspx

Brown, S. E., Santiago, D., & Lopez, E. (2003). Latinos in higher education: Today and tomorrow. *Change: The Magazine of Higher Learning, 35,* 40–47.

Carolan-Silva, A., & Reyes, J. R. (2013). Navigating the path to college: Latino students' social network and access to college. *Educational Studies, 49,* 334–359.

Cohen, A. M., Brawer, F. B., & Kisker, C. (2014). *The American community college* (5th ed.). San Francisco, CA: Jossey-Bass.

Cowan Pitre, C., & Pitre, P. (2009). Increasing underrepresented high school students' college transitions and achievements: TRIO educational opportunity programs. *NASSP bulletin, 93*(2), 96–110.

de los Santos, A. G., & Vega, I. I. (2008). Hispanic presidents and chancellors of institutions of higher education in the United States in 2001 and 2006. *Journal of Hispanic Higher Education, 14*(2), 693–727.

Easley, N., Bianco, M., & Leech, N. (2012). Ganas: A qualitative study examining Mexican heritage students' motivation to succeed in higher education. *Journal of Hispanic Higher Education, 11*(2), 164–178.

Fry, R., & Lopez, M. H. (2012). *Hispanic student enrollments reach new highs in 2011.* Retrieved from Pew Research Center website: http://www.pewhispanic.org/2012/08/20/hispanic-student-enrollments-reach-new-highs-in-2011

González, K. P. (2015). Increasing college completion for Latino/as in community colleges: Leadership and strategy. In M. L. Freeman & M. Martinez (Ed.), *Special issue: College completion for Latino/a students: Institutional and system approaches* (New Directions for Higher Education, No. 172, pp. 71–80). San Francisco, CA: Jossey-Bass.

Gross, J. P. K., Zerquera, D., Inge, B., & Berry, M. (2014). Latino associate degree completion: Effects of financial aid over time. *Journal of Hispanic Higher Education, 13*(3), 177–190.

Gutierrez, M., Castaneda, C., & Katsinas, S. G. (2002). Latino leadership in community colleges: Issues and challenges. *Community College Journal of Research and Practice, 26*(4), 297–314.

Harper, S. R. (2013). *Five things student affairs administrators can do to improve success among college men of color.* Washington, DC: NASPA–Student Affairs Administrators in Higher Education.

Harper, S. R., & Hurtado, S. H. (2007). Nine themes in campus racial climates and implications for institutional transformation. In S. R. Harper & L. D. Patton (Eds.), *Responding to the realities of race on campus* (New Directions for Student Services, No. 120, pp. 7–24). San Francisco, CA: Jossey-Bass.

Hernandez, I., Jr. (2013). *Latina/o leadership: Transforming community colleges* (Unpublished doctoral dissertation). Retrieved from http://lib.dr.iastate.edu/etd/13445

Hernández, I., Hernández, S., & de la Teja, M. H. (2017). *Five things student affairs professionals should know about supporting Latinx students in community colleges.* Washington, DC: NASPA–Student Affairs Administrators in Higher Education.

Improving college access and completion for low-income and first-generation students: Hearing before the Subcommittee on Higher Education and Workforce Training, of the House Committee on Education and the Workforce, 114th Cong. 7 (2015) (testimony of Laura Perna). Retrieved from https://www.gpo.gov/fdsys/pkg/CHRG-114hhrg94315/pdf/CHRG-114hhrg94315.pdf

Juszkiewicz, J. (2016, March). *Trends in community college enrollment and completion data, 2016.* Washington, DC: American Association of Community Colleges.

Krogstad, J. M. (2016, July). *5 facts about Latinos and education Hispanic trends.* Retrieved from Pew Research Center website: http://www.pewresearch.org/fact-tank/2016/07/28/5-facts-about-latinos-and-education

Krogstad, J. M., & Fry, R. (2015, January). *Hispanics to benefit from Obama's community college plan*. Retrieved from Pew Research Center website: http://www.pewresearch.org/fact-tank/2015/01/20/hispanics-to-benefit-from-obamas-community-college-plan

Kurlaender, M. (2006). Choosing community college: Factors affecting Latino college choice. In C. L. Horn, S. M. Flores, & G. Orfield (Eds.), *Latino educational opportunity* (New Directions for Community Colleges, No. 133, pp. 7–16). San Francisco, CA: Jossey-Bass.

Lopez, M. H. (2009). *Latinos and education: Explaining the attainment gap*. Retrieved from Pew Research Center website: http://www.pewhispanic.org/2009/10/07/latinos-and-education-explaining-the-attainment-gap

Marquez Kiyama, J., & Luca, S. G. (2014). Structured opportunities: Exploring the social and academic benefits for peer mentors in retention programs. *Journal of College Student Retention, 15*(4), 489–514. doi:10.2190/CS.15.4.b

Martin, G. L., & Seifert, T. A. (2011). The relationship between students' interactions with student affairs professionals and cognitive outcomes in the first year of college. *Journal of Student Affairs Research and Practice, 48*(4), 389–410.

Martinez, M., & Fernandez, E. (2004). Latinos at community colleges. In A. M. Ortiz (Ed.), *Addressing the unique needs of Latino American students* (New Directions for Student Services, No. 105, pp. 51–62). San Francisco, CA: Jossey-Bass.

Martinez, T. J., & Herney, S. A. (2017). Hispanic leadership pipeline. *Diverse: Issues In Higher Education, 34*(6), 25.

McDonough, P. M., & Calderone, S. (2006). The meaning of money: Perceptual differences between college counselors and low-income families about college costs and financial aid. *American Behavioral Scientist, 49*(12), 1703–1718.

National Center for Education Statistics. (2015a). Table 302.6: Percentage of 18- to 24-year-olds enrolled in degree-granting postsecondary institutions, by level of institution and sex and race/ethnicity of student: 1970 through 2015 [Data set]. Retrieved from https://nces.ed.gov/programs/digest/d16/tables/dt16_302.60.asp

National Center for Education Statistics. (2015b). Table 302.65: Percentage of 18- to 24-year-olds enrolled in degree-granting postsecondary institutions, by race/ethnicity and state: 2014 [Data set]. Retrieved from https://nces.ed.gov/programs/digest/d15/tables/dt15_302.65.asp

National Center for Education Statistics. (2015c). Table 306.20: Total fall enrollment in degree-granting postsecondary institutions, by level and control of institution and race/ethnicity of student: Selected years, 1976 through 2014 [Data set]. Retrieved from http://files.eric.ed.gov/fulltext/ED570993.pdf

Nuñez, A.-M. (2009). Latino students' transition to college: A social and intercultural capital perspective. *Harvard Educational Review, 79*(1), 22–48.

Nuñez, A.-M., Sparks, P. J., & Hernandez, E. A. (2011). Latino access to community colleges and Hispanic-serving institutions: A national study. *Journal of Hispanic Higher Education, 10*(1), 18–40.

Ortiz, A. M. (2004). Promoting the success of Latinos students: A call to action. In A. M. Ortiz (Ed.), *Addressing the unique needs of Latino American students* (New Directions for Student Services, No. 105, pp. 84–97). San Francisco, CA: Jossey-Bass.

Perez, P. A., & McDonough, P. M. (2008). Understanding Latina and Latino college choice: A social capital and chain migration analysis. *Journal of Hispanic Higher Education, 7*(3), 249–265.

Pérez, D., & Sáenz, V. B. (2017). Thriving Latino males in selective predominantly white institutions. *Journal of Hispanic Higher Education, 16*(2), 162–186.

Pérez, D., II, & Taylor, K. B. (2015). Cultivando logradores: Nurturing and sustaining Latino male success in higher education. *Journal of Diversity in Higher Education, 9*(1), 1–19.

Perna, L. (2000). Racial/ethnic group differences in college enrollment decisions. In A. Cabrera & S. La Nasa (Eds.), *Understanding college choice among disadvantaged students* (New Directions for Institutional Research, No. 107, pp. 65–83). San Francisco, CA: Jossey-Bass.

Person, A. E., & Rosenbaum, J. E. (2006). Chain enrollment and college enclaves: Benefit and drawbacks of Latino college students enrollment decisions. In C. L. Horn, S. M. Flores, & G. Orfield (Eds.), *Latino educational opportunity* (New Directions for Community Colleges, No. 133, pp. 51–60). San Francisco, CA: Jossey-Bass.

Rendón, L. I. (1994). Validating culturally diverse students: Toward a new model of learning and student development. *Innovative Higher Education, 19*(1), 33–51.

Rodriguez, F. C. (2015). Why diversity and equity matter: Reflections from a community college president. In E. L. Castro (Ed.), *Understanding equity in community college practice* (New Directions for Community Colleges, No. 172, pp. 15–24). San Francisco, CA: Jossey-Bass.

Roorda, M., & Brown, S. E. (2015). *The condition of college & career readiness 2015: Hispanic students.* Retrieved from ACT website: https://www.act.org/content/dam/act/unsecured/documents/CCCR_National_2016.pdf

Ross, M., & Green, M. F. (2000). *The American college president 2000 edition.* Washington, DC: American Council on Education.

Sáenz, V. B. (2002, September). *Hispanic students and community colleges: A critical point for intervention.* Los Angeles, CA: ERIC Clearinghouse for Community College.

Santiago, D. A. (2011, September 25). All together: The role of Latino families in higher education. *The Chronicle of Higher Education.* Retrieved from http://www.chronicle.com/article/All-Together-the-Role-of/129100

Snyder, T. D., de Brey, C., & Dillow, S. A. (2016). *Digest of education statistics 2015* (NCES 2016-014). Washington, DC: National Center for Education Statistics, Institute of Education Sciences, U.S. Department of Education.

Solórzano, D. G., & Delgado Bernal, D. (2001). Examining transformational resistance through a critical race and latcrit theory framework. *Urban Education, 36*(3), 308–332.

Solórzano, D. G., Acevedo-Gil, N., & Santos, R. E. (2013). *Latina/o community college students: Understanding the barriers of developmental education* (Policy Report No. 10). Retrieved from UC/ACCORD PATHWAYS to Postsecondary Success: Maximizing Opportunities for Youth in Poverty website: http://pathways.gseis.ucla.edu/publications/DevEdPolicyBrief.pdf

Stanton-Salazar, R. D. (2011). A social capital framework for the study of institutional agents and their role in the empowerment of low-status students and youth. *Youth & Society, 43*(3), 1066–1109.

Stepler, R. (2016). *Hispanic, black parents see college degree as key for children's success.* Retrieved from Pew Research Center website: http://www.pewresearch.org/fact-tank/2016/02/24/hispanic-black-parents-see-college-degree-as-key-for-childrens-success

Stone, F. (2004). *Mentoring advantage: Creating the next generation of leaders.* Chicago, IL: Dearborn Trade Publishing.

Strayhorn, T. L. (2012). *College students' sense of belonging: A key to educational success for all students.* New York, NY: Routledge.

Torres, V., Reiser, A., LePeau, L., Davis, L., & Ruder, J. (2006). A model of first-generation Latino/a college students' approach to seeking academic information. *NACADA Journal, 26*(2), 65–70.

Tovar, E. (2014). The role of faculty, counselor, and support programs on Latino/a community college students' success and intent to persist. *Community College Review, 43*(1), 46–71.

Valenzuela, A. (1999). *Subtractive schooling: U.S.-Mexican youth and the politics of caring.* Albany, NY: State University of New York Press.

Valverde, L. A. (2003). *Leaders of color in higher education: Unrecognized triumphs in harsh institutions.* New York, NY: Altamira Press.

West, C. (2016, April 4). Excelencia: Community colleges need to embrace Latino role. *Diverse: Issues in Higher Education.* Retrieved from https://diverseeducation.com/article/83286

Williams, D. A. (2013). *Strategic diversity leadership: Activating change and transformation.* Sterling, VA: Stylus.

Zamani-Gallaher, E. M. (2007). The confluence of race, gender, and class among community college students: Assessing attitudes toward affirmative action in college admissions. *Equity and Excellence in Education, 40*(3), 241–251.

CHAPTER 8

REVOLUTIONIZING HONORS

A Model for Transformation and Success

Marta Elena Esquilin

I n the United States, higher education is perceived as the great equalizer (Benedict & McClough, 2010; Dougherty, 1994; Kerckhoff, 1995; Knottnerus, 1987; Sewell & Hauser, 1972; Torche, 2011). There are staggering numbers of talented, critically minded, and academically promising young people who are experiencing real structural barriers to higher education (Solórzano, Villalpando, & Oseguera, 2005). While Latina/os represent the largest racial/ethnic group in the United States, they also have the lowest educational transition rates from elementary to advanced degrees in comparison with

Whites, Native Americans, Asian Americans, and African Americans (Solarzano et al., 2005). As Solarzano et al. (2005) contended, "This lack of achievement and attainment . . . has resulted in both a loss of talent to U.S. society and a loss of important role models for the next generation of Latina/o students" (p. 277). These structural inequities have devastating implications for Latinx/a/o communities.

Critical race theory (CRT) provides an important framework for understanding the ways in which racism has created real barriers to access and success for Latinx/a/o students (Delgado Bernal & Villalpando, 2002; Solórzano & Delgado Bernal, 2001; Solórzano & Villalpando, 1998; Villalpando, 2003; Villalpando & Delgado Bernal, 2002; Yosso, 2000). Within the field of higher education, "CRT . . . explores the ways in which 'race-neutral' laws and institutional structures, practices, and policies perpetuate racial/ethnic educational inequality" (Solórzano et al., 2005, p. 274). This theoretical framework provides a nuanced critique of how structural racism operates within higher education and offers a road map for high-impact initiatives that seek to eradicate these inequities.

The Honors Living-Learning Community (HLLC) at Rutgers University–Newark (RU-N), created by Shirley M. Collado—former executive vice chancellor and chief operating officer of RU-N and the ninth president of Ithaca College—aims to address educational inequities by fostering the holistic development of talented students who wish to contribute positively to society. Similar to other U.S. urban centers, Newark, New Jersey, has considerable educational and racial/ethnic inequities. In 2010 Newark had the largest number of Latino (93,746) and Black (145,085) residents of any municipality in New Jersey (American Community Survey, 2017). In 2016, of all Newark Public School students, 44% were Hispanic and 47% were Black (Newark Public Schools, 2017). Districtwide, only 73.47% of Newark high school students graduated, compared with the 90% of students statewide (American Community Survey, 2017). Furthermore, in 2015 only 16% of Newark residents who were 25 years of age or older had attained a bachelor's degree or higher; the statewide average was 38% (American Community Survey, 2017). Within this context, only 10% of Newark residents who identified as Latino or Hispanic had attained a bachelor's degree (American Community Survey, 2017).

At the HLLC, administrators and faculty are committed to removing structural barriers that deter low-income Latinx/o/a and Black students in Newark from pursuing higher education. The HLLC utilizes a multilayered admissions process focused on measuring academic potential, resiliency, and multiple intelligences to identify students who may be missed when traditional metrics (e.g., grades, SAT scores) are used to determine academic promise (Guinier, 2015; Miller, 2005). Furthermore, the HLLC employs various best practices—including intensive strengths-based academic advisement, residential living-learning communities, intergenerational mentoring, and culturally relevant pedagogy—to support students. Research on student success in college, specifically in terms of students from underrepresented communities, highlights the importance of wraparound services that include strong and seamless relationships among faculty, student services, and the community in order to support emotional, developmental, and academic achievement (Williamson, Goosen, & Gonzalez, 2014).

The HLLC's commitment is grounded in a belief that admitting students from underrepresented communities will enhance not only their lives but also the educational environment at RU-N as well as the local, national, and global community. In *The Tyranny of the Meritocracy,* Guinier (2015) elaborated on the invaluable perspectives that diverse students add both to college classrooms and to democracy. She asserted, "True diversity that brings together a group of individuals more representative of the world we live in can help all of us rethink tasks, synthesize information better, and innovate creative ways to solve problems" (p. 38). Arguably, there is no one better equipped to help solve local and global problems than students who may have experienced the impact of these issues firsthand. As a result of their life experiences, these students offer keen insights that make them indispensable assets to the college campus and to their fields of study.

The HLLC capitalizes on students' assets by providing them with opportunities and resources to become leaders in their fields of study, collaborators in their communities, and change agents in the world. This is consistent with Guinier's (2015) argument to reconceptualize merit within higher education:

If our society truly values education as a means of preparing citizens to participate in the decisions that affect their lives as individuals and the society they create as a collective, as well as to enable individuals to improve their lots and their society, then we need to reexamine exactly how we define "merit." (Introduction, para. 18)

Ultimately, Guinier's conceptualization of merit as an individual's ability to optimally contribute to democracy is consistent with the HLLC's mission to cultivate students who will change their communities and the world. Given the structural inequities plaguing Latinx/a/o communities nationally, Latinx/a/o students are in a unique position to provide innovative and culturally grounded solutions to ameliorate some of these issues. Yosso (2005) contended that people of color have accumulated unique resources in the form of community cultural wealth, or "an array of knowledge, skills, abilities and contacts possessed and utilized by Communities of Color to survive and resist macro- and micro-forms of oppression" (p. 77), which can increase their success in college but also allow them to optimally contribute to the public good (Pérez, 2016; Rendón, Nora, & Kanagala, 2014).

Research shows that educational ideologies based on deficit models can be harmful to the self-esteem, psychological well-being, and academic potential of those who are disenfranchised by systems of inequity (Irizarry, 2009; Pérez, Ashlee, Karikari, Do, & Sim, in press; Valencia, 1997, 2010). More specifically, Ford's (2014) research elucidated how deficit paradigms contribute to the underrepresentation of Black and Hispanic students in gifted programs. She asserted, "Too many African American and Hispanic students do not achieve to their potential because they are stifled by society's deeply ingrained bias of equating Whites and whiteness with superiority" (p. 150). This dynamic limits opportunities for Latinx/a/o students to take part in the high-quality educational experiences available in honors programs.

The HLLC at RU-N seeks to eradicate structural barriers while critiquing deficit-based ideologies that fail to recognize the talent, academic potential, and intellectual abilities of students from under-resourced communities. Utilizing a strengths-based model, the HLLC was implemented under the leadership of chancellor Nancy Cantor, who is nationally recognized for her research on the role that universities play as *anchor institutions* within communities. According to Cantor (2017), the RU-N's mission centers on not just being *in* Newark, but of Newark. This partnership with the Newark community includes interdependence, sharing of resources, and prioritizing work and scholarship that is mutually beneficial and focused on the public good (Cantor, 2017).

Part of realizing this vision is increasing access to higher education for Newark residents. To this end, the HLLC has broadened the ways that academic potential and intellect are identified and utilizes culturally relevant pedagogy and practices to create infrastructures that best support the intellectual, ethical, and psychosocial development of students who have been viewed through a deficit lens. Strengths-based perspectives assume that every individual has resources that can be mobilized toward success in many areas of life (Saleebey, 1996). More specifically, this approach is characterized by "efforts to label what is right" within people and organizations (Buckingham, 2007, p. 6). The HLLC has adopted a strengths-based model for identifying and cultivating academic talent and potential.

BACKGROUND

The HLLC disrupts narratives rooted in racist, classist, and deficit-based ideologies that create and maintain barriers to student success. These barriers often materialize as microaggressions that undermine the success of Latina/o college students (Yosso, Smith, Ceja, & Solórzano, 2009). Racial microaggressions are daily, brief, and commonplace verbal, behavioral, or environmental indignities—intentional or unintentional—that communicate hostile or derogatory racial slights and insults toward people of color (Sue et al., 2007). Narrow admissions metrics and culturally biased curriculum and pedagogical practices can perpetuate microaggressions.

Racial microaggressions diminish the emotional well-being and academic success of students who have a collective history of marginalization and disenfranchisement within the academy (Sue et al., 2007). Furthermore, Yosso et al.'s (2009) research on Latinx/a/o students revealed how microaggressions in the form of interpersonal, institutional, and racial jokes can be detrimental to student success. These ongoing verbal and psychological assaults influence students' self-efficacy and their perception of themselves as scholars and leaders within their disciplines. Studies indicate that ideologies related to the intellectual inferiority of Black and Latinx/a/o students permeate even the most progressive environments—that is, those in which White people often perceive themselves to be free of bias—and can be invisible to students of color who internalize these messages (Pérez et al., in press; Rivas-Drake & Mooney, 2009; Sue et al., 2007).

Strengths-Based Approaches to Latinx/a/o Student Success

Researchers have highlighted several best practices in supporting the success of Latinx/a/o students, such as high-touch mentoring, wraparound services, intensive academic advising, culturally specific communities of support, and curricular models (Museus, 2014; Museus & Jayakumar, 2012; Museus & Smith, 2016; Oseguera, Locks, & Vega, 2009; Solórzano et al., 2005; Swail, 2004; Yosso et al., 2009). Furthermore, the positive psychology movement and strengths-based approaches to student success, including attribution theory and appreciative inquiry, have focused heavily on helping students identify their own internal resources instead of emphasizing their deficits (Demetriou, & Schmitz-Sciborski, 2011; Pérez & Sáenz, 2017; Schreiner, 2010). This research can be used to inform student affairs practice and inspire innovative approaches to student success for those who have been racially and economically disenfranchised. By operationalizing best practices and innovative approaches grounded in research that is focused on what Paris (2012) characterized as resource pedagogies, or "approaches to teaching and learning [that] draw upon the cultural resources and strengths of students" (p. 1), the HLLC advances strengths-based praxis within higher education.

THE HLLC IS REDEFINING HONORS

The HLLC is redefining the notion of *merit* by creating diverse intergenerational and interdisciplinary learning communities that cultivate Latinx/a/o students' academic talent and potential to effect positive social change in Newark. The HLLC's learning communities are composed of students, faculty, and community partners who are engaged in rigorous scholarship centered on addressing the nation's most pressing social issues, including, but not limited to, poverty, xenophobia, racism, sexism and heterosexism, and climate change.

The HLLC was purposefully designed to help students thrive at RU-N. The HLLC's admissions processes and retention practices are culturally specific and responsive to the educational needs of students who have been disenfranchised by systems of inequity in education. In designing the HLLC, faculty and staff reflected on several questions: What would it mean to truly value and recognize the assets that Latinx/a/o and other HLLC scholars bring to the RU-N college campus? How might HLLC administrators center their experiences within the curriculum? What infrastructures are needed to create a model for student success that identifies and cultivates their unique strengths, talents, and skill sets?

Approximately two-thirds of the soon-to-be 400 HLLC scholars are residents of greater Newark who demonstrate potential to succeed academically, think critically, and become positive change agents on campus and in the larger community. HLLC scholars are selected to join a diverse living-learning community focused on cultivating knowledge; fostering understanding across and within groups; and activating social, institutional, and cultural change. The demographic trends within the HLLC are significant given its stark contrast with traditional honors communities, which admit students primarily based on test scores and grades.

Approximately 80% of HLLC students identify as Black or Latinx/a/o. More than 65% of these students are eligible for Pell Grants, and almost 50% are first-generation college students. Traditionally, honors colleges disproportionately admit students who identify as White and come from the upper socioeconomic quartiles (Ford, 2014; Pittman, 2001). Ford (2014) documented racial segregation that exists within gifted and honors programs at the secondary level: "There is no denying that gifted education classes and services are disproportionately represented by and serving White, higher-income, and privileged students, and gifted education gives them a boost up the social and fiscal hierarchy" (p. 149). Demographic trends in advanced placement courses and gifted programs have a direct correlation to college honors (Quinton, 2014). Lack of access to pre-college honors opportunities often results in the underrepresentation of Black, Latinx/a/o, and low-income students in honors programs at the college level. Therefore, the HLLC is utilizing alternative metrics to assess students' academic potential.

IDENTIFYING ALTERNATIVES TO THE SAT

The HLLC recognizes that the SAT is not an adequate assessment tool for measuring the unique skills, knowledge, or multiple intelligences necessary to be successful in college or to contribute optimally to society. Researchers consistently highlight racial and economic biases inherent in standardized testing and how this negatively impacts admissions rates among low-income students of color (Astin, 1982, 1993; Miller, 2005; Solórzano et al., 2005). Solórzano et al. (2005) attributed the disproportionate representation of Latinx/a/os in two-year versus four-year institutions to the use of standardized testing.

SAT scores do not assess a student's ability to critically analyze social inequities or use innovative methods to address them. These scores do not assess the skills necessary to have difficult dialogues about identity and community in diverse settings. Finally, standardized tests will not allow us to assess a student's orientation toward failure and his or her unique ability to exhibit the resiliency necessary to navigate challenges within a college environment. Guinier (2015) expanded on the dangers of relying exclusively on the SAT in college admissions process:

> When we redefine merit by those characteristics that indicate a student's potential for future success in our democracy—leadership, the ability to collaborate with others, resiliency, and a drive to learn, among others—then we might be able to make use of actions that prioritize such traits. If we commit to mentoring and nurturing that potential in our students, universities might more successfully cultivate potential leaders. (p. 20)

Given the HLLC's distinctive mission and focus on social change and community engagement, expanding the admissions rubric to measure traits like leadership and resiliency are imperative. The HLLC has designed a comprehensive rubric that measures student characteristics including critical thinking skills, social and emotional intelligence, leadership skills, academic potential, artistic and intellectual abilities, resiliency, passion for social change, and the ability to dialogue across difference. The metrics for these attributes center on the realities of students whose social identities and life experiences position them to contribute innovative perspectives to local issues.

Each year, the HLLC engages approximately 900 students in a series of interactive activities designed to assess their abilities. This holistic admissions process includes large group interviews, individual interviews, holistic assessment of transcripts, and essays focused on students' passions related to social issues. The large group interview process requires students to operate in teams and to engage in group simulations focused on conceptualizing community development plans and allocating resources based on community needs. This process allows faculty and staff to assess orientation toward social justice, ability to operate in a group, leadership skills, and critical thinking skills.

The individual interview process focuses heavily on understanding the student's life experiences and identifying individual strengths, resiliency, coping skills, resourcefulness, values, and passions. These attributes are assessed through a series of questions that allow students to share stories and articulate how these concepts have emerged in their lives. More specifically, consistent with attribution theory (Demetriou & Schmitz-Sciborski, 2011), there is a focus on understanding how students make meaning of their failures and successes. The HLLC looks for students who can adapt to failure and not give up and those who have an internal locus of control. Students who believe they have some level of control over the outcomes of their lives and those who have a deep sense of purpose or responsibility that allows them to persevere through obstacles will be more successful in college (Demetriou & Schmitz-Sciborski, 2011). Yosso's (2005) community cultural wealth theory, a strengths-based framework for understanding the unique cultural assets and resiliency that students who have been disenfranchised by systems of inequity bring to a college environment, supported how these attributes foster success within college.

Each year, the HLLC admits 90 first-year and transfer students. Including transfer students from local community colleges in the pool fulfills two priorities—increasing college access for under-resourced students and creating intergenerational learning communities. Many of the transfer students admitted into the HLLC are older students with varied life experiences. Research related to the benefits of intergenerational learning communities highlights the value for both older and younger students in the co-creation of knowledge (Marquez Kiyama & Luca, 2014; Pstross et al., 2017). Most Latinx/a/o students' initial exposure to college is through the community college system (Solórzano, Acevedo-Gil, & Santos, 2013). However, holistically identifying and admitting students to the HLLC is just the beginning. The HLLC utilizes culturally specific pedagogy and practice to create infrastructures that best support students' intellectual, ethical, and psychosocial development.

THE HLLC CURRICULUM

The HLLC builds on students' knowledge and lived experiences, increases cultural competency, and teaches students to approach local challenges from historical, philosophical, and comparative perspectives. The HLLC curriculum builds upon Ladson-Billings (1995) assertion that instituting a culturally relevant pedagogy will "produce students who can achieve academically . . . demonstrate cultural competence, and . . . who can both understand and critique the existing social order" (p. 474). The HLLC curriculum provides students with a framework to explore social inequities and themes related to citizenship as they emerge within various academic disciplines. All students take 18 credits of HLLC courses that are interdisciplinary, are taught by faculty and community leaders from various sectors, and explore themes related to local citizenship in a global world. Courses offered in the 2016–2017 academic year focused on a variety of topics—from tackling juvenile justice to illustrating Newark's oral histories through the arts, to critiquing images of crime in the media.

High academic expectations of students are at the core of culturally relevant pedagogy (Ladson-Billings, 1995). One of the HLLC's core courses, HLLC 303: Local Citizenship Within a Global World, is a writing-intensive course focused on the historical and contemporary role that local citizens have played in fostering social change in Newark and beyond. By design, the 300-level course combines students of various academic experiences and preparedness and sets high expectations for academic rigor, critical thinking, and intensive reading and writing; at the same time, the course offers high levels of individualized academic support for those who need it.

The HLLC curriculum focuses on creating learning communities of scholars, activists, community members, and students engaged in critical discourse about some of the world's most pressing social issues. Many of the faculty are engaged in public scholarship to improve the lives of underserved communities. This central pedagogical approach is reflected in bell hooks's concept of critical thinking as transformation. She explained this concept as follows:

> I think thinking critically is at the heart of anybody transforming their life. . . . In a certain kind of patronizing way, education just says, all these people need is tools for survival, basic survival tools, like their degree so they can get a job and not, in fact, that we enhance their lives in the same way we've enhanced our lives by engaging in a certain kind of critical process. (Patierno, Jhally, & Hirshorn, 2002, p. 3)

Faculty and staff strive to engage students in experiences that help them critically reflect on what it means to be an agent of change in their families, communities, and the world.

INTERGENERATIONAL MENTORING AND COHORT MODEL

The HLLC has built a retention infrastructure based on national best practices to support HLLC students from admission through graduation. Students of color are more likely to stay in school and graduate when they develop strong social ties and are integrated into smaller cultural communities (Marquez Kiyama & Luca, 2014; Solórzano & Yosso, 2000). The HLLC is made up of multiple learning communities and utilizes a cohort model. In addition to smaller intergenerational learning communities that center on the curriculum, students live together in residence halls and are assigned to cohorts of 10 students, creating social support systems that are critical during the first two years—when students are most likely to drop out of college. HLLC cohorts meet biweekly with peer mentors, who are older HLLC scholars and who have been trained and supported to facilitate cohort meetings that deal with acclimating to the RU-N community, learning about campus resources, and providing a safe space for HLLC scholars to process their collegiate experiences. Peer mentoring and encouraging intergenerational support systems are powerful tools for community building, retention, and student success.

In addition, all HLLC scholars meet biweekly with a faculty mentor during the first two years of college. The HLLC purposefully select mentors who are comfortable engaging diverse student populations. Faculty mentors provide holistic support, addressing personal, academic, and social matters. Faculty mentors are supported by HLLC deans via biweekly group meetings, where they receive guidance and work collaboratively to connect students with such resources as learning centers, counseling services, financial aid, and crisis intervention. Additionally, the HLLC provides academic advisors and deans who offer individualized advising to students based on their level of academic preparedness and major field of study.

IMPLICATIONS FOR PRACTICE

The HLLC is an innovative model for designing honors programs that accurately reflect the demographics of the nation and that prepare future leaders to address social inequity on multiple levels. The first implication for practice relates to shifting how academic potential, abilities, and intellect are measured by utilizing a more holistic admissions process. The second implication—and perhaps one of the most challenging aspects of the HLLC's work—focuses on cultivating Latinx/a/o student talent, particularly when students have internalized deficit-based ideologies related to intelligence and worth. The HLLC challenges faculty and staff to reflect critically on the norms and assumptions that undergird the culture of the institution and examine what it would mean to truly shift structures, policies, and environments to be inclusive and supportive of all students (Pérez et al., in press; Valencia, 2010). Central to this concept is culturally relevant pedagogy that privileges the experiences of Latinx/a/o students and frames teaching and learning through that lens (Museus & Jayakumar, 2012). The HLLC curriculum focuses on community-engaged scholarship and examines what it means to be active citizens and positive change agents in the world.

The third implication is the importance of intergenerational mentoring in supporting the success of Latinx/a/o students—both through individualized support from faculty and staff mentors and through cohort-based peer mentoring. This multilayered support system helps students acclimate to the campus environment and aids in their psychosocial development. For Latinx/a/o students in particular, culturally based support systems and strong community ties are critical to their success on campus (Museus, 2014; Museus & Jayakumar, 2012; Museus & Smith, 2016; Oseguera et al., 2009; Solórzano et al., 2005; Swail, 2004; Yosso et al., 2009). Residential living-learning communities and shared interdisciplinary learning communities aid in this support.

Lastly, the HLLC has prioritized placing Latinx/a/o faculty and staff in leadership positions throughout the organization. For far too long, students marginalized by systems of inequity have been forced to the sidelines while their identities, needs, and potential for success were defined by others. The lack of Latinx/a/o role models in leadership positions, the undervaluing of their intellectual abilities or potential, and the centering of Eurocentric hetero-patriarchal histories, values, and experiences are nothing less than alienating. Latinx/a/o students need to see themselves reflected at the highest levels so that they may aspire to reach their fullest potential.

CONCLUSION

Established in 2015, the HLLC has served as an incubator for innovation on issues of access, equity, inclusion, and pedagogy at RU-N. Through this initiative, the HLLC has been able to creatively engage students, faculty, and staff to increase access to higher education for Latinx/a/o students, cultivate their academic potential and leadership abilities through culturally relevant and publicly engaged pedagogical practices, and utilize best practices for retention and student success.

REFERENCES

Advocates for Children of New Jersey. (2017). *New Jersey kids count report.* Retrieved from http://acnj.org/downloads/2017_03_16_KidsCount_Newark_8Education.pdf

American Community Survey. (2017). Retrieved from https://www.census.gov/programs-surveys/acs

Astin, A. W. (1982). *Minorities in American higher education.* San Francisco, CA: Jossey-Bass.

Astin, A. W. (1993). *What matters in college? Four critical years revisited.* San Francisco, CA: Jossey-Bass.

Benedict, M. E., & McClough, D. (2010). Is education the great equalizer? An examination of race and higher education attainment on earnings. *Pennsylvania Economic Review, 17*(1/2), 77–97.

Buckingham, D. (2007). *Beyond technology: Children's learning in the age of digital culture.* Cambridge, United Kingdom: Polity.

Cantor, N. (2017). *Anchor institution—community engagement in Newark: Striving together.* Retrieved from http://www.newark.rutgers.edu/sites/default/files/camden_anchors_panel—final_formatted.pdf

Delgado Bernal, D., & Villalpando, O. (2002). An apartheid of knowledge in academia: The struggle over the "legitimate" knowledge of faculty of color. *Equity & Excellence in Education, 35*(2), 169–180.

Demetriou, C., & Schmitz-Sciborski, A. (2011). Integration, motivation, strengths and optimism: Retention theories past, present and future. In R. Hayes (Ed.), *Proceedings of the 7th National Symposium on Student Retention, 2011, Charleston* (pp. 300–312). Norman, OK: The University of Oklahoma.

Dougherty, K. (1994). *The contradictory college: The conflicting origins, impacts, and futures of community colleges.* Albany, NY: SUNY Press.

Ford, D. Y. (2014). Segregation and the underrepresentation of blacks and Hispanics in gifted education: Social inequality and deficit paradigms. *Roeper Review, 36*(3), 143–154.

Guinier, L. (2015). *The tyranny of the meritocracy: Democratizing higher education in America* [Kindle version]. Retrieved from Amazon.com

Irizarry, J. G. (2009). Reinvigorating multicultural education through youth participatory action research. *Multicultural Perspectives, 11*(4), 194–199.

Kerckhoff, A. C. (1995). Institutional arrangement and stratification processes in industrial societies. *Annual Review of Sociology, 21,* 323–347.

Knottnerus, J. D. (1987). Status attainment research and its image of society. *American Sociological Review, 52*(1), 113–121.

Ladson-Billings, G. (1995). Toward a theory of culturally relevant pedagogy. *American Educational Research Journal, 32*(3), 465–491.

Marquez Kiyama, J., & Luca, S. G. (2014). Structured opportunities: Exploring the social and academic benefits for peer mentors in retention programs. *Journal of College Student Retention, 15*(4), 489–514.

Miller, L. S. (2005). Exploring high academic performance: The case of Latinos in higher education. *Journal of Hispanic Higher Education, 4*(3), 252–271.

Museus, S. D. (2014). The Culturally Engaging Campus Environments (CECE) Model: A new theory of college success among racially diverse student populations. In M. B. Paulsen (Ed.), *Higher education: Handbook of theory and research* (Vol. 29, pp. 189–227). New York, NY: Springer.

Museus, S. D., & Jayakumar, U. M. (2012). *Creating campus cultures: Fostering success among racially diverse student populations.* New York, NY: Routledge.

Museus, S. D., & Smith, E. J. (2016). *The culturally engaging campus environments: Model and survey.* Washington, DC: NASPA–Student Affairs Administrators in Higher Education.

Newark Public Schools. (2017). *Newark public schools: District summary (2016-2017).* Retrieved from http://www.nps.k12.nj.us/departments/data-research/district-summary

Oseguera, L., Locks, A. M., & Vega, I. I. (2009). Increasing Latina/o students' baccalaureate attainment: A focus on retention. *Journal of Hispanic Higher Education, 8*(1), 23–53.

Paris, D. (2012). Culturally sustaining pedagogy: A needed change in stance, terminology, and practice. *Educational Researcher, 41*(3), 93–97.

Patierno, M., Jhally, S., & Hirshorn, H. (Eds.). (2002). *bell hooks: Cultural criticism & transformation.* Northampton, MA: Media Education Foundation.

Pérez II, D. (2016). Over the ivy wall: Latino male achievers nurturing community cultural wealth at a highly selective, predominantly white institution. In V. B. Sáenz, L. Ponjuán, & J. López Figueroa (Eds.), *Ensuring the success of Latino males in higher education: A national imperative* (pp. 130–146). Sterling, VA: Stylus.

Pérez, D., II, Ashlee, K., Karikari, S., Do, V. H., & Sim, C. (in press). Re-conceptualizing student success in higher education: Reflections from graduate student affairs educators using anti-deficit achievement framework. *Journal on Excellence in College Teaching.*

Pérez, D., II, & Sáenz, V. B. (2017). Thriving Latino males in selective predominantly white institutions. *Journal of Hispanic Higher Education, 16*(2), 162–186.

Pittman, A. A. (2001). Diversity issues & honors education. *Innovations in undergraduate research and honors education: Proceedings of the Second Schreyer National Conference.* Retrieved from http://digitalcommons.unl.edu/nchcschreyer2/25

Pstross, M., Corrigan, T., Knopf, R. C., Sung, H. K., Talmage, C. A., Conroy, C., & Fowley, C. (2017). The benefits of intergenerational learning in higher education: Lessons learned from two age friendly university programs. *Innovative Higher Education, 42*(2), 157–171. doi:10.1007/s10755-016-9371-x

Quinton, S. (2014, December 11). The race gap in high school honors classes. *The Atlantic.* Retrieved from https://www.theatlantic.com/politics/archive/2014/12/the-race-gap-in-high-school-honors-classes/431751

Rendón, L. I., Nora, A., & Kanagala, V. (2014). *Ventajas/assets y conocimientos/knowledge: Leveraging Latin@ strengths to foster student success.* San Antonio, TX: The University of Texas at San Antonio, College of Education & Human Development, Center for Research and Policy in Education.

Rivas-Drake, D., & Mooney, M. (2009). Neither colorblind nor oppositional: Perceived minority status and trajectories of academic adjustment among Latinos in elite higher education. *Developmental Psychology, 45*(3), 642–651.

Saleebey, D. (1996). The strengths perspectives in social work practice: Extensions and cautions. *Social Work, 41*(3), 296–305. doi:10.1093/sw/41.3.296

Schreiner, L. A. (2010). The "thriving quotient": A new vision for student success. *About Campus, 15*(2), 2–10.

Sewell, W. H., & Hauser, R. M. (1972). Causes and consequences of higher education: Models of the status attainment process. *American Journal of Agricultural Economics, 54,* 851–861.

Solórzano, D. G., Acevedo-Gil, N., & Santos, R. E. (2013). *Latina/o community college students: Understanding the barriers of developmental education* (Policy Report No. 10). Retrieved from https://pathways.gseis.ucla.edu/publications/DevEdPolicyBrief.pdf

Solórzano, D. G., & Delgado Bernal, D. (2001). Critical race theory and transformational resistance: Chicana/o students in an urban context. *Urban Education, 36*(3), 308–342.

Solórzano, D. G., & Villalpando, O. (1998). Critical race theory, marginality, and the experience of minority students in higher education. In C. Torres & T. Mitchell, (Eds.), *Emerging issues in the sociology of education: Comparative perspectives* (pp. 211–224). Albany, NY: SUNY Press.

Solórzano, D. G., Villalpando, O., & Oseguera, L. (2005). Educational inequities and Latina/o undergraduate students in the United States: A critical race analysis of their educational progress. *Journal of Hispanic Higher Education, 4*(3), 272–294.

Solórzano, D. G., & Yosso, T. (2000). Toward a critical race theory of Chicana and Chicano education. In C. Tejeda, C. Martinez, & Z. Leonardo (Eds.), *Demarcating the border of Chicana(o)/ Latina(o) education* (pp. 35–65). Cresskill, NJ: Hampton Press.

Solórzano, R. W., & Solórzano, D. G. (1999). Beginning teacher standards: Impact on second-language learners and implications for teacher education. *Teacher Education Quarterly, 26*, 37–70.

Steele, C. M., & Aronson, J. (1995). Stereotype threat and the intellectual test performance of African Americans. *Journal of Personality and Social Psychology, 69*(5), 797–811.

Sue, D. W., Capodilupo, C. M., Torino, G. C., Bucceri, J. M., Holder, A., Nadal, K. L., & Esquilin, M. (2007). Racial microaggressions in everyday life: Implications for clinical practice. *American Psychologist, 62*(4), 271–286.

Swail, W. S. (2004). *The art of student retention: A handbook for practitioners and administrators.* Austin, TX: Educational Policy Institute.

Torche, F. (2011). Is a college degree still the great equalizer? Intergenerational mobility across levels of schooling in the United States. *American Journal of Sociology, 117*(3), 763–807.

Valencia, R. R. (1997). *The evolution of deficit thinking: Educational thought and practice.* The Stanford Series on Education and Public Policy. Bristol, PA: Falmer Press.

Valencia, R. R. (2010). *Dismantling contemporary deficit thinking: Educational thought and practice.* New York, NY: Routledge.

Villalpando, O. (2003). Self-segregation or self-preservation? A critical race theory and Latina/o critical theory analysis of a study of Chicana/o college students. *International Journal of Qualitative Studies in Education, 16*(5), 619–646.

Villalpando, O., & Delgado Bernal, D. (2002). A critical race theory analysis of barriers that impede the success of faculty of color. In W. Smith, P. Altbach, & K. Lomotey (Eds.), *The racial crisis in American higher education* (pp. 243–270). Albany, NY: SUNY Press.

Williamson, L. V., Goosen, R. A., & Gonzalez, G. F., Jr. (2014). Faculty advising to support student learning. *Journal of Developmental Education, 38*(1), 20–24.

Yosso, T. J. (2000). *Critical race and LatCrit approach to media literacy: Chicana/o resistance to visual microaggressions* (Unpublished doctoral dissertation). University of California, Los Angeles.

Yosso, T. J. (2005). Whose culture has capital? A critical race theory discussion of community cultural wealth. *Race Ethnicity and Education, 8*(1), 69–91.

Yosso, T. J., Smith, W. A., Ceja, M., & Solórzano, D. G. (2009). Critical race theory, racial microaggressions, and campus racial climate for Latina/o. *Harvard Educational Review, 79*(4), 659–786.

PART IV

LATINX/A/O PROFESSIONAL PATHWAYS

Mid-level
Professional Narrative

Using "I" Statements

Identity, Involvement, and Intentionality in a Latinx/a/o Professional's Journey

Juan Carlos Matos

Becoming a student affairs professional was not my initial career goal. Neither of my parents attended a four-year university, and I knew of only two cousins who attended college. Additionally, I didn't have much guidance in high school on how to combine a passion for drawing, a desire to be an architect, and a love for science. Ultimately, however, this eclectic mix of interests and motivation converged into applying to the University of Miami (UM) with an architectural engineering major.

As an undergraduate, I remember conversations with other students about school "getting in the way" of being involved with clubs and wishing that being a student leader counted as a class. Through my involvement at UM, my exposure to the field of student affairs increased, and my desire to pursue a graduate degree in higher education became a lot clearer. What I experienced is described in Taub and McEwen's (2006) research investigating why individuals enter the field of higher education. Because "no undergraduate major leads directly to graduate study in student affairs and because so few individuals are aware of the field as a career possibility" (p. 206), developing an interest and ultimately desiring to join the profession continues to be a game of chance. As in my case, it is often through student leadership roles and interactions with administrators that undergraduate students become interested in student affairs as a career.

Reflecting back on my journey led me to think critically about which experiences had the most impact on the professional I am today. In this narrative, I will share how I was able to navigate my development as a student and professional as a result of three major factors: (a) engaging in opportunities to explore my intersecting identities, (b) getting involved, and (c) acting intentionally at each step along my journey. I believe that these three factors have helped me to navigate my journey and can be helpful to other Latinx/a/o professionals as they, too, pursue success in higher education.

INTERSECTING IDENTITIES

In my own journey, success as a student and professional has been shaped by a marked attention to and reflection about my intersecting identities. I was born in the Dominican Republic, was brought to the United States by my parents when I was less than a year old, and grew up in Brooklyn. The only Dominicans I knew growing up were my family members and a few students at my school and their families. I went to Catholic school all the way through high school and spent most of my life being called Juan, pronounced as "won," like in wonton. College was the first time I had the opportunity to ask to be called Juan Carlos, as opposed to just by my first name. It was the first step in reclaiming my Latino identity.

Ferdman and Gallegos (2001) developed a way to understand the matrix of Latinx/a/o identity orientation and to describe the complexity of Latinx/a/o cultural identity. As a freshman, I navigated existing between being "sub-group identified," expanding on my Dominican identity, and being "Latino-identified," acknowledging Latinos as "a distinct racial category across all Latino subgroups" (Ferdman & Gallegos, 2001, p. 51). As detailed in this matrix, through the orientation process, Latinx/a/o identity becomes fully integrated with other intersecting identities, including gender, race, ethnicity, class, professional level, and other dimensions. As a result, many Latinx/a/os are also able to understand, explain, and use the inherent interconnections to understand and identify with many parts of themselves and others. For me, understanding my different identities and their intersections has certainly facilitated connecting with others and building relationships.

Along the way, the "Latino-integrated" orientation described by Ferdman and Gallegos (2001) has helped me to understand my identity development and exploration process—and to become more self-aware. While at UM, I was involved with the Hispanic Heritage Month committee through the Office of Multicultural Student Affairs. This experience led me to explore my Dominican roots more deeply and to understand that Dominicans identify as a mix of African, indigenous/ Taíno, and European racial ancestry. The learning I experienced as part of the committee deepened my connection to my Latino identity. As a result of my experience and self-discovery, I then shifted from self-identifying as Latino to being Afro-Latino. Although I had never denied my

African ancestry, formally identifying as Afro-Latino was a way to officially acknowledge this heritage. Along with rediscovering and accepting my racial and ethnic identity, I also had to tackle my coming-out process. Although my parents and family were not outwardly homophobic, their connection to Christianity made me afraid to explore my sexual orientation while living at home. Going away for college granted me the freedom to explore being gay and also the opportunity to come out to the majority of my family members at my own pace.

But despite my ability to navigate coming out and being accepted by my family, it has been hard, at times, to feel included and accepted culturally, given that the Latino culture and language are inherently structured and gendered male and female. It was not until recently, after serving as a full-time professional for five years, that I learned about the new gender-inclusive term *Latinx/a/o* gaining popularity in various sectors of the Latina/o community. The term recognizes the intersection of gender identity with *Latinidad,* the cultural and social attributes connected to Latin American people, and captures the intersections of my racial/ethnic, gender, and sexual identities. That being said, I acknowledge that others in the Latinx/a/o community may disagree and that I am privileged as a cisgender male who can use the terms *Latino* and *Latinx/a/o* interchangeably within the community. It is equally important to consider that many transgender, gender-queer, and gender nonconforming people feel that Latinx/a/o is the most inclusive way to identify themselves, given their intersecting identities and the established gendered norms of the culture.

INVOLVEMENT

My participation in clubs as a college student—and connecting to identity-specific communities and professional organizations—has helped me to develop stronger leadership skills as well as camaraderie with other professionals who also have marginalized identities. Growing as a leader and gaining professional colleagues through participation in identity-based communities was only possible because of my increased understanding of the importance of the multiple dimensions of my own identity. According to Jones and McEwen (2000), it is critical for individuals to have a core set of attributes and characteristics and various intersecting identity circles, all within a contextual space influenced by family background, sociocultural conditions, and career decisions, to name a few. If one thinks about the communities one is involved in as the contextual space in which one navigates social identities, being able to connect with others based on these various identities is essential to professional growth.

In my case, engaging with others who share similar social identities has continued to be the best way to find new paths for involvement. Astin (1999) defined involvement as "the amount of physical and psychological energy [a student] devotes to the academic experience" (p. 518). Thus, the amount of time devoted to various forms of involvement can shape one's trajectory. My passion for being involved led to taking leadership roles in cultural clubs, founding a campus chapter of Sigma Lambda Beta, and joining the Hispanic Heritage Month committee. Throughout that involvement, I was exposed to interactions with student affairs professionals, and this increased my desire to translate undergraduate involvement into a profession. After meeting with an administrator from career services my senior year, I realized that I had a passion for student affairs. The next logical intentional step was to apply to graduate school.

INTENTIONALITY

The third factor that has been critical in my ability to navigate higher education successfully has been acting intentionally, especially when making decisions about the future, including my decision to attend graduate school at New York University (NYU). For example, internship opportunities in the NYU Higher Education Program helped me to gain experience as an academic advisor, support students of color, study abroad in South Africa, and work at the campus's Lesbian, Gay, Bisexual, Transgender and Queer Center. Being intentional when it came time to start my job search meant exploring entry-level positions—ideally, those focused on diversity and inclusion work, which was my main area of interest—in New York City. Fortunately, my combination of interests, passions, and experiences gained at NYU made me a viable candidate for the position of assistant director of multicultural affairs at Fordham University.

The director, who was the hiring officer, was attending the ACPA–College Student Educators International Convention in Philadelphia, and I made it a priority to meet her in person. This was a chance to introduce myself before the on-campus interview. I honestly feel that our informal interactions at the conference aided me in becoming a top candidate for my first professional position. Once hired, it was beneficial to work with a director who valued collaboration and professional development. This exposed me to staff from various areas of the university and allowed me to be involved in and outside of my institution.

While at Fordham, my committee involvement ranged from divisional staff development to heading civility programming, participating in the Jesuit Association for Student Personnel Administrators conference and the Conference on Diversity and Equity. Outside of my institution, attending conferences such as the National Conference on Race and Ethnicity and the National Intergroup Dialogue Institute also enhanced my professional growth and helped me to reach various milestones, including presenting at local and national conferences. Later, membership and taking a volunteer leadership role in NASPA–Student Affairs Administrators in Higher Education's Knowledge Communities (KCs), specifically the Latinx/a/o KC and the Gender and Sexuality KC, have enhanced my professional support networks as well as energized me and enhanced my professional development.

Another way that I have exercised intentionality during my professional journey has been through my interactions with senior staff. When the director position in my department became vacant, for instance, I expressed a desire to apply for the position, and I later landed the promotion. After transitioning to the position, I shared with my supervisor my interest to advance to a senior role in higher education, strategically aligning the timing with the NASPA Escaleras Institute's inaugural cohort application process. My learning experience at the institute, along with the opportunity to be in a space with other aspiring Latinx/a/o professionals, remains a highlight of my career. I later decided to pursue a doctoral degree and enrolled in the administration and supervision program in Fordham University's School of Education.

CONCLUSION

I hope that sharing a few snapshots of my journey toward becoming a mid-level professional demystifies the process for some and possibly inspires others. Each step and experience added schools of thought to my developing professional philosophy. Whether it was a growing understanding of social justice and intersections of identity, making the most of professional involvement, or understanding how powerful it can be to strategically share my intentions and desires with my colleagues, I have become a better professional because of it. Lastly, navigating these experiences has made me feel open to having a more fluid career path. My ultimate goal may remain becoming a college or university president someday or change to becoming a faculty member in a higher education program, or I could choose to leave the field entirely to pursue other passions. But regardless of what I ultimately end up pursuing, identity, involvement, and intentionality will continue to be key components of my journey. I believe these concepts are a natural fit with the norms and values of the Latinx/a/o culture and should be taken into consideration by all Latinx/a/o professionals as they navigate their own journeys as students and higher education professionals.

REFERENCES

Astin, A. W. (1999). Student involvement: A developmental theory for higher education *Journal of College Student Development, 40*(5), 518–529.

Ferdman, B. M., & Gallegos, P. I. (2001). Identity development and Latinos in the United States. In C. L. Wijeyesinghe & B. W. Jackson III (Eds.), *New perspective on racial identity development: A theoretical and practical anthology* (pp. 32–66). New York, NY: New York University Press.

Jones, S. R., & McEwen, M. K. (2000). A conceptual model of multiple dimensions of identity. *Journal of College Student Development, 41*(4), 405–414.

Taub, D. J., & McEwen, M. K. (2006). Decision to enter the profession of student affairs. *Journal of College Student Development, 47*(2), 206–216.

CHAPTER 9

YO TAMBIEN!

Pathways for Latinx/a/o Undergraduate
Students Into Student Affairs

Tonantzin Oseguera

T
he Latinx/a/o population is expected to increase to 106 million in the United States by 2050 (U.S. Census Bureau, 2015). The accelerating increase of ethnic and racial minorities in the general population is similarly reflected in the student population of colleges and universities. In the past decade alone, the number of underrepresented students enrolled in higher education has nearly doubled to 27% of the total student population, and this figure is expected to double again by 2019 (Almanac of Higher Education, 2011). For Latinx/a/os, the number is expected to grow to 39% percent

of college-eligible students, up from 2011 estimates that Latinx/a/os made up 18% of college-age students (Santiago, 2011).

However, the workforce within higher education has been slow to mirror the diversity of its student population. Presently, 14% of university presidents and executives are from underrepresented backgrounds; faculty and staff fare slightly better in reflecting ethnic and racial diversity, with 21% of faculty and 23% of staff being from underrepresented backgrounds (Aguirre, 2000; Ross, Green, & Henderson, 1993). Only about 2.6% of college and university presidents and 4.2% of faculty are Latinx/a/o (Aguirre, 2000; Almanac of Higher Education, 2011; National Center for Education Statistics [NCES], 2015). While strides have been made in hiring Latinx/a/o faculty into tenured lines, higher education leadership—that is, presidents, deans, and vice presidents—still lags behind faculty and the student population in terms of employing Latinx/a/o individuals.

The field of student affairs is particularly behind the curve in reflecting the nation's ethnic diversity (Komives & Kuh, 1988; Sagaria & Johnsrud, 1991; Talbot, 1996; Taub & McEwen, 2006). Research from the late 1980s and early 1990s revealed that 86% of student affairs practitioners were White (Sagaria & Johnsrud, 1991; Task Force on Professional Preparation and Practice, 1989). Current studies indicate that little progress has been made in this area, as, on average, only 20% of the nation's student affairs practitioners are underrepresented minorities (Talbot, 1996; Taub & McEwen, 2006). Because student affairs professionals have the most contact with students throughout their college experience, it is imperative that the field mirrors the diversity of the student population it serves.

This chapter examines the existing disparity between the numbers of underrepresented students attending higher education and the ethnic diversity of the student affairs profession, as well as some ongoing efforts to close this gap. The chapter further explores how cultural agents who affirm students' ethnic heritage have a significant impact on and shape students' ultimate choice to pursue careers in student affairs. Conclusions indicate that involvement in cocurricular activities, participation in pipeline programs, and the influence of mentors act as a socialization process to effect underrepresented students to enter the student affairs profession.

PATHWAYS INTO STUDENT AFFAIRS

Student affairs professionals aspire to inform and enlighten every facet of college students' lives and promote the value of student learning (ACPA–College Student Educators International, 1996; American Council on Education, 1937; Keeling, 2004, 2006). The application and admissions process includes contact with admissions counselors, financial aid advisors, housing staff, and other student affairs professionals. Throughout college, students will increasingly interact with student affairs professionals in a variety of ways, ranging from brief interactions during campus activities programs to more significant exchanges during counseling or mediation of roommate conflicts. By graduation, cumulatively, these interactions will have contributed significantly to a student's college experience and success (Pascarella & Terenzini, 1991, 2005; Terenzini, Pascarella, & Blimling, 1996).

It is because of this interaction with student affairs professionals that many undergraduate students become interested in the field. In fact, for many student affairs educators, working in the field started with a personal connection. I was encouraged by the vice president of student affairs at my undergraduate institution. At the time, a group of student leaders within our Chicano/Latino resource center was advocating for a cultural celebration for the first time on campus. Because of my other leadership roles on campus, I was the one to spearhead conversations with appropriate administrators. Initially, I was told that such a cultural celebration could cause segregation among students, that it was a break from tradition, and that—of course—there was no funding. But I was relentless and worked with several student organizations to hold fund-raisers, and we agreed to pay for meals for the event. We came back to the conversation and laid out a program proposal that included no contributions from the university other than space, and if necessary, we were willing to host the event off-campus. The proposal earned me a meeting with the university president during which I shared our groups' rationale, and the university ultimately agreed to host the event. It was after this meeting that the vice president asked me if I had ever considered student affairs as a career, and this sparked my interest enough to change my plans and pursue graduate school in student affairs.

STUDENT AFFAIRS ASSOCIATIONS AS A PIPELINE

My interest in the field resulted mostly by happenstance and because someone in student affairs shared her experience with me. My point of entry is not unique; however, this is not a sustainable model for recruiting new professionals. Studies examining the existing entry points into student affairs are limited, and there is disagreement as to the primary decision points used as an entrance into the field. Some in the profession see randomness in the process; others believe it is the influence of a mentor or a personal calling (Brown, 1987; Forney, 1994; Komives & Kuh, 1988; Richmond & Sherman, 1991; Taub & McEwen, 2006).

Over the years a number of programs by higher education associations have invested in promoting student affairs to undergraduates. Most tout getting involved in student activities and working in a college setting as a reason to choose student affairs. All major student personnel associations—including ACPA–College Student Educators International, the Association of College Unions International, the Association of College and University Housing Officers–International, and NODA: Association for Orientation, Transition, and Retention in Higher Education—have developed programs to encourage undergraduate students to enter the field. Current undergraduate programs are designed to enhance students' leadership skills and promote participation in a relevant national association; however, only NASPA–Student Affairs Administrators in Higher Education has developed a program that acts as a pathway for undergraduate students from historically underrepresented populations to pursue a career in student affairs (Rodriguez, 2006). This program is unique not only because of its singular priority but also because of its diversifying effect on student affairs and, ultimately, the university workforce (Brown, 1997; Hunter, 1992; Sagaria & Johnsrud, 1991).

NASPA UNDERGRADUATE FELLOWS PROGRAM

In 1989, NASPA developed the Minority Undergraduate Fellows Program (MUFP) with a mission to increase the number of ethnic minority professionals in the field of student affairs and higher education. The stated objective was to introduce undergraduate students to the field of student affairs, provide mentors currently in the field, and develop students' leadership skills as a means of encouraging them to pursue a master's degree in student affairs administration. The program grew steadily throughout the 1990s by approximately 50 participants per year. By 2004, the MUFP program had 784 alumni, with a majority having pursued a career in student affairs (NASPA, 2014).

Initially, the intent of MUFP was to serve only ethnic minorities, but the program has undergone two significant revisions of its mission. In 1999, the MUFP Board and the NASPA Board of Directors began conversations to include students with disabilities into the MUFP program, and in the 2000–2001 academic year, the MUFP mission was broadened to include students with disabilities. In 2005, the MUFP Board was asked to broaden the program's scope to include other historically underrepresented student populations, including first-generation students as well as lesbian, gay, bisexual, and transgender college students (NASPA, 2005). In 2006, MUFP was renamed the NASPA Undergraduate Fellows Program (NUFP). Today, the program's mission is "to increase the numbers of underrepresented ethnic minorities, LGBT, and disabled professionals in the fields of student affairs and higher education" (NASPA, 2017, para. 3).

In recent years, participation in NUFP has continued to grow. The number of participants increased from 166 in 2008 to 219 in 2010, with the most significant surge in 2013, when there were 527 students in the program (N. Victoria, personal communication, May 2, 2017). The program's overarching goal is twofold: to provide an understanding of the student affairs field and to serve as an entry point into a student affairs career. Program components include on-campus mentoring, regional and national conference attendance, paid summer internships, and a summer leadership institute (NASPA, 2017). Throughout the years, these components have evolved in response to newly identified learning outcomes and as additional needs have arisen. Within each component, the fellows' activities are semi-structured to facilitate important learning outcomes through curriculum and training.

Mentorship and Conferences

Connecting mentors and fellows has been a mainstay of the NUFP program since 1989. On-campus mentorship is provided to participating students by a current NASPA member in order to familiarize the student with student affairs' structure and what a career in the field may entail. Mentorship responsibilities are informal, with few recommendations for mentors and mentees. NASPA suggests that the mentor and fellow meet monthly for advice on setting yearly goals and on developing a project that shows an understanding of the responsibilities of a student affairs professional (NASPA, 2017).

Fellows initiate contact with established professionals and are familiarized with the student affairs culture by attending regional and national conferences. Since the 2003 national conference in St. Louis, there has been a preconference track designed for fellows to learn more about student affairs as a possible career choice (NASPA, 2004). Currently, fellows have the opportunity to network with professionals who mirror their demographic in NUFP-specific workshops, attend preconference training, and enjoy a reception for alumni and current fellows during all NASPA conferences (NASPA, 2017).

Summer Internships and Leadership Institutes

Universities may also provide NUFP fellows with internship opportunities during the summer break. Funded by the host institution, internships vary in duration from six to eight weeks, but they must be appropriate work for an undergraduate student interested in student affairs (NASPA, 2017). These opportunities bring an immediate reality to the practice of student affairs—something unavailable in classroom settings.

In 1993, a summer leadership institute was incorporated into NUFP in an effort to attract students who had participated in the fellows program during the academic year; students are nominated by mentors, and participants are selected by the Fellows Advisory Committee (NASPA, 2017). The Dungy Leadership Institute is an intensive five-day seminar hosted by a different university each year; it focuses on the skills necessary for developing a career in student affairs. A highly selective process determines the yearly cohort of 32 fellows (NASPA, 2017). During the seminar, students are exposed to a variety of student affairs administrators who serve as the institute's faculty. Workshops tackle such important topics as identity development, student development theories, personal competencies, current issues in student affairs, and the graduate school application processes. Although less than 15% of the total NASPA membership identifies as Hispanic/Latinx/a/o, each year a little more than 50% of fellows identify as Hispanic/Latinx/a/o (N. Victoria, personal communication, May 2, 2017).

As with the projected growth of the overall Latinx/a/o student population by 2025, the makeup of participants in NUFP can be expected to reflect an increased number of Latinx/a/o students over the next few years. With a notable number of fellows identifying as such, it can be supposed that the number of Latinx/a/o student affairs administrators will also likely increase. NUFP stands out in terms of helping to close the gap between Latinx/a/o students attending college and Latinx/a/os entering the field of student affairs. Although I was not a fellow, I have witnessed the benefit of such a program—how it shaped the inspiration, preparation, and yield of Latinx/a/o students into the field. On a personal note, I have officially mentored six fellows, five of whom self-identified as Latinx/a/o. All five have gone on to graduate programs in student affairs; two of them graduated with master's degrees in 2017. I also know that across several universities and colleges, former MUFP/NUFP fellows are working to continue the legacy of recruiting talented undergraduate students from underrepresented backgrounds into the field of student affairs.

PROMISING PATHWAYS

Research supports the assertion that student affairs is not as widely recognizable as other professions (Richmond & Sherman, 1991; Taub

& McEwen, 2006), and thus many students may not initially consider it as a viable professional option. It cannot be expected that everyone who encounters student affairs professionals will become interested in the field; thus, as student affairs professionals, we must spend some time sharing information about careers in student affairs. Conveying the benefits of a career in student affairs—such as working with college students and being employed in a university setting—may spark undergraduate students' interest in student affairs. Outreach efforts may be particularly effective for students majoring in the human sciences—that is, psychology, human development, family studies, sociology, and ethnic studies. Emphasizing the opportunity to serve others, the benefits of working at a university, and possible research prospects may also attract students already interested in human sciences. Further, how practitioners discuss student affairs can shape how aspiring students perceive the profession. Student affairs practitioners could articulate the values of a career in student affairs in a manner that speaks to the values and mission of the profession. As a field, student affairs professionals could augment efforts beyond Careers in Student Affairs Week/Month, including participation in career fairs by student affairs divisions as a means to expose students to the multitude of relevant jobs (Oseguera, 2013).

The value of education and service for the greater good can be connecting points to attract Latinx/a/o students to student affairs. These values already play a role in the community (Stanton-Salazar, 1997) and can help stress the importance of seeking a college degree and selecting social service careers (U.S. Bureau of Labor Statistics, 2015). Like other service careers, student affairs counts among its benefits working in a meaningful environment, enjoying possible advancement, reaping educational benefits, and enriching society (NASPA, 2017).

CONCLUSION

As higher education nears an impending increase of Latinx/a/o students, it is more essential than ever to strive to increase the number of Latinx/a/os serving in student affairs leadership roles. This is an important step to increase outreach to and role modeling for Latinx/a/o students who are not aware of student affairs as a potential career choice. While some professional organizations have made efforts to address this gap, initiatives such as the NASPA Undergraduate Fellows Program are successfully advancing student affairs as a viable option for Latinx/a/os and other students of color. By providing critical resources such as mentoring and learning opportunities delivered through conferences, internships, and institutes, this program aims to change the face of student affairs. Nevertheless, there is still much work to be done—especially if higher education is to reflect the demographics of U.S. colleges and universities now and in the coming decades. Therefore, Latinx/a/os and allies in higher education must actively bring about this much-needed change in order to improve success for both Latinx/a/o students and professionals.

REFERENCES

ACPA–College Student Educators International. (1996). *The student learning imperative: Implications for student affairs.* Retrieved from http://www.myacpa.org/files/acpas-student-learning-imperativepdf

Aguirre, A., Jr. (2000). *Women and minority faculty in the academic workplace: Recruitment, retention, and academic culture.* ASHE-ERIC Higher Education Report, Vol. 27, No. 6. San Francisco, CA: Jossey-Bass.

Almanac of Higher Education. (2011). *Chronicle of higher education.* Retrieved from http://www.chronicle.com/almanac

American Council on Education. (1937). *The student personnel point of view.* Retrieved from https://www.naspa.org/images/uploads/main/Student_Personnel_Point_of_View_1949.pdf

Brown, R. D. (1987). Professional pathways and professional education. In L. V. Moore & R. B. Young (Eds.), *Expanding opportunities for professional education* (pp. 5–18). San Francisco, CA: Jossey-Bass.

Forney, D. S. (1994). A profile of student affairs masters's students: Characteristics, attitudes, and learning styles. *Journal of College Student Development, 35*(5), 337–345.

Hunter, D. E. (1992). How student affairs professionals choose their careers. *NASPA Journal, 29*, 181–288.

Keeling, R. P. (Ed.). (2004). *Learning reconsidered: A campus-wide focus on the student experience.* Washington, DC: ACPA–College Student Educators International & NASPA–Student Affairs Administrators in Higher Education.

Keeling, R. P. (Ed.). (2006). *Learning reconsidered 2: Implementing a campus-wide focus on the student experience.* Washington, DC: ACPA–College Student Educators International, Association of College and University Housing Officers–International, Association of College Unions International, National Academic Advising Association, National Association for Campus Activities, NASPA–Student Affairs Administrators in Higher Education, & National Intramural-Recreational Sports Association

Komives, S. R., & Kuh, G. (1988). "The right stuff": Some thoughts on attracting good people to student affairs work. In R. B. Young & L. V. Moore (Eds.), *The state of the art of professional education and practice* (pp. 1–20). Washington, DC: Commission on Professional Education in Student Affairs.

NASPA–Student Affairs Administrators in Higher Education. (2004). *Minority Undergraduate Fellows Program February 2004 annual report.* Washington, DC: Author.

NASPA–Student Affairs Administrators in Higher Education. (2005). *NUFP transition report.* Washington, DC: Author.

NASPA–Student Affairs Administrators in Higher Education. (2014). *13–14 NASPA Undergraduate Fellows Program: Program handbook.* Retrieved from https://www.naspa.org/images/uploads/main/NUFP1314Handbook_FINAL.pdf

NASPA–Student Affairs Administrators in Higher Education. (2017). NASPA Undergraduate Fellows Program. Retrieved from https://www.naspa.org/constituent-groups/professionals/nufp/history

National Center for Education Statistics. (2015). *Digest of education statistics, 2015.* Retrieved from https://nces.ed.gov/programs/digest/2015menu_tables.asp

Oseguera, T. (2013). *Coloring the pipeline: An analysis of the NASPA undergraduate fellows program as a path for underrepresented students into student affairs* (Doctoral dissertation). Retrieved from ProQuest Dissertations and Theses database. (UMI No. 598310)

Pascarella, E. T., & Terenzini, P. T. (1991). *How college affects students: Findings and insights from twenty years of research.* San Francisco, CA: Jossey-Bass.

Pascarella, E., & Terenzini, P. (2005). *How college affects students (Vol. 2): A decade of research.* San Francisco, CA: Jossey-Bass.

Richmond, J., & Sherman, K. J. (1991). Student-development preparation and placement: A longitudinal study of graduate students' and new professionals' experiences. *Journal of College Student Development, 32*(1), 8–16.

Rodriguez, A. A., (2006). *From MUFP fellow to alum: The experience and impact of the minority undergraduate fellows program* (Master's thesis). University of Vermont, Burlington, VT.

Ross, M., Green, M. F., & Henderson, C. (1993). *The American college president.* Washington, DC: American Council on Education.

Sagaria, M. A., & Johnsrud, L. K. (1991). Recruiting, advancing, and retaining minorities in student affairs: Moving from rhetoric to results. *NASPA Journal, 28*(2), 105–120.

Santiago, D. A. (2011). *Ensuring America's future: Benchmarking Latino college completion to meet national goals: 2010 to 2020* (Research Report). Retrieved from Excelencia in Education website: http://www.edexcelencia.org/sites/default/files/benchmarkingeaf2011edition.pdf

Stanton-Salazar, R. D. (1997). A social capital framework for understanding the socialization of racial minority children and youth. *Harvard Educational Review, 67*(1), 1–40.

Talbot, D. M. (1996). Master's students' perspectives on their graduate education regarding issues of diversity. *NASPA Journal, 33*(3), 163–178.

Task Force on Professional Preparation and Practice. (1989). *The recruitment, preparation, and nurturing of the student affairs profession.* Washington, DC: National Association of Student Personnel Administrators and American College Personnel Association.

Taub, D. J., & McEwen M. K. (2006). Decision to enter the profession of student affairs. *Journal of College Student Development, 47*(2), 206–216.

Terenzini, P. T., Pascarella, E. T., & Blimling, G. S. (1996). Students' out-of-class experiences and their influence on learning and cognitive development: A literature review. *Journal of College Student Development, 37*(2), 149–162.

U.S. Bureau of Labor Statistics. (2015). *Hispanics and Latinos in industries and occupations.* Retrieved from https://www.bls.gov/opub/ted/2015/hispanics-and-latinos-in-industries-and-occupations.htm

U.S. Census Bureau. (2015). *United States quick facts, Hispanic or Latino, percent, July 1, 2015* (V2015). Retrieved from http://www.census.gov/quickfacts

CHAPTER 10

JOURNEY TO THE VICE PRESIDENCY

Camino y Consejos

Anthony Cruz

"*S*i, se puede" ("Yes, someone can") is one of my favorite slogans. It was popularized in the 1960s by civil rights activist and labor leader Cesar Chavez, and I have personally used it to motivate myself on my path toward senior leadership in student affairs; it has also allowed me to overcome many obstacles and block out the negativity of others by keeping me positive and focused. The path to senior leadership is full of landmines—but also full of amazing rewards. Throughout my journey, the values and experiences that have shaped my identity as a Hispanic male have also helped me to reach success as a senior leader in higher education.

This chapter will demonstrate how my experiences have defined who I am and why higher education is so important to me. Moreover, it describes the twists and turns of my journey to the vice presidency. It will also detail my most valued pieces of advice in the hope that it may help future student affairs leaders have a smoother journey to the vice presidency.

BECOMING "HISPANIC"

My earliest memories are of me as a 5-year-old child walking the streets of the north side of Chicago and serving as an interpreter for my Cuban grandmother. I enjoyed being her interpreter as we went from store to store shopping for the ingredients to make the perfect *arroz con pollo* (chicken and rice) for dinner that night. Both of my parents immigrated to the United States with their parents and settled in Chicago, Illinois, in the early 1960s. I was part of the first generation in our family to be born in the United States, and I was constantly reminded by my parents that I was an American. I had no doubt that I was an American, but I also knew that I was different than the other kids at my Catholic elementary school. My parents spoke limited English, and we ate many different foods—and conversations with my classmates emphasized these differences from an early age. I knew my parents were from Cuba and very proud of their country and its traditions. They also worked very hard, and I have always been very proud of their dedication to our family and their labor in tough blue-collar jobs to give me the best education possible.

But it was at the beginning of second grade that my world was rocked when I was introduced to a new term that would forever change my sense of identity. It was an early September morning when I was called to the school office to complete some survey paperwork. To this day I'm not sure the purpose of the survey, but I was not the only student in the office, as there was a line of my schoolmates waiting in front of several tables to speak with strangers. As I approached the front of the line, I could overhear the lady asking my classmate questions from the form. I stepped up when it was my turn, and they asked me for my name. I clearly said, "Anthony Cruz." I spelled out Cruz to avoid any confusion with the spelling.

I was then presented with a form and asked to answer several questions. I did my best as a second grader and started to write down the answers. The first few questions were geared toward collecting demographic data, and when I reached the race/ethnicity question, I saw that the options available were White, Black, Asian, Hispanic, American Indian, and Pacific Islander. I read through the options and confidently marked "White" on the form. When the woman reviewed my answers, she remarked that I had made a mistake. I looked at her with astonishment. She then said that I was supposed to have checked the box for Hispanic, and I completed the rest of the survey and left the line puzzled. I had been brought up thinking that I was a White kid of Cuban descent and still had no idea what the term *Hispanic* meant. Because of my experience that day—and countless others since then—I was slowly conditioned to think of myself as Hispanic.

Although I understand that members of our community may have mixed feelings about the term *Hispanic* because of the way it was assigned and how it has been used by the government, I personally don't have a huge issue with it; however, I recognize that the term reduces my identity to one single word and that it was created by the Nixon administration to lump all Latinx/a/o people together in one convenient category. I believe strongly that each of us is more than a word, and it is important to remind ourselves of this fact as we work to advance through our careers. In my case, my Latinx/a/o heritage, my unique experiences, my culture and values, and my sense of family have shaped my sense of identity and influenced me as a developing professional in higher education. Thus, I continue to be proud of being Hispanic even though that term was imposed on me.

My Hispanic identity, initially shaped by my family and school experiences, has continued to expand and change over the years. My sense of self has been deeply influenced by the intersections in my parents' immigrant experience, my being a first-generation Hispanic college student at a Hispanic-serving institution, and my living in the Midwest for the past nine years as an underrepresented person of color. Over time, these factors have helped me to develop a lens through which I see higher education and its purpose. Like my parents, I believe that the American dream can be achieved through education. However, Latinx/a/os and members of other underrepresented groups have a difficult time achieving their educational goals because of antiquated immigration policies, multigeneration poverty, segregation, discrimination, and failed economic policies. Over the years, as I have climbed the career ladder and served in a variety of roles, I have kept both my culture and my cultural experience in mind, continuing to examine the work through this unique lens. For example, at the cabinet level, I feel that it is my obligation to represent the interests of students and particularly those who are disenfranchised. My recent experience in the Midwest has shown me that we still have a long way to go to achieve a basic understanding of the issues facing Latinx/a/o students and their parents. Therefore, as a Hispanic professional in higher education, I feel that it is my obligation to educate and inform others on the issues that Latinx/a/o students face.

THE IMPORTANCE OF PURSUING A COLLEGE EDUCATION

Like many Latinx/a/o immigrants in the United States, my parents got up at dawn every morning and worked long hours in poor conditions to provide me with a safe home environment and the best education possible. Although neither one of my parents had the opportunity to finish high school, they knew the value of education and instilled in me the importance of pursuing learning. I admired their tenacity and determination, and I feel very proud that they both taught themselves to read and write in English, helped me with my homework when they could, and were always open to meeting with my teachers. My parents always told me that a factory job was not in my future—and if it was, it would be me wearing the shirt and tie and giving the orders. They paid for private education for most of my schooling, and even though they had to sacrifice even the smallest of luxuries, they always made that tuition payment with the expectation that I would eventually go the college. I knew that college was important, and I didn't want to let them down. By the time I was a senior in high school, I was ready for college—both academically and socially. Both my parents' emphasis on college and my experience as a first-generation college student had a great deal to do with my ultimate decision to work in higher education and motivated me to make sure that students have the support services and networks necessary to be successful.

MY JOURNEY/*MI CAMINO* INTO STUDENT AFFAIRS

My journey to becoming a senior student affairs officer was unorthodox and happened without much planning. After graduating with a master's degree in public administration from Florida State University, I began looking for a job in local government, with the goal of becoming a city or county manager. Unfortunately for me—and millions of other Americans—the country had entered a recession and jobs were very scarce. During my job search, I happened to stumble upon a job listing for an assistant director of admissions position at my undergraduate alma mater, Florida International University (FIU). I read the job description and felt that my education and experience were a good fit. I applied, interviewed, and was given the job a few weeks before graduation. This position opened my eyes to a career in higher education, and I realized that I loved working with students and enjoyed being back at FIU. From that point on, I knew that my future was in higher education, and in only a couple of years, at the age of 26, I became the youngest assistant dean in FIU history.

I was very happy with how my career was progressing, and my wife was pregnant with our second child; however, my growing family made me reassess my financial situation, and when my best friend's cousin offered me a financial services position with more earning potential, I chose to take it. My decision to leave FIU to pursue this position was a significant detour from my higher education path, and I spent the next three years as a financial advisor—until the financial markets' meltdown following the 9/11 attacks. The ensuing turbulence in the financial sector sent me back to higher education.

My attempt to reenter the higher education world was very difficult, but eventually I landed at a private proprietary college as director of advising and retention. I learned a great deal in that position, but left after only a year because I didn't feel comfortable with the college's preoccupation with finances and their bottom-line mentality. On a positive note, however, it was the first time that I had been given the opportunity to supervise and manage a team, which boosted my marketability as an administrator. Soon afterward, I was fortunate to be given the opportunity to return to FIU, and I worked there in several student services–related positions.

Notwithstanding my joy about being back at FIU, the more time went by, the more I felt like I really belonged at a community college.

I remembered my admissions days and how much I had enjoyed working with the transfer students from the local community college. With excitement and after being back at FIU for five years, I made a very deliberate decision to go to work at a community college. This is where I felt that I could make the most difference in serving students, and I also committed myself to work toward a senior leadership position. My rationale was that the higher I ascended in the organization, the greater the impact I could have on students' lives. I loved working with students on an individual level but felt I could do more to affect student outcomes by creating programs and systems on a larger scale.

I decided to apply for an associate dean of student affairs position at Broward College in Florida. It took a few attempts, but eventually I was offered the position and spent a couple of years learning the community college environment and sharpening my student affairs skills. After a few years, I felt that I was prepared for the next stage in my career, as a dean of student affairs. I knew that I would most likely not find a dean position locally, and after consulting with my wife, I started a nationwide search.

My search led me to Cincinnati, where I accepted my first senior student affairs officer position. During my four years at Cincinnati State Technical and Community College, I was responsible for both the enrollment management and student development functions, and I oversaw multiple direct reports and a division of more than 100 student services professionals. By my fourth year, I felt that I needed to move on and pursue a vice presidency. I was very fortunate that nearby Sinclair Community College was looking for a new vice president of enrollment management and student affairs. In this role, I was part of the president's cabinet and had the opportunity to interact with members of the board of trustees, and I was finally able to see how decisions were made by the president and the other cabinet members.

My new position also helped me to understand institutional politics and the complexity of the decision-making process. Senior leadership must consider the political realities of meeting the needs of students, faculty, staff, local elected officials, state legislatures, and community members. Public community colleges are particularly involved with the community and concerned about perceptions of how public dollars are used. As a senior student affairs leader in that setting, I learned that it is essential to look beyond the needs of one's own division and consider how one's decisions impact others throughout the entire organization.

About a year ago, I decided to leave Sinclair Community College and accepted a new position as the vice chancellor of student affairs at St. Louis Community College in St. Louis, Missouri. This new position gives me the opportunity to lead student affairs from the district system level and expand my approach to effectively lead four campuses and two centers in St. Louis County. Working in a district system has broadened my portfolio of responsibilities and challenged me to work with multiple campuses, each with its own distinct culture and traditions. I find that the biggest challenge is to create consistency across the campuses and improve the student experience holistically while allowing each campus to maintain its own identity.

Though I began to work in higher education by happenstance, I eventually chose to work in the field of student affairs because I felt that it brought me the closest to students and the student experience. I believe that what students experience outside the classroom is just as important as the things they learn in it. My own time as an undergraduate shaped these beliefs. As an undergraduate student, I highly valued my experiences in my fraternity, student government, and student organizations. I also saw that there was a great deal of room for improvement for other student services. My work in student affairs has been varied and not traditional by any standard; I did not start in a residence hall or in an orientation office, for example. As a result, I have been fortunate to work in a variety of student services–related jobs that have increased both the breadth and depth of my experience. My career and my particular trajectory in student affairs have been directly influenced by my work in both student development and enrollment management, and my experience at community colleges has made it necessary for me to master both areas, because these responsibilities are core competencies for community college senior student affairs leaders.

Working in higher education has provided continuous opportunity for self-exploration and growth. A couple a years ago, for example, I was engaged in self-reflection and trying to gain a better understanding of who I am and my purpose. While sharing my thoughts with a colleague, she suggested that I watch Simon Sinek's YouTube video on "start with why" (https://startwithwhy.com/find-your-why). I watched the video and started to think about why I had devoted the past 21 years of my life to working in student affairs. What did I discover as a result of my reflection? My why is simple: I want to change lives. I want to change lives the same way my parents changed my life. As Cuban immigrants, they sacrificed everything to give me a better life, and I am grateful for the opportunities I have had. It is now my chance to support others in that pursuit as well.

LESSONS LEARNED: MY ADVICE/*MI CONSEJOS*

During my 21 years in higher education, I have learned many things that have helped me become a better student affairs leader. Latinx/a/o student affairs leaders should consider the following advice in preparing to pursue a vice presidential role.

- **Get your doctorate.** Whether you choose to go the PhD or the EdD route, it is never too early to start working on your doctorate. It took me seven years to complete my doctorate while I was working full-time in several student affairs leadership roles. Community colleges as well as four-year colleges and universities are looking for student affairs professionals with advanced degrees. You could have gotten away without one 20 years ago, but today it is a requirement for senior leadership roles in student affairs.

- **Get out of your comfort zone.** Do at least one thing every day that makes you uncomfortable. We all have things that make us feel uncomfortable. Some people don't like to speak in public, for example; others don't like confronting staff members when they have done something wrong, and some are afraid of numbers and the budgeting process. You will need to overcome these and many other fears to become an effective senior leader. From my experience, the best way to overcome these challenges is to confront them directly and take action regardless of how you feel. I truly believe that you will not really grow as a leader unless you experience these growing pains for yourself. The good thing is that you can work with supervisors, peers, and others to help you on your quest.
- **Don't bring your supervisor problems; bring your supervisor solutions.** The first time I heard, "Don't bring me problems; bring me solutions!" come out of my boss's mouth, I was devastated. "How can he say that to me, knowing the problem I'm facing?" I said to myself. I thought he was heartless and didn't care about me and my situation. It took me some time and much thought, but I found a solution to that problem. I was a very young administrator and expected my supervisor to solve my problems without me devoting the necessary time and energy to find a solution on my own. It took me about 10 years to realize that he was 100% correct. As student affairs leaders, we have very demanding professional lives, and we need to

make multiple complex decisions daily. When we need to solve a problem, we can't simply burden our supervisors or peers with finding the answers for us; we need to think long and hard about viable solutions. Once we have crafted some possible solutions, we can take those ideas to our supervisors and peers for some meaningful dialogue and vetting. We can then rely on their experience and expertise to guide us to the best option. To date, I use this technique with my teams to make sure that they are getting the most out of their creative energies.

- **Say it three times.** During the past five years, I have continually collaborated and closely communicated with my senior-leadership peers, board of trustee members, and other constituent groups. I have learned a great deal about various communication styles and the importance of communicating effectively across all levels of a college. One of the techniques that I have learned is to present ideas at least three different times to make sure you secure buy-in from the appropriate person or group you are trying to persuade. At first you may think this seems redundant and completely unnecessary, but what you will find is that people are hearing and not necessarily listening when you present an idea to them the first time and maybe even the second time. By the third time, however, they will start listening and start thinking about whether your idea has merit. While it may ultimately get rejected, at least they have listened and decided. This technique will feel very awkward when you first try it, but it can be very effective—especially for those more complex ideas.

- **Be fair and listen to all sides.** Very early in my career, I had the great fortune of having a very wise supervisor who had been working in higher education for more than 30 years. She gave me the opportunity to sit in on meetings and shared her thought process as she made difficult decisions. I was struck by how well she listened to everyone regardless of their point of view or particular stance on an issue. Although her final decisions were not liked by all, everyone respected her because she was fair. I have always tried to model myself after her style of leadership. She was authentic and everyone could see that throughout her interactions. Making decisions about student and staff matters can be very difficult at times, but we need to listen to others—whether they are students, peers, or supervisees. As the leaders, we will be respected only if we truly respect the views of others.

- **Learn the culture and politics of your institution.** Throughout my formal education, I have never taken a class that has talked about how to navigate the turbulent waters of institutional culture and politics. Every college and university has its own culture, which we must understand to be effective student affairs leaders. If we understand the culture, we will be much better at avoiding the pitfalls and obstacles that prevent us from excelling in our profession. Many times, we are sheltered from the politics by our supervisors or because we are deep in our student affairs departmental cocoons. As you take on larger leadership roles and eventually the vice presidency, you will realize that institutions are much more complex than the student affairs world. We must work across organizational divisions to become genuinely effective leaders. This is essential because most critical decisions are often made outside of your domain and you must try your best to be part of that decision-making process. This will require you to form alliances within your division and across the entire institution.

These relationships can also help you to see beyond the scope of your everyday routine into a world that is much larger and more complex than you ever expected.

- **Be ready to move.** Many newer student affairs professionals are naïve enough to believe that they will remain at their institutions for the rest of their careers. It is much more likely that as you progress through your career, you'll find it necessary to move from your institution, from your region, and even to a different state in order to advance your career. I think many Latinx/a/o professionals have a difficult time with this because they feel that they are betraying their communities, or they have a difficult time leaving family or friends. I have gone from living in south Florida, which is majority Latinx/a/o, to living in the Midwest, where the Latinx/a/o population is less than 3%. These moves have opened my horizons to learning new things and meeting new people. It is important for all Latinx/a/o student affairs leaders to consider opportunities as they arise across the country.

CONCLUSION

Without a doubt, my journey to the vice presidency has been interesting and challenging at times. My identity as a Hispanic male has unquestionably shaped who I am as a senior student affairs leader. My family, my experiences as a first-generation college student, and my residence in areas of the country with large and small Latinx/a/o populations have also influenced my career choices and trajectory. My 21 years working in student affairs have taught me several valuable lessons that I was happy to share in this chapter, and I hope that Latinx/a/o student affairs professionals will glean some strategies that can help them on their paths to the vice presidency.

CHAPTER 11

PATHWAY TO THE PROFESSORATE

The Solitude of the Long-Distance Runner

William Luis

As a youngster, I was fast but hated to run long distances. When I joined the school track team, there was no doubt that I would be a sprinter. However, when we trained, the coach made me work on endurance and that meant running long distances. My thing was the sprint; I wanted to get the race over with as quickly as possible, rather than endure the agony that accompanied a long-distance run. You could see the pain in the runner's face! I was always athletic, and the culture of my neighborhood supported physical fitness over intellectual prowess. In fact, strength and speed could save your life, especially in a neighborhood where, for some, joining a gang was more important than going to school. Even in school, if you didn't defend yourself, you became the object of abuse. That happened to José Mieles, a short, skinny, pale Puerto Rican who wore huge black-frame glasses that turned him into a geek before it became fashionable to be one. Without provocation, John Weeks would grab Mieles by the seat of his pants and walk him down the hallway. I graduated from junior high school with a Gold Seal Diploma, but more important, I received the much-coveted Gym Award.

Earlier that year, our quarter-mile relay team qualified for the city finals. This was the largest event of its kind, with schools from all five boroughs and kids who lived in more dangerous neighborhoods than ours and ran faster to stay away from trouble. Our coach, Mr. Reeves, had a plan. He assigned George Johnson to start, Michael Moore to run the second leg, George Rivera to the third, and me to anchor. Even though I was faster from the blocks, the coach wanted me to run for the finish line. We won our qualifying heats, but the coach appeared dissatisfied. He reluctantly told us that another team had a time faster than ours. He was more upset than any of us, because our expectations were not that high. Mr. Reeves told us that if we won, he would take us to the Olympic trials that summer in Manhattan. That news provided the motivation to try harder.

We all smiled when George Johnson drew an inner lane. As the anchor, I had a front-row seat to the race. We heard the gunfire, and George Johnson got off to a fast start; he passed the baton flawlessly to Michael, then Michael to George Rivera, who continued to maintain a slight lead around the turn, and I was the runner no one could catch. This was the story the coach delivered at the student assembly the day we were recognized for setting a school record.

GROWING UP IN THE LOWER EAST SIDE

Born and raised in the Lower East Side of Manhattan, I became a product of my environment. After my father died, my mother, Petra, had the daunting task of raising two young boys in a hostile inner-city environment. As a single-parent family, the odds were stacked against us. We were not expected to survive. I still can't explain how she managed to pull us through. She never learned English; she didn't have to because all her friends spoke Spanish, and so did most everyone else, including the Jewish merchants on Orchard Street and the vendors in the *marketa* on Essex Street.

High school was not very exciting, and even track lost its magic. I often felt that I peaked in junior high school. My competitors were no longer students; they looked like men. At Seward Park High, I received an average education from teachers who were more interested in educating students who looked like them. We, who didn't look like the White students and teachers, weren't expected to be smart. With my high average, I was placed into honors homeroom but not into any of the honors classes. In all the subsequent homerooms, the non-White students could be counted on one hand. Many of them were placed in general, nonacademic, classes. While in college, I returned to the school to visit my teachers. When I reintroduced myself, one of the teachers asked which community college was I attending.

In high school, I did my school work, but I was more attracted to extracurricular activities: student government, track and field, martial arts (which came in handy in our rough neighborhood), and church. However, in one English class I was exposed to Salinger's *Catcher in the Rye* and Sillitoe's "The Loneliness of the Long-Distance Runner," and their protagonists helped me understand something about myself: I felt like they did. Society wanted to mold the protagonists and me, and we didn't fit in. My environment did not tolerate difference. I had to be one thing or another, Black or White, smart or dumb, fat or skinny, fast or slow. My mother was Afro-Cuban, my father was born in China and raised in Cuba, and I had African American, Puerto Rican, Jewish, Chinese, and Italian friends. Each group saw in me not who I was but a vision of themselves. With my African American friends, I was Black; with my Puerto Rican *compadres*, I was Latino; with my Jewish friends, I was smart. Was I all of them, parts of them, or someone else? They never accepted the racial and ethnic complexity of my own identity. Salinger's Holden Caulfield showed me that I didn't belong, and I became a nonconformist.

PATHWAY TO COLLEGE

Seward Park provided an academic pathway to college, and for me it became a road out of the neighborhood. I strove to be a little better than the average student, and I felt I could make up ground by getting involved in student government. So I became the junior class president, and the following year I was elected president of the student government. These leadership positions connected me to other organizations and communities. I joined the National Conference of Christians and Jews, which held events at the Waldorf Astoria, a place my circle of neighborhood friends knew only by name. I also participated in urban–suburbia student exchanges that placed inner-city kids with suburban families. In turn, the suburban kids would come to our schools, though I don't recall any of us being asked to open our apartments to them. My suburban host lived in a big house located in a beautiful neighborhood, just like the ones I saw on television. His parents had installed a white, shag carpet, and we had to take off our shoes when we entered the house. The school was also immaculate in comparison to ours, with all the facilities we could only hope for. It didn't take me long to realize that even though these kids had all the material things they wanted, they had other types of problems. My host, who had it all, was doing drugs. When his parents weren't home, he grabbed a ladder to show me where he hid his pot, underneath the roof shingles. In the suburbs, I was exposed to things that were unfamiliar to me in the city.

Leadership became a part of my life, and gave meaning to my college experiences. I was part of an experimental program initiated by John Benson, one of the admissions officers of Harpur College (Binghamton University), who was "crazy" to think someone could read admissions applications and find strengths beyond the traditional numerical markers. A group of us became candidates for his program, and he convinced me to attend an all-White college. My entering class was the second in his experiment; the first had six students and the second, another 18, all from New York City and of African American and Latino descent. These were the turbulent 1960s and John believed in us. We sought each other out, and along with the only five or six regularly admitted Black students, we formed the Afro-Latin Alliance. As one of three co-chairs, I saw us as a black dot on a large white sheet of paper. We were expected to fail or forget our past and assimilate, but we resisted. Rather, it became our mission to educate the college community about who we were and where we came from. One such person was our English professor, Larry Gottheim, who was intrigued by the challenge. With a 16-mm movie camera in hand, Larry and student co-director Rodney Young followed some of us back to New York City to capture aspects of our neighborhoods.

The film opens with members of the Afro-Latin Alliance engaged in a vibrant discussion about racism in our communities. The conversation about the death of Black people at the hands of the police serves as an audible background to the vivid and disturbing images of newspaper clippings juxtaposed with scenes from Harlem and the Lower

East Side. While filming in Harlem, all of us in attendance cram into Rodney's VW Beetle convertible while Larry operates the camera. Someone launches a bottle that explodes near us. Rodney stops the car, reaches into the glove compartment, and pulls out a gun. At that moment, we realize, yet again, the volatility of life in our environment. We also filmed at the Lower East Side, where my mother founded the Movimiento Hispano Unido and was director of a sewing program for newly arrived immigrants, sponsored by Mobilization for Youth.

Who would have thought that the idea of the long-distance race would take on a metaphorical meaning, or that 40 years later I would still be involved with working to make university life a more inclusive environment? My path would cross Larry's again, when I joined the faculty at Binghamton as director of the Latin American Studies Program, the same program I fought to establish as a student. Larry's life had also changed. He had left the English Department to found the Department of Cinema.

DEVELOPING NEW SOCIAL CAPITAL AND PURSUING A GRADUATE EDUCATION

My interest in education sparked while working on my master's degree at the University of Wisconsin, in the traditional way with a few caring professors, but also through friends like Irene. The daughter of chemistry and mathematics professors, Irene was raised in an academic and supportive environment. She was brilliant; she had skipped a few grades in high school and was on track to graduate from college at a young age. Graduate school was in her DNA. She pursued a graduate program in linguistics at Princeton and completed her doctorate at Stanford. Her Jewish parents welcomed me into a home full of books, magazines, and newspapers, with vibrant political, historical, social, and philosophical discussions. Language required precision, and ideas were nuanced—they had to be backed by facts and articulated correctly. Her environment was totally different from the one I was familiar with. The family expected their children to do graduate work at leading institutions. Learning and education became a road to success. Those were the years of Watergate and my introduction to acronyms like PBS and NPR, very different programming from the variety shows that captivated my family. The atmosphere was contagious and it was only a matter of time before I began to internalize the same values and started to consider a doctoral program. I asked Irene if she thought I was smart enough to work on a PhD. She supported my decision. Years later I would learn that being smart had little to do with talent; it was all about learning how to work hard. This type of work required little inspiration and much perspiration.

Some three years of dating Irene brought me closer to her family. I was invited to family excursions and activities, broke bread with them on the Sabbath and other Jewish holidays, and became a known fixture in their household, or so I thought. During that time, Irene had transferred to Stanford while I worked in a community school in East Harlem. But I felt the need to do more with my life and decided to enroll at Cornell University. Although I didn't know it when I applied, Cornell offered the best program possible for me.

Irene had been studying in England during the fall term. When it was time for her to return for the holidays, I called her mother to make arrangements to meet her daughter at the airport. But something had changed. My enthusiasm turned somber when her mother explained that the family would meet Irene at the airport, and they would fly me to California for her return to Stanford. The response caught me by surprise, and a flurry of questions sped through my head. Was this a bribe? Had I been voted out of the family and the relationship? Did Irene's mother think that our relationship was getting too serious?

Had her liberal values changed when it got too close to home? Was her daughter expected settle down with someone of their culture? Had Irene met someone else while studying abroad?

I didn't go to the airport, but I didn't fly to Palo Alto either. We did meet, but everything had changed. She had changed, the family had changed, and, perhaps, I had changed too. I left the city before the end of the vacation period and returned to Cornell to ponder my future. When classes began, I met with my mentor, Roberto González Echevarría, to explore my options. Roberto had become my role model. However, he always found ways of showing me how little I knew and how much I needed to learn. He even claimed he was a faster sprinter than me. I shared with him my uncertainty about wanting to be at Cornell. After all, I was there not for me but for Irene. Her future had been determined by her parents before she came into the world, and I had assimilated ideas and expectations that were more proper of her family's values than those of my loved ones.

Nevertheless, my relationship with my family also continued to be important. My mother was a saint and a trouper. She wanted the best for her children, always supported us, and never doubted our decisions. Even when we needed money and she had none, she found ways to borrow it to meet our needs. But she was unfamiliar with the language, culture, and laws of her adopted country, and there were things about the education system she didn't understand. So, I explained to Roberto the backdrop to my concerns in painstaking detail. He let me talk, and I like to believe that he listened intently. After I finished, he responded with a grunting sound, *"Déjate de comer mierda y ponte a trabajar"* (literally, "Stop eating shit, and get to work"). Roberto, who was careful to conceal his compassionate side, gave me the best advice possible. At that moment, I decided that the PhD was not for someone else but for me.

Graduate school became the best experience of my life. I was being paid to learn! More important, I was ready to immerse myself in theoretical discussions and tackle thorny subjects. I read from early in the morning until late at night, and also on weekends. The days ran into each other and after a while they all seemed the same. I went to class and attended conferences armed with questions that made even the most self-assured professors think before they responded. It was another beginning, one that was full of exciting new ideas, many challenges, and new friends. We were committed to the learning process and supported each other. I took the usual classes and some that were not so usual. A seminar on Marxism shattered the mold. The students met with the professor off campus late at night, and it wasn't unusual for us to go and watch the sunrise at the end of the class. In graduate school, I polished my knowledge of structuralism and embraced poststructuralism, but I also realized that they did not provide answers to all my questions. I moved into historical discourse to ground my work, but I was also aware that this field had its own limitations. I searched for new approaches to old questions.

IN PURSUIT OF TENURE

I was fortunate to begin my career at Dartmouth College, especially because I was hired without a PhD in hand. I joined the faculty with the same attitude, passion, and sense of justice I nurtured as a graduate student. There was a sense of excitement in the air. The Department of Spanish and Portuguese had just separated from the Department of Romance Languages, and recently hired faculty were all invited to help set the groundwork for building a dynamic department. I was surprised and elated that the same considerations provided to White faculty were also offered to someone like me. I organized talks and conferences and contributed to the academic life of the department. I also became the first university professor to take U.S. students and faculty to Cuba. With time, I also learned about matters that are not part of the graduate school culture and curriculum. Students are taught about research and teaching, and also about honesty and academic integrity. I learned later that some individuals adhere to a different standard.

Still, my recollection of those early years is very positive. I had a job, and not just any job, but employment at a top-tier institution and with colleagues who had graduated from some of the best graduate programs in the country! Many of my colleagues, both new and seasoned, believed that they had arrived, and Dartmouth would be their first and only employer. Just as I had previously accepted living in Ithaca without relying on New York City, I maintained the same attitude about Hanover. I felt like a tourist traveling in a different country and adapting to a different culture. As with my other foreign travels, I embraced the opportunity to explore a new environment. I got involved in outdoor life, went on winter and summer hikes, participated in downhill and cross-country skiing, purchased eggs and milk from the local farmer who raised his own cows and chickens, and picked my own fruits and vegetables. I acquired a chimney brush and ladder, and climbed onto the steep roof to sweep the chimney. I bought a chainsaw and a truckload of logs, which I cut, split, and piled for the upcoming winter. Not bad for a city slicker!

I didn't look or speak like a Vermonter or others from that part of New England. My skin was dark, my hair and beard were long and curly, I spoke with a different accent, and I dressed like a student, which I was. Nevertheless, the university environment was deceptively informal and students and professors addressed each other by given name. Slowly, I learned that not everyone could or would be treated the same. It took me a while to understand that if a White colleague and I dressed the same, we were still treated differently. Some of my White colleagues at this and other institutions wore T-shirts, jeans, and sneakers. However, if a person of color did the same, that person would be viewed differently. I would even go as far as to say that it was acceptable to be a White mediocre professor or administrator, but it was a different experience if the professor or administrator were a person of color. For Black or Afro-Latino faculty members to be respected, they had to be equal or better than their White colleagues. Being better sometimes had negative repercussions and made some coworkers feel insecure. I could even imagine some of them whispering under their breath, "Who does he think he is?" Several went out of their way to keep me closer than their friends, as the saying goes. There was no refuge; not even the sacred library could protect me.

At Cornell, I had lived in the library; at Dartmouth, I did the same. I was a regular visitor, always searching for books to read and checking them out. I kept the interlibrary loan office staff busy. But in the library, I experienced something that would be repeated in different ways at Dartmouth and at other institutions. I still remember the day I waited in line to check out a pile of heavy books that I held in both arms. When my turn arrived, the attendant working behind the counter turned her back and walked away to take care of other duties. Her actions caught me by surprise and questions started rumbling in my head. Did I just become invisible to her? Did she not see me waiting in line? Was I not the next person to be attended? Not wanting to believe what had just happened, I called out to her that I was next in line. I also added the magical phrase that I was a member of the faculty. When she heard the status of my appointment, she changed her expression and approached me with lightning speed to assist me with a smile. I shared my experience with my White colleagues and asked them if that had ever happened to them. The answer was a resounding no. They wondered if the reaction was motivated by my youthful look or by the way I was dressed. "Why? Because some Dartmouth faculty don't look like me?" I added. Even if that were the case, even if I were a student, why should that be a reason to refuse assistance to the next person in line? Weren't we all members of the same Dartmouth family?

NAVIGATING ACADEMIC POLITICS

But the biggest betrayal came from people I knew, members of the Department of Spanish and Portuguese and college administrators. I had joined the faculty under the presidency of John Kemeny, a giant in the field of mathematics and computer science and a man of unquestionable integrity, and Fred Berthold, who was the first dean of the William Jewett Tucker Foundation and the first Preston H. Kelsey Professor of Religion; he served as Kemeny's dean of arts and sciences. In time, things changed, and the Dartmouth faculty were presented with new administrators. The first two chairs, who had welcomed me to the department, left to explore options at other institutions and a different person assumed their place. The new chair was very different from the previous ones. The others embraced my contributions to the department, but she demanded loyalty from her faculty. Other junior colleagues saw the writing on the wall and, in due time, each left the department before his time of tenure. I didn't. I was idealistic, believed in academic freedom, and decided to stand on my record, which was much stronger than that of others in the department who had been awarded tenure. Although I considered myself to be a team player, perhaps there was something in my blood that forced me to oppose any form of abuse. My grandfather was the son of a slave, fought in Cuba's Liberation Army, and also stood up for what he believed.

Predictably, the chair and I had our differences. When we interviewed finalists for the positions we advertised, as in the past, I asked poignant questions. However, when we met to discuss their performance, I often wondered if we were talking about the same people. I heard glowing remarks about applicants whose talks I considered to be weak and, in some cases, disastrous. These candidates, who in my estimation were not the most qualified, were the ones we were encouraged to support.

A surreal incident occurred in which the chair stormed into my office and demanded that I confirm that the chair who hired me had accepted a position at the Library of Congress. At that time, I was an advisor and contributing editor to the Library of Congress Hispanic Division's *Handbook of Latin American Studies*, which made me privy to confidential information that I felt I was not at liberty to divulge. The chair insisted that I provide her with that information so she could use it to expel that person from the department, before the previous chair who hired me was ready to resign her faculty appointment from Dartmouth.

Everything came to a head one afternoon when the chair requested that we meet in her office. First she berated me for creating problems in the department and not agreeing with her position. Then, in what I tried to understand as a symbolic expression of unity, she invited me to physically embrace her. I do not recall how long the embrace lasted, but it made me feel very uncomfortable—uncomfortable enough for me to document the incident and send it to the dean. I wrote to the new dean with the confidence that he would look into the matter. How could he not? We knew each other, and we were both members of the Black Caucus. He, and all the faculty of color, had shared concerns about issues that interfered with our ability to work at the institution, issues that pertained to race and racism on campus. Some concerns stemmed from the birth of the *Dartmouth Review* and its staffers' persistence in attacking a faculty member of color in the Music Department. I thought that all of us were working to change the culture of Dartmouth College. Regrettably for me, the new dean had other interests. In due time rumors circulated that he was having an affair with the chair of my department. This was alarming to me for the obvious reasons, and more so as it pertained to their respective partners, since each was married with children. I found it disturbing that at the precise moment when I was confiding in the dean what I considered to be a form of harassment and discrimination, the dean and my chair were sharing the same pillow. For me that meant a potential violation of my privacy and confidentiality. Everything I was sending to the dean could potentially be provided to the woman who oversaw my department. In response, he asserted that too much noise was coming from the Department of Spanish and Portuguese.

NAVIGATING AND
OVERCOMING DISAPPOINTMENT

While at Dartmouth, I came up for tenure twice. The first time, I requested an early tenure decision. I wanted to move quickly through the system, not only because I exceeded all of the requirements outlined by the previous deans to the faculty for my entering class, but also because I had perceived a change in the department's climate as the new chair attempted to consolidate her power. This was about the same time department colleagues sought employment at other universities. I felt alone, but I also trusted the institution to uphold the highest standards and judge me on my record. However, the Department of Spanish and Portuguese lacked the minimum number of senior members to render a tenure decision, so an outside ad hoc committee was formed with representatives from other departments. I also knew them; we shared a common interest in literary theory and criticism. One committee member had even shared how his tenure experience had been affected by racism in his department, which he brought to the attention of some members of the Board of Trustees. But it soon became apparent that I did not know my colleagues well enough; rather, my chair knew them better than I did, and they became her accomplices.

I had every reason to believe that the chair and her co-conspirators had tampered with my tenure file and some of the outside evaluators. I was provided with confidential information that the overwhelming majority of evaluations supported my promotion with tenure, but the ad hoc committee paid more attention to two negative letters that criticized my work, and these evaluators were friends of the chair. The ad hoc committee focused on a few sentences to build a narrative that played into the hands of the chair. It did not matter that I had published in top-tier journals or that I was the only Dartmouth advisor to the Hispanic Division of the Library of Congress, or that I was the only Latino faculty member at Dartmouth. They had no qualms about abandoning their academic integrity and giving into peer pressure. Did my singular accomplishments at the start of my career threaten them? Was it their desire to seek or maintain membership in an incestuous community? The ad hoc committee rendered its decision: All but one voted to deny tenure and promotion. A code of silence was imposed and the Affirmative Action Office continued its investigation.

Non-committee members did speak to me about my case as the silence turned into rumors that engulfed the college, and I learned that, ironically, the colleague who had shared with me his own fight for tenure chose to be loyal to the same people who wanted to exorcise him from the college. It seemed that he had been granted membership into a club that could wield power indiscriminately against the most vulnerable. Had he been placed on the ad hoc committee because he was Black, to diminish any accusation of racism? He found solace in telling me that the ad hoc committee could only recommend and not

decide tenure. Perhaps he was right. I was promoted to associate professor without tenure, to be evaluated again in two years' time. I was not
pleased with the decision, but the chair, ad hoc committee, and dean
did not get their way either. That is how I understood the decision back
then. I now believe that it was a grace period that provided me with the
time to leave Dartmouth.

LESSONS LEARNED AND
MAKING SENSE OF IT ALL

Yet I refused to depart because I was convinced that my teaching and
publication records were strong. I proceeded to finish one book while
I continued to work on two others. When I had joined the faculty,
we were told it was not necessary or useful to publish your dissertation. Institutions like Dartmouth preferred to see new work beyond
the dissertation. I had the required articles and had also submitted a
monograph that was different from my dissertation. Members of the
ad hoc committee could not attack the quantity of my work, so they
went after the quality. In the end, it really did not matter. By the time
I came up for tenure a second time, the once newly appointed dean
was now more experienced and called in favors, especially because he
knew he had to recuse himself from the deliberations. I suspect that
my strongest advocate was also asked to do the same. On my second
review, all the letters were positive, except for one from a visible institution not known for its humanities programs. As in the first deliberations, a few negative sentences became the centerpiece of the one
that was drafted and forwarded to the promotions committee. All the
other supporting documents were ignored or suppressed. And as in
the first evaluation, the same member of the department resisted the
pressure to make the recommendation unanimous. He was the only

one who refused to surrender to the demands of belonging to that community. He must have felt as lonely as I did.

During that two-year period, the dean and the chair had formalized their love affair. Now they were husband and wife. The next rumor that circulated reached members of the higher levels of the administration, who were concerned that I might litigate the case in a court of law. I did consider that option. I spoke with someone who had sued Dartmouth and won, but the fight had not been pretty and all the college had done, in the end, was to give her the position she had earned. Would that really be a win for me? There was a universal sigh of relief when I decided not to pursue the matter. I opted to move forward—it was time to undergo another rebirth. That was the best decision for me. I realized that it would have been more destructive to continue to work under the same conditions in that department and with little or no support from that or any other dean. But in my heart of hearts, I fought for the right to decide when to leave. Thus, I may have earned the dubious distinction of being the only faculty member in the academic profession to survive two tenure rejections at the same institution.

What does my case say about the people who engage in unethical behavior? What does it mean when they look like you or me? My dean was African American and, at first, he appeared to share the same beliefs and value system as other people of color in higher education, who were committed to working toward a more ethical institution and society. My chair was Hispanic, from the Iberian Peninsula. In other words, she was not a Latina, and she did not care how difficult it was for Latinx/a/os entering higher education. More important, she was not willing to protect those who spoke the same language she did. In her case, language or culture was not a motivating factor. Perhaps it had nothing to do with race, language, or ethnicity. To me, it felt like something more sinister was happening, something more cultural, political, social, or even psychological. Their actions were more egocentric—a manifestation of a quest for unbridled power. It was the same type of abuse John Weeks wielded against José Mieles back in junior high school. John used it to humiliate José and make himself feel superior, enlarge his stature, and seek acceptance by those at the center of power. Is this not the same structure we see in dictatorships, from the right or the left, when people of the same nationality or ethnic identity are driven to oppress their fellow citizens?

At a young age, my brother and I made frequent trips to Cuba to meet our family and nurture our Spanish. After Fidel Castro's triumph, my mother left us with family in Havana while she returned to work in the United States. This was a period in which we lived with Eva, my brother's godmother. Aunt Eva, *la más negra* (the darkest) member of the Santos family, practiced *santería*; she was a *santera*. She had, what seemed to me back then, a large house, with animals in the backyard and dogs we loved to play with; she had everything we lacked in New York City. At night, we slept in the spare room, the same one that housed her saints. We were scared of the masks, the horsetail used for cleansing, and the *soperas* where the saints resided, but we were also fascinated by the rituals of positioning oneself on the straw mat to pay respects, first on one side, then on the other, and the sacrifices of pigeons, chickens, and goats. Slowly, we became more accepting of the *santos* and saw the rituals as a way of life. Ironically, *santeras* and *espiritistas* in both New York and Puerto Rico predicted that I would be victorious with my tenure at Dartmouth and I believed them. Were they wrong? Did I misunderstand them? I questioned my faith in them.

Maybe my victory was to leave Dartmouth, or perhaps the victory would come later with my professional accomplishments: two endowed chairs, American Council of Learned Societies and Guggenheim fellowships, and numerous publications. But I still wonder: Is destiny fixed or can it be altered? Because the predictions failed to come true, had my destiny been altered? On a trip to Cuba a few years after the second tenure decision had been rendered, I spent time with my uncle Tin, and my cousin Zenaida, who was older than my uncle. During this visit, Tin, who was not a *santero*, channeled my godmother's spirit. Aralia was the eldest of my grandmother's 10 children. When my grandfather passed away, she became the surrogate mother of her brothers and sisters. She never had children, and I became the son she always wanted. Suddenly, my uncle stopped being himself; his voice, facial expressions, and mannerisms had changed. He now spoke slowly and softly, and he moved and gestured as if he had been transformed into my godmother. Zenaida made sure that I observed what was taking place before us. She wanted me to notice my uncle's behavior. Aralia spoke delicately but with determination and explained that it was she who had intervened in my tenure decision. She didn't want me to be at that college, to live in that environment. It was she who altered the predictions to award me tenure, and she had changed the course of my life. I had to travel to Cuba to receive this message, maybe to bring closure to my doubts or obtain spiritual tranquility.

CONCLUSION

My path from my neighborhood to college, then to graduate school, and into the profession has been solitary. I use the words *solitary* and *solitude* to reference the works that moved me when I was in high school but also to describe a journey taken by very few people who come from where I started and have walked the roads I have, without a map or even a compass, making mistakes, figuring things out (or not), falling but then getting up, dusting themselves off, and continuing the journey.

I have gone on with my career. I used the energy I could have spent documenting all the injustices I had experienced and directed it to my teaching, research, and service, and to helping others. It felt liberating. I decided if I could survive that experience, I could endure anything. Life possessed few challenges I couldn't handle. In context, I wasn't the only professor who had been mistreated. There were others and they went on to establish successful careers. Despite everything that happened, I am proud to state that I started my career at Dartmouth.

Nashville and Vanderbilt University have become my new home. I still say that I am from New York, but I have lived in Nashville longer than any other place. I travel to New York City with some regularity, but it seems only vaguely familiar to me. I recognize the areas where I lived on the Lower East Side, but the city has also changed. It is not the same place I knew in my youth.

Initially, I was a little hesitant about moving to the South, for all the reasons anyone can imagine, especially for someone from New York City. I found Nashville to be a well-kept secret, but Vanderbilt and Nashville are not the same places I knew when I first arrived. We have all grown together. As I reflect on these memories, it is clear that I have become, in the metaphor of life as a long-distance race, a long-distance runner. A colleague at Binghamton University once said: "The higher you go, the lonelier it gets." I often wish I had a community that could understand me, but I have become more accepting of my solitude. It is a lonely journey and yet there is no other, for the other roads are not worth traveling. I now embrace the solitude of the long-distance runner.

CHAPTER 12

How Passion and Commitment to Equitable Higher Education and Many Diverse Champions Led Me to the Presidency

Mildred García

> *I took my father to see* Rogue One *today. I wanted my Mexican father, with his thick Mexican accent, to experience what it was like to see a hero in a blockbuster film speak the way he does.* (Time & Space, 2017, para. 1)

I ndeed, actor Diego Luna's choice to keep his Mexican accent for *Rogue One: A Star Wars Story* was part of a bold and calculated effort to illustrate what we in higher education have always known and the research continues to show: Diversity matters, representation matters, and when the heroes and sheroes of the new majority are leading our institutions at home, abroad, and in galaxies far, far away, there is a new hope for all of us.

For me and the Latinx/a/o higher education leaders of my generation, this representation was almost nonexistent when we began our academic journeys; not just on the silver screen, but at the head of the classrooms and in administrative buildings at schools, colleges, and universities across the United States. We were, however, no stranger to accents in our homes and neighborhoods, and their omnipresence reflected the magnetic pull of the American Dream and the many diverse peoples who came to this country aspiring to achieve it.

BEGINNINGS

My parents, who had migrated to New York City from Puerto Rico before I was born, were two of those people. As a child, I was fascinated by my father's accent when he spoke English. It represented both the rich culture from which he came and the possibility of a new future he envisioned for his children. And he was not alone. I'll never forget our family trips to Delancey Street on the Lower East Side of Manhattan where my father, with his thick Puerto Rican accent, would negotiate with Hassidic Jews, with their thick Yiddish accents, over the price of the outfits my siblings and I would have the privilege of wearing on Easter Sunday.

To me, the sound of those two starkly contrasting accents, along with the myriad other dialects floating along the open storefronts on those crisp, spring mornings, was America personified. It was the sound of possibility, a beautiful melody that can be orchestrated only by the many diverse peoples who call this country home. Unfortunately, as my journey in education progressed, that music slowly disappeared, and the diversity I so fondly remembered was no longer prevalent, especially in positions of leadership. In the absence of such role models, I learned to seek out like-minded individuals who shared my dream to break higher education's glass ceiling—not just fellow Latinx/a/os, but all people of color and women working to be the change we wanted to see in higher education. We lifted each other up, invested in each other's talents, and collaborated in ways that made it impossible for the old guard to deny the validity of our voice—even if it did come with an accent.

This practice was a precursor to our entire careers, and even though nearly all of us now hold leadership roles or are leading universities or colleges, and even though we collectively represent the new majority in this country, the need for us to continue to support each other— and those who aspire to follow in our footsteps—has not diminished. All of us, particularly women and people of color, need the support structures of trusted colleagues wherever we are in our careers, but it is most critical at the beginning of it for two reasons: (a) This is when we are most vulnerable to the adversity and doubt that comes with being underrepresented in higher education, and (b) this is when we establish a network of colleagues with whom we will fight through that adversity while ascending the leadership path.

As a first-generation college student, a woman of color, and the daughter of factory workers with no more than an eighth grade education (not for lack of intelligence, but for lack of opportunity), the strength of my support network was critical for my success. This began, of course, with my parents, who instilled in me the value of a diverse community. In our tenement alone lived Italians, African Americans, and other Puerto Ricans, and while we were all poor economically, we were rich in cultures, customs, and languages, giving us an invaluable introduction to the importance of being global citizens.

This diverse community also gave my parents a platform to instill in us that no matter how far we climbed, we would always represent a group who have to fight for opportunity rather than those in the majority who are often born into it. And despite the uniqueness of each of the cultures throughout our community, it was also clear that we would always be lumped together as one homogenous group. With this, too, my parents saw an opportunity to teach us not only that our tenement represented many differences, but that together we were a community of differences that equally embraced the commonalities of our plight and the uniqueness of our cultures.

We worked together to help and support other immigrant and migrant families that were new to New York, determined to show that we were an integral part of this new world and that, together, we could achieve the American Dream through education and hard work. My parents established the Culebra Social Club in which people from my father's town would gather to help each other translate this new world. He was the club's first president and was actively involved in the creation of the Puerto Rican Day Parade in New York. Seeing him in this role made a significant impression on me, although I was unable to fully comprehend it for many years.

THE POWER OF EDUCATION

What I did comprehend, partially because my parents said it to me so often, is the mantra by which I lead today: *"La unica herencia que una familia pobre le deja a sus hijos es una buena educacion,"* which means, "The only inheritance a poor family leaves its children is a good education." Together, my mom and dad wielded the power of that profound truth to push each of their seven children to look beyond what society expected of them. When my father died when I was 12 and we moved to the Brooklyn housing projects, my mother kept that message alive, using her job in the factories to not only provide for us, but also to ensure we understood that education—and only education—could propel us to a brighter future beyond those factory walls.

This collaborative and supportive spirit grounded in the importance of education became the foundation for my ascension to higher education leadership, and while there is no precise pathway to any presidency, especially for women and people of color, my path was illuminated when I first witnessed the power of equitable access to quality public education. It came on the heels of *Brown v. Board of Education* (1954), which made me, the youngest girl in my family, the first to be thrust into a middle-class educational environment rather than the underserved schools in the projects that some of my older brothers and sisters attended. I was taught French, received music lessons, and was taken on field trips to the Metropolitan Museum of Art and Broadway plays—opportunities we now recognize as *high-impact practices* that none of my older siblings had. I am thus a living, breathing manifestation of the transformative power of equitable access to higher education—no smarter than my parents or siblings, simply the benefactor of opportunities they never had, opportunities that continue to be scarce for millions of low-income and underrepresented students and working professionals across this country today.

PURSUING A CAREER IN HIGHER EDUCATION

With this in mind, it is no wonder that I pursued education as a career, first as a faculty member, and then, when I was mentored to have a broader impact on the diverse students of our nation, an administrator. For me, a presidency seemed like an impossibility, so I never thought to pursue one. Like many women and people of color, I suffered from *imposter syndrome* and continue to wrestle with it to this day. But by staying driven by the one thing that should drive all educators regardless of title, position, or salary—our diverse students and passionately serving their needs—I was able to cast off the belief that these positions were not for people who looked like me.

And therein lies an important ingredient for every step of an aspiring president's journey: Show up as who you really are and remain vigilant about keeping the best interest of your students at the heart of everything you do. The time of this writing is a difficult one for our country, and those who are suspicious of diversity and fear the changing face of our nation have been emboldened to speak and lash out against it. I am amazed at how many higher education leaders haven't publicly condemned this movement by making stated and demonstrated commitments to protect their students from it. When I speak with these leaders, I hear the same reasoning for their lack of action: "I disagree with what's happening, but I can't risk upsetting our donors and constituents." I politely remind them to review their institution's mission statement, where they will most certainly find language stating that their university aims to welcome all racial, geographic, and ethnic groups in ways that foster respect for and understanding of the cultural differences of an increasingly diverse country and global economy. When Deferred Action for Childhood Arrivals (DACA) students are threatened, or Muslim community members are subjected to religious-based travel bans, or the Black Lives Matter movement is called into question, or lesbian, gay, bisexual, transgender, queer, intersex, and asexual communities fear losing their well-earned rights, or any other number of social justice crises occur on college and university campuses, higher education leaders are obligated to speak out not just on moral grounds, but also by the very tenets we agreed to uphold when we accepted our leadership roles.

OVERCOMING BARRIERS

Speaking up can be difficult, especially for women and people of color who must check all the boxes, have all the credentials, and be up to date and published on all the latest research and grants just to get a seat at the table. Never forget, there are those looking for reasons to silence and exclude us from becoming student advocates and leaders. Don't give them that chance, but don't lose yourself in the process. Yes, you must find an institution where you can comfortably be yourself and work collaboratively across every college and division for the betterment of all students, but above all else, you must take care of self. Just as flight attendants instruct us to don our own oxygen mask before assisting others, we must first take care of mind, body, heart, and soul before we can effectively lead on behalf of the students we serve.

It's not fair that we are held to a higher standard, or that we are expected to "code-switch" in certain settings, or that one mistake can derail our chances at a presidency, or that expectations decrease the moment a woman or person of color enters the room—but that is our reality. I've been told to cut my hair, take off my ankle bracelet, and dress more conservatively. I had a high school counselor say I wasn't "college material," had a former colleague say I was aiming "too high" in pursuing a doctorate, and was told several times not to conduct research or publish on issues of social justice because it is a "self-interest." All of this is an everyday reality for women and people of color who dare to dream beyond what society expects of them, compounding their collective responsibility to widen equitable access to not just higher education, but also board of director representation, leadership opportunities, and presidencies for those who aspire to reach them.

Earlier I mentioned that for my generation of Latinx/a/o leaders in higher education, there were few women and people of color in leadership positions to whom we could look for mentorship and support. Of course, much like my parents having no more than an eighth grade education, this was not because of lack of intelligence or ability, but rather lack of opportunity. To put this into context, the American Council on Education (2012) began surveying college presidents in 1986, and at that time, the vast majority of college and university leaders were White men. However, as I progressed in my journey from tenure-track instructor at LaGuardia Community College, to assistant vice president at Montclair State University, to tenured professor and vice provost for academic personnel at Arizona State University, those numbers slowly began to change—not nearly at the pace of the nation's demographic shift, but small and measurable improvements nonetheless. As this happened, mentors did begin to emerge for women and people of color who aspired to lead institutions.

THE POWER OF MENTORING

I had many such mentors, beginning with Flora Mancuso Edwards, president of Hostos Community College, City University of New York, for whom I served first as executive assistant/chief of staff and then as dean of students. Mancuso Edwards taught me the importance of finding an institution that suits your skills, matches your passion, and supports the students you want to serve. A Cuban immigrant, Mancuso Edwards drew strength from leading an institution populated with students whose lives mirrored her own—at the time, the institution was 85% Latino, and the majority of those students emigrated from the Dominican Republic or Puerto Rico. There was also a strong population of African American students as well as single mothers. Indeed, Mancuso Edwards was both an inspiration to the diverse students she served and, because of her passion, an effective champion of their upward mobility through academic success.

As I worked my way toward a presidency through myriad faculty and administrative positions, including visiting professorships at The Pennsylvania State University and Teachers College, Columbia University, I learned that strong colleagues and supporters didn't necessarily have to look and sound like me; they just needed to share my passion for equitable access to higher education. My mentors included White men as well as women who were not Latina, and their support and influence was equally transformative throughout my journey. As I often say, diversity includes White men, and if we want the power of diversity to truly lift our institutions and students, then we must ensure everyone has a seat at the table, not just underrepresented groups who traditionally struggle to get there.

This applies not only to your own support network, but also to the leadership teams you join or build as you progress toward a presidency. Learn to collaborate with and create diverse teams of talented individuals whose skills and passions both complement and contrast with yours. My degrees are in higher education and business, so I seek out leaders with backgrounds in engineering, the arts, humanities, or communications—any discipline that varies from mine and those of the other team members. I also proactively search for and work with colleagues outside higher education and find their perspectives to be as insightful as they are refreshing. Recognize that our diverse campus communities are made up of some of the most intelligent and innovative minds in the world—bright, creative faculty, staff, students, alumni, and constituents whose potential transcends their job descriptions, résumés, backgrounds, or degrees. Tap into those minds, work to transform their ideas into strategic initiatives that align with the university's mission, and ask for their support in achieving your mutual goals.

Yes, risks are involved in all of these practices, but listening to your heart and going against what some people think you should do—as long as you've done your research, explored all facets of every solution, and consulted with trusted colleagues and mentors—is often the best course of action. I took a risk in accepting my first presidency at Berkeley College, one that a trusted colleague advised me not to take. Berkeley is a for-profit institution, and there was a fear that I would be pigeonholed in a way that would prevent me from one day returning to "traditional" higher education. But with the help of other mentors, my thoughts returned to the most important consideration when making any decision in a career in higher education: the students. Berkeley was populated with the student body I was passionate about serving—low-income, underserved, and first-generation students from diverse backgrounds—and that alone cemented my decision to take the job.

On one of my first strolls across campus, two African American students approached me and said, "We heard you're from the Brooklyn housing projects."

"I am," I replied as they exchanged looks of doubt. Sensing their skepticism, I rattled off the name of my old street and the number of the building I grew up in. Their jaws hit the floor; they lived on the same street, in the same building. After a pleasant exchange about the neighborhood, I reminded them of the importance of finishing their degree and gave them some advice on how to see their academic goals to fruition.

Leading Berkeley College was a wonderful experience, one I will forever be grateful for. Had I turned my back on that opportunity, I would have been surrendering to the very elitism of higher education that I set out to avoid. Moreover, the aforementioned risk of not getting the opportunity to one day lead a public university was mitigated through the constant upkeep of my research. I continued to write, publish, and drive national conversations about equitable access, inclusivity, and diversity in higher education—so much so that when the California State University (CSU) system began its search for new presidents to lead from this perspective, my name kept popping up. This prompted a phone call from then CSU chancellor, Charles Reed, who proved to be a mentor and champion of my candidacy and career. My mother had just passed away, so I was unable to apply to CSU at that time, underscoring yet another critical factor when pursuing a presidency: Not only must it be the right institution with the right students that align with your passion and skill set, it must also be the right time. Alas, when I got the first phone call, it was not the right time. But, again, because I continued to stay relevant in my research and publications, I was nominated a second time a year later, and this time everything aligned.

REFLECTING ON LESSONS LEARNED

After 10 years of leading two different CSU institutions (CSU Dominguez Hills from 2007 to 2012 and CSU Fullerton from 2012 to the present), I have learned countless other lessons, and a day doesn't go by that I don't encounter at least one teachable moment for my colleagues or myself. I have also found that my advisors and confidantes continue to be equally important in helping me see and navigate these moments. I also enjoy having a constant and ongoing group of mentees, from members of my own leadership team to those I support through the American Association of State Colleges and Universities' Millennium Leadership Initiative. In the past three years alone, three of my former mentees—all women and/or people of color—began their own presidencies and will now begin mentoring a new generation.

In my current presidency of CSU Fullerton, the most populated campus in the largest system of higher education in the country, I am honored to have what is likely the most impactful role of my career. I have found the institution that matches me and my passion and, above all, has the students I want to serve. Fifty-five percent of CSU Fullerton's more than 40,000 students are the first in their family to attend college, more than 60% are students of color, and nearly half are Pell Grant-eligible. These diverse students—some of whom work two jobs and catch three buses just to get to class—are at the heart of every decision I make. While some may see doing higher education's heaviest lifting with the least amount of resources an impossible task, we at CSU Fullerton see it as an opportunity for greatness.

At present, I have assembled a very diverse team composed of individuals who are not only educated in a variety of disciplines but also ethnically diverse and gender balanced. They are African American, Latino, Caucasian, Asian American, and Middle Eastern, from lower socioeconomic backgrounds to upper-class upbringings. Four of my six vice presidents are people of color and of our nine academic deans, six are women and one is openly gay. Each of these diverse leaders is empowered to offer their unique perspective, and together, we work across all divisions and colleges to hold each other accountable and to collaboratively achieve our goals with the faculty, staff, and students.

Since my arrival at the institution in 2012, this inclusive, equitable, and collaborative environment has helped the university facilitate a 30% improvement in six-year graduation rates for first-time freshmen and a 65% improvement in four-year graduation rates for first-time freshmen; the elimination of the achievement gap for transfer students while cutting it in half for first-time freshmen; the conferral of more than 10,000 degrees to one graduating class for the first time in university history; a near tripling of annual total new gift commitments; the hiring of 270 diverse tenure-track faculty members; and a shift from our longstanding "top regional university" ranking with *U.S. News & World Report* to a "top national university" ranking—a first in the school's history. Today, the university is first in the CSU system in graduating women, first in California in graduating Latinos, and fifth in the nation in graduating students of color.

CONCLUSION

To think that the inspiration that led me here began with a simple phrase from two Puerto Rican parents who migrated to New York to

see their children achieve the American Dream: *"La única herencia que una familia pobre le deja a sus hijos es una buena educación."*
Throughout my entire journey from first-generation college student to the first Latina president in the largest system of higher education in the United States, I've continued to believe in that phrase, not just for low-income students of color, but for all students regardless of where they are from, how they got here, who they love, what gender they identify with, how much money is in their bank account, or what god they pray to. We all need an inheritance that includes equitable access to a good education, not just for the private good of our graduates, but also for the public good of the global economy in which they will build careers and raise families. Our collective success hinges on our ability to work toward a common mission, not in silos or in separate colleges, divisions, or institutions, but collaboratively in ways that tap into the power of our diversity.

I am so grateful to the diverse champions whose mentorship led me and so many other Latinx/a/o leaders to the right institutions at the right time for the right reasons. Together, we stand as a testament to the transformative power of equitable access to higher education, and I am proud that a new generation of diverse students and higher education professionals now look to us to see what is possible. No, we are not movie stars in a blockbuster film, but like Diego Luna in *Rogue One*, we represent a new possibility in a new world in which the limitations of the old one are being abolished by the new majority.

Mom and Dad, with their thick Puerto Rican accents, would be proud.

REFERENCES

Brown v. Board of Education, 347 U.S. 483 (1954).

American Council on Education. (2012). *The American college president: 2011 edition* (10th ed.). Washington, DC: Author.

Time & Space. (2017, January 2). I took my father to see *Rogue One* today [Tumblr post]. Retrieved from http://riveralwaysknew.tumblr.com/post/155327892192/i-took-my-father-to -see-rogue-one-today-ive

Chapter 13

Exploring the New Latinx/a/o Faculty Pathway

Lucy Arellano

As a faculty member, I am often asked, "Did you always want to be a professor?" These inquiries often come from current graduate students who are contemplating their future career paths. Much to their surprise, my answer is a resounding, "No." It was not until my final year as a doctoral student that I set this career goal. I thought about why this aspiration had not emerged before. I realized that I did not see myself as a faculty member exactly because I did not see myself as a faculty member. It was not until I saw another Latina professor in the field of higher education stand in front of a class, whose personal experiences and background resembled mine, that I could visualize that career trajectory as an option for me. This professor was also a Chicana, first-generation college student, and from a low-income background. Up until that point, I had only two other Latina professors as an undergraduate student—a Puertorriqueña in Spanish, and a Cubana in sociology. When I served as a teaching assistant for the Chicana professor in my doctoral program, I saw myself in that role as she professed in front of the classroom. I could anticipate the lecture she was going to deliver and predict the answer she would provide to students' questions. At that moment, I felt the *"tú eres mi otro yo"* ("you are my other me") connection that Luis Valdez (1990) described in *In Lak'ech*. My decision to become a faculty member came from the ability to see myself—a version of myself—in front of the classroom.

This was not the first time I felt a connection with a Latina professor. As a graduate student at the University of Michigan, I was inspired after reading *From the Barrio to the Academy: Revelations of a Mexican American "Scholarship Girl"* by Laura Rendón (1992). Her description of academic shock mirrored my own as a young scholar:

> A feeling of alienation that moves the student from concrete to abstract experience and that takes the student from an old culture that is vastly different in tradition, style, and values to a new world of unfamiliar intellectual conventions, practices, and assumptions. . . . If the student persists in using past experience to affirm himself or herself, not only do rewards become more difficult to attain but the student is also riddled with the guilt, pain, and confusion that arise from daring to live simultaneously in two vastly different worlds while being fully accepted in neither. (Rendón, 1992, p. 56)

I felt painfully validated. She was telling my story in her voice. In retrospect, it is ironic that I traveled the same hallways she navigated two-and-a-half decades earlier as a graduate student in the School of Education Building at the University of Michigan. Yet the struggles remain the same. Today, Latinx/a/o students continue to experience alienation, a hostile campus climate, and a lack of role models as they pursue higher education. As a master's student, I carried Rendón's journal article with me. I would reread it whenever I questioned what I was doing in graduate school or thought I could not finish. Even now, it remains a source of inspiration. I wondered how many Latinas had traveled the pathway through the doctorate and into the professoriate.

BACKGROUND

The pathway to the professoriate becomes narrower at each subsequent step. This trajectory is significantly more constricting for Latinx/a/o faculty. To better understand the pathway, it is important to start at the very beginning of the journey. A seminal report (Pérez Huber, Huidor, Malagón, Sánchez, & Solórzano, 2006) highlighted the participation of Latinx/a/os as a group across the K–20 spectrum. According to the updated report, from 100 Latinx/a/os who begin elementary school together, 63 Latinas/60 Latinos graduate high school, 13 Latinas/11 Latinos graduate with a bachelor's degree, 4 Latinas/3 Latinos complete graduate school, and 0.3 Latinas/0.3 Latinos graduate with a doctoral degree (Pérez Huber et al., 2015).

Continuing to explore the pathway to the professoriate, there have been some gains in the number of Latinx/a/os joining the faculty ranks within the past three decades. Table 13.1 includes the percentages of full-time faculty in degree-granting postsecondary institutions by race/ethnicity for a span of 32 years. In 1981, only 6,899 of the 451,558 faculty were Hispanic—a mere 1.5%. In 2013, 33,217 of the total 791,391 (4.2%) were Hispanic faculty (National Center for Education Statistics [NCES], 1986, 1993, 2000, 2006, 2015). Although Hispanics have experienced some gains in the professoriate, the percentage is not on par with the representation of the national population demographics for this community—currently at 17.6% (U.S. Census Bureau, 2015).

Table 13.1. *Percentage of Full-Time Faculty in Degree-Granting Postsecondary Institutions, by Race/Ethnicity*

	1981	1991*	1997**	2005**	2013**
Black, non-Hispanic	4.1%	4.7%	4.9%	5.2%	5.5%
Hispanic	1.5%	2.2%	2.6%	3.4%	4.2%
Asian or Pacific Islander	3.2%	5.1%	5.5%	7.2%	9.1%
American Indian/ Alaskan Native	0.3%	0.3%	0.4%	0.5%	0.4%
White, non-Hispanic	90.9%	87.7%	83.9%	78.1%	72.7%
Total (n =)	451,558	520,324	568,719	675,624	791,391

*Data for the target year of 1989 were not available.
**Percentages for 1997, 2005, and 2013 do not include nonresident and race/ethnicity unknown.

Note. Data from *Digest of Education Statistics, 1985–1986* (Table 100); *Digest of Education Statistics, 1993* (Table 219); *Digest of Education Statistics, 2000* (Table 230); *Digest of Education Statistics, 2006* (Table 232); *Digest of Education Statistics, 2015* (Table 315.20); by National Center for Education Statistics. Public domain.

Table 13.2 illustrates the percentages of full-time Hispanic faculty in degree-granting postsecondary institutions by rank and gender (NCES, 1986, 1993, 2000, 2006, 2015). The most startling finding in this data set is the discrepancy between the distribution of male and female faculty in various academic ranks. In 1981, Hispanic females constituted only about 30% of the faculty, while Hispanic males accounted for about 70% of the positions. Across the 30-year span, males are fairly evenly distributed at the ranks of assistant, associate, and full professors across. Females are less likely to be promoted to full professor (range of 9.2% to 12.8%) but more likely to be represented among assistant professors (range of 22.6% to 31.5%). Although this trend persisted between 1981 and 1997, a noticeable decline occurred in Hispanic female assistant professors in 2013 and an increase occurred in the "other faculty" category, which includes nontenure and non-instructional faculty. This finding is consistent with the general national trend across higher education institutions of decreased tenure and tenure-track positions (Eagan et al., 2014).

Table 13.2. *Percentage of Full-Time Hispanic Faculty in Degree-Granting Postsecondary Institutions, by Rank and Gender*

	1981		1991*		1997		2005		2013	
	Male	Female	Male	Female	Male	Female	Male	Female	Male	Female
Professors	20.2%	9.2%	22.5%	9.4%	24.5%	12.8%	21.5%	10.8%	21.3%	12.1%
Associate professors	22.9%	16.0%	20.3%	15.2%	21.5%	18.2%	20.4%	17.1%	20.5%	17.8%
Assistant professors	24.9%	27.6%	26.7%	31.5%	25.0%	29.3%	24.1%	26.4%	20.4%	22.6%
Instructors	24.2%	34.5%	19.3%	27.3%	15.8%	21.2%	20.7%	25.9%	16.8%	21.5%
Lecturers	1.5%	3.5%	2.5%	5.3%	2.9%	5.1%	4.0%	7.1%	4.8%	7.4%
Other faculty	6.4%	9.2%	8.7%	11.3%	10.4%	13.3%	9.4%	12.7%	16.1%	18.6%
Total (*n* =)	4,844	2,055	7,353	4,069	8,792	5,976	12,486	10,332	17,198	16,019

*Data for the target year of 1989 were not available.

Note. Data from *Digest of Education Statistics, 1985–1986* (Table 100); *Digest of Education Statistics, 1993* (Table 219); *Digest of Education Statistics, 2000* (Table 230); *Digest of Education Statistics, 2006* (Table 232); *Digest of Education Statistics, 2015* (Table 315.20); by National Center for Education Statistics. Public domain.

Contextualizing these data is also important. The numbers included in Tables 13.1 and 13.2 represent those Latinx/a/os who already find themselves in full-time faculty roles at colleges and universities across the country. However, it needs to be acknowledged that there is a pool of applicants who seek faculty roles but are unsuccessful. In 2015, 3,423 Hispanics/Latinos earned a doctoral degree (National Science Foundation [NSF], 2016). Each of the four years prior (2011, 2012, 2013, 2014), the average was about 3,000 graduates per year. The sum of all Hispanic/Latino doctorate earners between 2005 and 2015 is 31,010 (NSF, 2016).

These numbers of Latinx/a/o candidates earning doctorates also debunk the myth (Smith, 1996) that there simply are not enough qualified Latinx/a/o applicants to diversify higher education—the 31,010 individuals (NSF, 2016) prove otherwise. But a number of hurdles stand between graduate school and the professoriate. Very few Latinx/a/os are encouraged, advised, or even groomed to become professors (Castellanos, Gloria, & Kamimura, 2006). Thus, the self-doubt that "we are not good enough" becomes the narrative we believe when we do not hear positive affirmations to counter it (Gildersleeve, Croom, & Vasquez, 2011). Even when some do reach the door, they are filtered out during the search process due to lack of "fit" because they do not share the background of those in power, ultimately perpetuating systemic institutionalized racism (Feagin, 2006). Mentoring, advising, support, exposure to other faculty of color, and understanding the dynamics of the campus climate are all factors that play a vital role in the continued growth and success of Latinx/a/o faculty.

FACULTY RESPONSIBILITIES

Understanding the role of faculty is essential to Latinx/a/o success. All faculty members are judged on three components of their position: research, teaching, and service. Depending on the institutional type, the emphasis placed on each category may vary, but faculty are evaluated based on their productivity in the three areas. What "counts" as faculty workload within each of the categories is an assiduous negotiation between the faculty member, their unit, and the institution.

Research

Research encompasses a wide array of duties. At the broadest level, it includes the production of intellectual knowledge in advancement of an academic field. In higher education, this is typically measured as peer-reviewed journal publications. At research-intensive universities, research also comprises securing grants to offset salary costs and support graduate students. Through research, Latinx/a/o faculty can employ lines of inquiry and methods that center on community and campus engagement. On my own campus, a student of color speak-out was held in 2015. As a higher education researcher who studies campus climate issues, I considered how I could engage with events like this. A colleague and I decided to use our own institution as a case study and we conducted a critical discourse analysis about the event (publication forthcoming). This is one example of how Latinx/a/o faculty can strategically use their positionality to make an impact.

Teaching

Teaching encompasses many activities both inside and outside the classroom. First is the most obvious—to teach a course. Everything from syllabus preparation to lesson planning to meeting with students falls under the duties of the instructor on record. Advising and mentoring students can also be considered teaching and this can have a differential impact on Latinx/a/o educators who are generally called on to support Latinx/a/o students and students of color, particularly at predominantly White institutions (PWIs). In the classroom, Latinx/a/o faculty can make all students more critical thinkers about social justice issues and can play a vital role in educating future change agents and advocates who will shape the field of higher education. Collaborating with students is just as important for the faculty member as it is for the students. Scholars have demonstrated that mentorship is a two-way relationship (Griffin, 2008). Further, positive interactions with students can have a direct impact on faculty retention.

Service

Service functions also encompass a diversity of effort. Most typically, embedded within the faculty position is service to the department or unit. This includes such everyday administrative obligations as recruitment, admissions, curriculum development, attending faculty meetings, and so on. In addition, there is also the expectation to provide service to the college, the university (via campuswide committees), and the field (typically via professional associations). In the role of service, Latinx/a/o faculty can be strategic in where they invest their time. The most important thing to remember is that this area is where Latinx/a/o faculty can very easily overcommit. It is crucial to consider the implications of saying either yes or no to a request to serve. Who is making the request? Is it a high-level leader at the institution? Could political backlash result from a no? What current responsibility will receive less time or attention? Ultimately, what are the benefits from taking on this additional task? Can these benefits be documented for inclusion in promotion and tenure dossier?

ADDED (UNRECOGNIZED) WORKLOAD BURDENS

In addition to the standard responsibilities and expectations of the position, faculty of color have additional burdens to carry (that go unrecognized) that supplement the regular duties all faculty are charged with (Turner, González, & Wood, 2008). Faculty of color make up only about 20% of all faculty nationally (NCES, 2015). Their presence is even more scant at PWIs. In 2012 a groundbreaking book brought together the voices of 40 female faculty of color (Muhs, Niemann, González, & Harris, 2012). The narratives exalt the challenges at the intersection of race, gender, and class while in the professoriate. It brought to light experiences that are typically only examined in one dimension (either race, or gender, or class) but never all three that get at the core of the unrecognized workload. Another important aspect of faculty life is engagement with students—particularly students of color.

Advising Overload

If given an option, many students of color welcome the opportunity to work with faculty of color (Blake-Beard, Bayne, Crosby, & Muller, 2011), especially when research interests align. The burden for Latinx/a/o faculty here does not lie in the act of serving (or chairing) a student's committee; rather, it materializes in the number of committees a faculty member of color can be asked to serve. Service on administrative committees is another example of how minoritized faculty will be overburdened because of the need to increase the structural diversity of the membership (Moule, 2005; Tuitt, Hanna, Martínez, Salazar, & Griffin, 2009).

Community Engagement

What Latinx/a/os need as faculty members is similar to what they needed as undergraduate students: a welcoming environment, sense of belonging, motivation, and validation (Strayhorn, 2012). The major difference is that as undergraduates, they could meet these needs within the campus environment, while as faculty members they have to find them outside of the college, which can prove challenging. This is where finding community comes in. Ironically, junior faculty are often advised to wait until after they attain tenure to take on projects that will connect them in any significant way to the surrounding community (Foster, 2010). In other words, the very thing that can help them succeed during the most vital time in their academic career, they are often encouraged to postpone until after tenure.

ADDED (UNRECOGNIZED) PSYCHOLOGICAL BURDENS

Imposter Syndrome

A different type of burden—a psychological kind—also afflicts many Latinx/a/o faculty. The *imposter syndrome* that may have emerged at the beginning of college is omnipresent as a faculty member. It is there in the classroom, when meeting with the dean, in cross-campus committee meetings, when submitting a journal article or grant proposal, when reading student evaluations, and when submitting promotion and tenure dossier materials. No matter how many degrees earned or how many research or teaching awards won, Latinx/a/o faculty will always question whether they are good enough. Untenured faculty experience the highest levels of imposter phenomenon (Hutchins, 2015) and this feeling is even more intense among faculty of color (Zambrana et al., 2015).

Leaving "Home" Behind

For Latinx/a/o faculty, home symbolizes the comfortable, the familiar, and the place where they can be their true authentic self. Rendón (1992) described grappling with leaving home and entering academia as living with guilt, pain, and confusion. Anzaldúa (1987) termed this *nepantla*. In a later manuscript, she expanded on the concept:

Bridges span liminal (threshold) spaces between worlds, spaces I call *nepantla*, a Nahuatl word meaning *tierra entre medio*. Transformations occur in this in-between space, an unstable, unpredictable, precarious, always-in-transition space lacking clear boundaries. *Nepantla es tierra desconocida*, and living in this liminal zone means being in a constant state of displacement—an uncomfortable, even alarming feeling. (Anzaldúa, 2002, p. 1)

Living in *nepantla* has become a way of life for many Latinx/a/o faculty in academe. I am the first in my family born in the United States. I am the first to attend college. I am the first to move away from home. I am the first to earn a doctorate. I am the first to become a professor. Living a lifetime of "firsts," I have made *nepantla* my home. I left East Los Angeles at the age of 18 to go to college in Ann Arbor, Michigan. In that *tierra desconocida* is where I learned to live in a constant state of displacement and transformation on multiple levels. It is because of my experience as an undergraduate student that I am in the field of higher education today. Moreno (2016) interviewed first-generation Latinx/a/o college students and examined the guilt they face when leaving home for college. Her findings resonate with my experience. As a tenure-track faculty member, I am still living every day with the firsts and what it means to forge ahead on this new pathway. It feels as though I am constantly in search of puzzle pieces to complete this virtual map I am supposed to navigate whose dimensions are unknown to me. And the yearning to return "home" transcends at all layers and is ever-present.

NEW DEMANDS

But those educators climbing up the tenure ranks must keep going. The United States is in a new era of race relations that mirrors some of the struggles endured in the 1950s and 1960s. Societal policies directly affect campuses (Milem, Chang, & Antonio, 2005), and there is a new wave of student activism. Latinx/a/o faculty do not have the luxury of waiting until the security of tenure to speak up on behalf of targeted communities (Stanley, 2006). Latinx/a/o faculty must facilitate difficult conversations in classes (Cress, 2008) and among colleagues. Latinx/a/o educators must embody a social justice critical framework just to survive the daily attacks (Pittman, 2010; Villalpando & Delgado Bernal, 2002).

In order to move forward, Latinx/a/o faculty and student affairs professionals must consider how this type of environment is affecting (a) their personal well-being, (b) the students they serve, and (c) the campus climate. As much as Latinx/a/o faculty may wish to disconnect from what is happening in the world, they have a responsibility to educate and prepare the future higher education and student affairs scholars, researchers, practitioners, policymakers, and leaders. Higher education scholarship provides several frameworks (Hurtado, Alvarez, Guillermo-Wann, Cuellar, & Arellano, 2012) to understand this phenomenon. Even though the Latinx/a/o community lies in the crosshairs as a target, it is important to recognize that this work is tremendously difficult yet more crucial than ever.

ADVICE FOR PROSPECTIVE AND EARLY CAREER LATINX/A/O FACULTY

The Latinx/a/o culture instills a strong work ethic and a commitment to the values of community, interdependence, and the betterment of the collective. In direct contrast are the values upheld in academia (evolving from a White, male, Anglo-Saxon, Western perspective) that champion autonomy, independence, and a focus on individual success. This tension magnifies when the role of gender is considered because Latinx/a/o women are socialized to care for others before themselves.

(Don't) Wait Until After Tenure

Latinx/a/o faculty feel a moral obligation to take on Latinx/a/o issues yet are advised to wait until after tenure to do so. Community engagement (discussed earlier) is one example. Another is to wait to take on projects that are seen as critical, question the status quo, or focus on improving the climate for marginalized populations. Although I understand the self-preservation aspect of this advice, it can feel utterly frustrating for Latinx/a/o faculty who want to be agents of change (Laden & Hagedorn, 2000). At times, it feels as though I am being asked to leave a part of me behind with the promise to retrieve it in the future. Within our Latinx/a/o culture we are taught to serve others, to uplift our community, to put others before ourselves, and to think about those who will come behind us. Thus, delaying can be in direct opposition to our cultural values.

Protect Your Time

If readers of this chapter remember nothing else, I hope they remember this: Faculty work never ends! It is vital that Latinx/a/o faculty set, and stick to, limits. Time is the most valuable and finite resource, and there is always work to be done. I encourage Latinx/a/o faculty to think of their careers in the same way small business owners think about their companies. Although it is oppositional to cultural values, Latinx/a/o faculty must be their own advocate. They must always be thinking about ways to improve, how to invest their time, and what direction to head toward next while protecting their research and writing time. Because teaching and service have embedded accountability structures and research does not, it will be the first thing faculty postpone. Yet if they are at a research university, it will be the single most determining factor for earning tenure and promotion. Thus, even if a faculty member is the best teacher in the world, over committing their time to service endeavors will not ensure professional longevity and success.

Find Balance

Along with learning how to prioritize their time, it is also important for Latinx/a/o faculty to center their health and wellness as they make every attempt to live a balanced life. Understandably, sacrifices and difficult decisions will have to be made. Although I would argue that there is no such thing as a truly balanced life, it is important to keep working toward it. We are more than our professional role. As faculty members whose experience is influenced by Latinx/a/o cultural norms and values, our sense of wellness is heavily shaped by how well we balance family, community, spiritual, mental, physical, financial, social, and political pressures, both inside and outside our institutions.

Mentor Students

Finally, it is essential for Latinx/a/o faculty to be the mentors they needed when they were students. We are each experts in our own lived experiences. As such, we can also use that insight to infer what our students need to succeed, especially when it comes to supporting Latinx/a/o students. When Latinx/a/o faculty come across younger versions of themselves, they should offer the kind of support they needed but did not know how to ask for as students. I have been lucky enough to have Latina faculty members guide me throughout my educational and academic career. I would not be where I am today had it not been for these *mujeres*. Recognizing the importance of being a mentor and role model as a Latinx/a/o faculty member, I strive to serve and support the success of other Latinx/a/o students and professionals.

WHAT I LOVE ABOUT MY JOB

Although I have focused on challenges faced by Latinx/a/o faculty, in the spirit of being open, honest, and transparent, I must also share the positive aspects of faculty life. Very few careers in the world can situate an individual to have a noticeable impact and the potential to reach multiple audiences in diverse ways. At the core of a faculty position is the opportunity to make a difference while also being my own boss. The norm for most faculty positions is a nine-month appointment with the option to work during the summer. Although I am accountable to a department and a college, I have the freedom to set my own research agenda. No one else dictates how I choose to contribute to the field with my scholarship. As a Latina faculty member, I unapologetically and without reservation focus my research agenda on the success of Latinx/a/o students. I also have some flexibility in what I teach. Certain programs offer electives for students that open up the opportunity for alignment between teaching and research; others have prescriptive curriculums, but even in those spaces, I have a choice. Outside of class time and scheduled meetings, I have an extremely flexible schedule. Most important, I can have an impact in every facet of my job: research, teaching, and service. Additionally, there is constant engagement within an intellectual community and at an individual level; a certain amount of respect and deference comes with the rank of professor.

CONCLUSION

The new Latinx/a/o faculty pathway continues to widen as more and more Latinx/a/os seek this route. In 1981 a mere 1.5% of all faculty were Hispanic (NCES, 1986). In 2013 that percentage rose to 4.2% (NCES, 2015). Although some growth has occurred, as demonstrated in the numbers, the conditions of the campus environment remain just as challenging. Latinx/a/o faculty live in a constant state of *nepantla* (Anzaldúa, 1987), existing in between two worlds whose core values are in direct opposition. While being judged on research, teaching, and service alongside their peers, they must also continue to trek the path while carrying additional unrecognized workloads and psychological burdens.

The United States is in a new sociopolitical era, and higher education is not immune to its influence. Policies dictated at the federal level directly affect how the campus climate is shaped for students, faculty, and administrators. The new professoriate must embody a commitment to social justice while maintaining a critical lens. For Latinx/a/o faculty to remain on the path, they must be vigilant with their time and prioritize those aspects of their position that will ensure continued success. Centering health and wellness is integral throughout this process. Last, it is important for Latinx/a/o faculty to remember where they came from in order to know where they are going. In a culture that is rooted in the values of community and interdependence, mentoring and showing others the pathway is the only assurance that there will be future trailblazers.

REFERENCES

Anzaldúa, G. (1987). *Borderlands/La Frontera: The new mestiza.* San Francisco, CA: Aunt Lute Books.

Anzaldúa, G. E. (2002). Preface: (Un)natural bridges, (un)safe spaces. In G. E. Anzaldúa & A. Keating (Eds.), *This bridge we call home: Radical visions for transformation* (pp. 1–5). New York, NY: Routledge.

Blake-Beard, S., Bayne, M. L., Crosby, F. J., & Muller, C. B. (2011). Matching by race and gender in mentoring relationships: Keeping our eyes on the prize. *Journal of Social Issues, 67*(3), 622–643.

Castellanos, J., Gloria, A. M., & Kamimura, M. (2006). *The Latina/o pathway to the PhD: Abriendo caminos.* Sterling, VA: Stylus.

Cress, C. M. (2008). Creating inclusive learning communities: The role of student–faculty relationships in mitigating negative campus climate. *Learning Inquiry, 2,* 95–111.

Eagan, M. K., Stolzenberg, E. B., Berdan Lozano, J., Aragon, M. C., Suchard, M. R., & Hurtado, S. (2014). *Undergraduate teaching faculty: The 2013–2014 HERI Faculty Survey.* Los Angeles, CA: Higher Education Research Institute, University of California, Los Angeles.

Feagin, J. R. (2006). *Systemic racism: A theory of oppression.* New York, NY: Routledge.

Foster, K. M. (2010). Taking a stand: Community-engaged scholarship on the tenure track. *Journal of Community Engagement and Scholarship, 3*(2), 20–30.

Gildersleeve, R. E., Croom, N. N., & Vasquez, P. L. (2011). "Am I going crazy?!": A critical race analysis of doctoral education. *Equity & Excellence in Education, 44*(1), 93–114.

Griffin, K. A. (2008). *Can reaching back push you forward?: A mixed methods exploration of Black faculty and their developmental relationship with students* (Unpublished doctoral dissertation). University of California, Los Angeles.

Hurtado, S., Alvarez, C. L., Guillermo-Wann, C., Cuellar, M., & Arellano, L. (2012). A model for diverse learning environments: The scholarship on creating and assessing conditions for student success. In J. C. Smart & M. B. Paulsen (Eds.), *Higher education: Handbook of theory and research* (Vol. 27, pp. 41–122). New York, NY: Springer.

Hutchins, H. M. (2015). Outing the imposter: A study exploring imposter phenomenon among higher education faculty. *New Horizons in Adult Education & Human Resource Development, 27*(2), 3–12.

Laden, B. V., & Hagedorn, L. S. (2000). Job satisfaction among faculty of color in academe: Individual survivors or institutional transformers? In L. S. Hagedorn (Ed.), *What contributes to job satisfaction among faculty and staff* (New Directions for Institutional Research, No. 105, pp. 57–66). San Francisco, CA: Jossey-Bass.

Milem, J. F., Chang, M. J., & Antonio, A. L. (2005). *Making diversity work on campus: A research based perspective.* Washington, DC: American Association of Colleges and Universities.

Moreno, R. (2016). *The guilt of success: Looking at Latino first generation college students and the guilt they face from leaving their home and community to pursue college* (Unpublished doctoral dissertation). California State University, Long Beach.

Moule, J. (2005). Implementing a social justice perspective in teacher education: Invisible burden for faculty of color. *Teacher Education Quarterly, 32*(4), 23–42.

Muhs, G. G., Niemann, Y. F., González, C. G., & Harris, A. P. (2012). *Presumed incompetent: The intersections of race and class for women in academia.* Logan, UT: Utah State University Press.

National Center for Education Statistics. (1986). *Digest of education statistics, 1985–1986.* Retrieved from https://eric.ed.gov/?id=ED270903

National Center for Education Statistics. (1993). *Digest of education statistics, 1993.* Retrieved from https://nces.ed.gov/pubsearch/pubsinfo.asp?pubid=93292

National Center for Education Statistics. (2000). *Digest of education statistics, 2000.* Retrieved from https://nces.ed.gov/programs/digest/2000menu_tables.asp

National Center for Education Statistics. (2006). *Digest of education statistics, 2006.* Retrieved from https://nces.ed.gov/programs/digest/2006menu_tables.asp

National Center for Education Statistics. (2015). *Digest of education statistics, 2015.* Retrieved from https://nces.ed.gov/programs/digest/2015menu_tables.asp

National Science Foundation, National Center for Science and Engineering Statistics. (2016). *Survey of earned doctorates, doctorate recipients from U.S. universities: 2015* (NSF 17-306). Retrieved from https://www.nsf.gov/statistics/2017/nsf17306

Pérez Huber, L., Huidor, O., Malagón, M. C., Sánchez, G., & Solórzano, D. G. (2006). *Falling through the cracks: Critical transitions in the Latina/o educational pipeline* (CSRC Research Report No. 7). Los Angeles, CA: University of California, Los Angeles Chicano Studies Research Center Press.

Pérez Huber, L., Malagón, M. C., Ramirez, A. R., Gonzalez, L. C., Jimenez, A. & Vélez, V. N. (2015). *Still falling through the cracks: Revisiting the Latina/o education pipeline* (CSRC Research Report No. 19). Los Angeles, CA: University of California, Los Angeles Chicano Studies Research Center Press.

Pittman, C. T. (2010). Race and gender oppression in the classroom: The experiences of women faculty of color with White male students. *Teaching Sociology, 38*(3), 183–196.

Rendón, L. I. (1992). From the barrio to the academy: Revelations of a Mexican American "scholarship girl." In L. Zwerling & H. London (Eds.), *First-generation students: Confronting the cultural issues* (New Directions for Community Colleges, No. 80, pp. 55–64). San Francisco, CA: Jossey-Bass.

Smith, D. G. (1996). *Achieving faculty diversity: Debunking the myths.* Washington, DC: Association of American Colleges and Universities.

Stanley, C. A. (2006). Coloring the academic landscape: Faculty of color breaking the silence in predominantly White colleges and universities. *American Educational Research Journal, 43*(4), 701–736.

Strayhorn, T. L. (2012). *College students' sense of belonging: A key to educational success for all students.* New York, NY: Routledge.

Tuitt, F., Hanna, M., Martínez, L. M., Salazar, M. D. C., & Griffin, R. (2009). Teaching in the line of fire: Faculty of color in the academy. *Thought and Action, Fall,* 65–74.

Turner, C. S . V., González, J. C., & Wood, J. L. (2008). Faculty of color in academe. What 20 years of literature tells us. *Journal of Diversity in Higher Education, 1*(3), 139–168.

U.S. Census Bureau. (2015). *United States QuickFacts, Hispanic or Latino, percent, July 1, 2015* (V2015). Retrieved from http://www.census.gov/quickfacts

Valdez, L. (1990). *Luis Valdez early works: Actos, bernabé and pensamiento serpentino.* Houston, TX: Arte Público Press.

Villalpando, O., & Delgado Bernal, D. (2002). A critical race theory analysis of barriers that impede the success of faculty of color. In W. Smith, P. Altbach, & K. Lomotey (Eds.), *The racial crisis in American higher education: Continuing challenges for the twenty-first century* (pp. 243–269). Albany, NY: State University of New York Press.

Zambrana, R. E., Ray, R., Espino, M. M., Castro, C., Cohen, B. D., & Eliason, J. (2015). "Don't leave us behind": The importance of mentoring for underrepresented minority faculty. *American Educational Research Journal, 52*(1), 40–72.

PART V

Looking to the Future and Advancing the Latinx/a/o Experience in Higher Education

BEING AN INSIDER-OUTSIDER

A Chicano Student Affairs Administrator's
Pathway in Higher Education

Jacob L. Diaz

I am Chicano and grew up in a bilingual home in San Diego, California. I loved learning and until high school earned pretty good grades. High school was the first time I received low grades, and as time passed, I stopped believing that I was smart—and the idea of college was something I thought impossible to achieve. Thankfully, my parents encouraged me to attend Southwestern Community College in San Diego, and although I had strong doubts that I could pass a college-level course, I decided to try.

I am indebted to the faculty and staff who mentored me and took time to understand who I was and where I came from. There were also faculty and staff who questioned whether I could achieve a college degree, which in turn caused me to doubt if I could. This narrative is about the impact that support and doubt has had on my career in higher education and how I have sustained myself in environments where being Chicano is neither reflected nor supported. I hope to share support for those who have the experience of being a leader at a college or university while at times being treated like an outsider. I argue that the leadership of Latinx/a/o professionals is critically important in attempting to help institutions behave more congruently with their aspirations to serve all students.

FAMILIA (FAMILY) AS A SOURCE OF HOPE

The initial seeds of hope were planted early in my life as a child, from spending many hours with *mi abuelos* (grandparents) during the summer. They shared many stories about their lives that fostered a deep sense of pride in me as a Chicano. They told me stories of working in the fields of the Midwestern United States, picking fruits, vegetables, and cotton. I learned about racism through stories they told me about not being allowed to speak Spanish in school or being laughed at by fellow students because their lunch was made of beans and tortillas. Each of my grandfathers served in the U.S. military, and each shared stories about growing up in south Texas near the border of Mexico. Through them, I learned about values such as loyalty and perseverance. I also was inspired by how they lived their lives and decided early on that I wanted to make them proud.

A moment that had a profound impact on me is when my father's mother, *mi abuela* Consuelo, told me a story about her experience as a custodian in the Texas public school system that continues to inspire my work to this day:

> *Mi'jo [son], I would go to work before 7:00 a.m. each day, and one of my responsibilities was to prepare the coffee and shine the conference room table where the administrators would work. Each morning, a group of Anglos [White men] would enter the conference room, serve themselves a cup of coffee, and talk with one another for the entire day. At the end of the day, I would clean up after they left so that the conference room table was clean and ready for them. One thing I noticed is that they wore a shirt and tie and didn't get dirty while working. Mi'jo, I want you to go to school and use your brain to work. Someday, I want you to be at this mesa [table], and to do that you need to go to school.*

I carry *mi abuela* with me as I serve as the dean of students and director of housing and residence life. Whenever I walk into a board room and sit at a shiny conference table, I can envision her smiling at me and am grateful because her vision of community included diverse voices, and this was passed to my father and on to me. The fact that she noticed the homogeneity of her workplace moved her to believe that education was a key to ensuring that those at the table would be more diverse in the next generation. These stories handed down from my family continually nurtured "the creation of a history that would break the links between parents' current occupational status and their children's future academic attainment" (Gandara, 1995, as cited in Yosso, 2005, p. 78).

FACING CHALLENGES ALONG MY EDUCATIONAL PATH

I wish I could share that being Chicano in higher education as a student and a professional has been smooth. Along the way there have been a number of educators who expressed doubt and directly discouraged me from pursuing a degree. For example, I vividly recall when an academic advisor at Southwestern Community College in Chula Vista, California, said to me, "I don't think you'd make it at a university." This was the first time an educator shared their professional opinion related to my educational aspiration. However, the support I received from family counterbalanced this negative experience and propelled me forward even when I felt most discouraged.

The pathway through college continues to be challenging for Chicana/o students who are affected by exchanges with faculty and staff that may cause them to doubt their goal of achieving a college degree. Researchers Yosso and Solórzano (2006) further illuminated these challenges in their work *Leaks in the Chicano and Chicana Educational Pipeline*:

> Of the 100 Chicana and Chicano students who start at the elementary level, 54 of them drop out (or are pushed out) of high school and 46 continue on to graduate. Of the 46 who graduate from high school, about 26 continue on toward some form of postsecondary education. Of those 26, approximately 17 enroll in community colleges and nine enroll at four-year institutions. Of those 17 in community colleges, only one will transfer to a four-year institution. Of the 9 Chicana/os attending a four-year college and the 1 community college transfer student, 8 will graduate with a baccalaureate degree. Finally, 2 Chicana/o students will continue on to earn a graduate or professional school degree and less than 1 will receive a doctorate. In contrast, of every 100 White elementary school students, 84 graduate high school, 26 graduate with a baccalaureate, and 10 earn a professional or graduate degree. (p. 1)

The underrepresentation of Chicana/o students in higher education is deeply troubling. The pathway is made more fragile due to educators who may not believe that Chicana/os should achieve a degree and as a result may cause doubt in these students' minds and hearts through such uninformed opinions.

Fortunately, I have felt the liberating power of faculty and staff who affirmed my identities. Yet, I have also felt the sting of racism from colleagues in my career that rendered me speechless and wondering if I belonged in the higher education community. I am grateful to my family and how they courageously cultivated hope and possibility within me to strive for my academic and professional dreams, and I rely on this source of wealth to sustain my motivation in my professional career.

MY PROFESSIONAL JOURNEY

As I transitioned into student affairs administration I began to notice that even with a full effort, proper credentials, and seemingly doing all the right things, I still would experience exclusion due to the color of my skin. As a professional, I have felt the conflict between being a hired member of the institution while simultaneously not being treated as a full participant. Collins (1986) described this as "the outsider within" and I utilize this concept to better understand what is happening and to lift my spirit when I experience racism in my leadership role.

Throughout my career, I have worked to resist the pressure to silence the powerful voice of my culture of origin. Yosso (2005) framed this as "resistant capital," and it has helped me to continue working toward transforming the spaces where I have the privilege of working to be more inclusive. As an example of this, throughout my 20-year career, I have experienced many moments in which supervisors have made microaggressions about Latinx/a/o people. An example of this is when I was meeting one-on-one with a supervisor and he said to me,

"Aren't Latinos your thing?" In the moment, I knew what I wanted to say in response but could not bring myself to be honest out of fear of reprisal. The thought quickly passed through my mind that this was the person who evaluates me, and I did not want to damage the relationship.

After this experience, I grew convinced that I was viewed solely as serving Latinx/a/o students. And while I certainly was committed to this effort, it was also important to me to lift up all students so that they could achieve their educational and professional dreams. In this environment I had already seen other colleagues experience consequences for speaking out; I worried I would lose my job if I confronted him, and I felt conflicted about silencing myself in order to survive. Yet, it was clear that I felt that I did not quite fit. In that moment, I could see that I was viewed as only capable of serving Latinx/a/o students even though my formal job title and position description indicated a duty to serve all students. The impact on me at that time was increased stress, worry, and exhaustion from the work it takes to receive these slights and continue to lead from a place of hope.

Sustaining oneself as a Latinx/a/o leader in higher education and nurturing possibility and hope within Latinx/a/o students is critical in environments where racism and exclusion consistently occur. As a Chicano, I entered higher education wondering if I belonged. I believe that we can and must do better than leave it to chance that the next generation of Latinx/a/o students doubts its rightful place in higher education. This is what inspires my work each day, and I expect institutions to behave differently and to welcome Latinx/a/o leadership to help ensure that institutions embody their written values.

REFERENCES

Collins, P. (1986). Learning from the outsider within: The sociological significance of Black feminist thought. *Social Problems, 33*(6), S14–S32. doi:10.2307/800672

Yosso, T. (2005). Whose culture has capital? A critical race theory discussion of community cultural wealth. *Race Ethnicity and Education, 8*(1), 69–91.

Yosso, T. J., & Solórzano, D. G. (2006). *Leaks in the Chicano and Chicana educational pipeline.* Los Angeles, CA: University of California, Los Angeles, Chicano Studies Research Center.

Chapter 14

Considerations for Improving Latinx/a/o Pathways to Faculty and Administrative Roles in Higher Education

Elizabeth D. Palacios

The development of Latinx/a/o university and college administrators and faculty is essential to addressing the lack of Latinx/a/o leadership in higher education. News across the country reports higher enrollment for Latinx/a/o students in higher education, even surpassing their White counterparts. Nonetheless, a disparity remains in graduation rates, graduate school enrollment, professional leadership, and college faculty and administrators (Pew Hispanic Center, 2016a). In response to the shortage of Latinx/a/o representation in leadership, universities and colleges continue to strategize for the recruitment and retention of first-generation, undocumented, transfer, and other underrepresented student groups to increase their graduation rates. Yet, despite emphasis on undergraduate completion, Latinx/a/o students are not being groomed for professional or graduate schools as successfully as their counterparts, thus making it less likely for Latinx/a/os to fill faculty and administration positions in higher education. Therefore, institutions of higher education must focus on building effective pathways from community colleges and universities to graduate and terminal degrees and from new professionals to senior administrators and tenured faculty members. This chapter will discuss the importance of reviewing such systemic barriers as admission policies, campus climate, research and internship opportunities, mentoring, campus involvement, and leadership development to achieve true educational reform and address this gap in higher education.

In my own journey, like many others who were first-generation students, just being admitted to college was an accomplishment. I focused so much on my acceptance to college that once I was accepted, I was faced with the question, "Now what?" When discussing my senior year class schedule, my high school counselor had been adamant that I was going to be a cosmetologist. She stated that I was going to be another welfare case like my other classmates in my predominantly Mexican American high school. I later learned during my freshman sociology class that my high school was in the second poorest school district in the state of Texas. Its dropout rate was among the highest in the state, and the families in the district, including mine, were among the poorest. When I told my counselor I wanted to go to college, she assured me that I was not college material. It took my parents, and one of my high school teachers, a few visits to convince her that I was indeed going to a university; in fact, I was applying to her alma mater! Forty years and three degrees later, I am still at her alma mater, which I now call my own. My personal axiom, which has been central to my journey, is "never allow others to define you." I have learned that there may be many naysayers in one's life, but it is up to the individual to hold true to oneself.

MAKING THE CASE FOR INCREASING EFFORTS TO INCREASE LATINX/A/OS IN ACADEMIA

My experience with my high school counselor trying to dissuade me from pursuing college is not a unique story. I later learned that many of my classmates were encouraged to pursue low-paying occupations rather than higher education. Because many first-generation students continue to poorly navigate the college experience, important data points should be referenced when making the argument for higher education to focus on improving both the student and professional experiences of Latinx/a/os. From 2004 to 2015, dropout rates for Latinx/a/os were cut in half to 13% (Excelencia in Education, 2015a). Despite the decrease in dropout rates, Latinx/a/o students are still faring at the lowest graduation rate at every level from high school graduation (67%) to advanced degrees (5%; U.S. Census Bureau, 2015). Today, Latinx/a/o students still struggle to be admitted into college, especially the more prestigious schools. Even when students are admitted, college completion becomes the next hurdle. Latinx/a/o students make up the largest ethnic group in college enrollment (70%), but they continue to face many obstacles and lag behind in completion rates (Excelencia in Education, 2015b).

As a senior administrator in higher education, I hear about this reality frequently. First-year students often share their concerns about feeling "lost" in college life. So many Latinx/a/o students are so busy working and attending class that they do not have the luxury of planning their academic experiences (e.g., internships, study abroad, leadership development, or community service opportunities). Whenever I ask seniors about graduate school, I often get a reply along the lines of, "Oh no, I'm taking a year off!" Just attaining a bachelor's degree is a feat for most and they can feel overwhelmed by the idea of planning on another three to five years of graduate or professional school. This is where faculty and professionals, especially in administrative roles, have the opportunity to work with Latinx/a/o students as they search for internships, apply for research grants, and prepare for graduate school. Administrators and faculty have not only the knowledge and experience but also a sphere of influence among their colleagues and staff, whom they can encourage to also serve as advocates and mentors to Latinx/a/o students.

An important consideration for increasing Latinx/a/o leadership in academia is the mentoring and nurturing of Latinx/a/o professionals. As the number of Latinx/a/o professionals in senior-level roles in higher education steadily increases, it is imperative that they keep the doors open for those coming behind. For Latinx/a/o students to see higher education as a viable professional option, mentoring and networking must be made available from the moment students sets foot on the college campus through their graduate education and even throughout their professional careers (Anaya & Cole, 2001; Bordes & Arredondo, 2005; Gonzalez-Figueroa & Young, 2005; Torres & Hernandez, 2010).

THE LATINX/A/O COLLEGE UNDERGRADUATE EXPERIENCE

Preparing undergraduate students to continue on to graduate and professional schools is an important pathway to increasing college faculty and administrators. Currently, 18% of the U.S. population is Latinx/a/o and is projected to grow to 28.6% of the U.S. population by 2060 (Excelencia in Education, 2015b). Although the growth rate for Latinx/a/os has slowed from 4.4% (2000–2007) to 2.8%

(2007–20014) owing to the 2007 recession, Latinx/a/os still make up more than half of the total U.S. population growth since 2000 (Pew Hispanic Center, 2016b).

As the number of Latinx/a/os living in the United States continues to rise, so will the opportunities to work with them during earlier years—from elementary through high school—to ensure successful high school graduation as well as college admissions and completions. High dropout rates have been a historical challenge for Latinx/a/os; however, during the past decade, high school completion rates have increased from 57% to 65%, high school dropout rates among this population have decreased by 50%, and record numbers of Latinx/a/o students are enrolling in colleges and universities (Excelencia in Education, 2015b). Many of these students may live in poverty, are more likely to be first in their family to attend college, and are least likely to take out loans to attend more prestigious universities, both public and private (Pew Hispanic Center, 2016a). According to recent statistics, Latinx/a/o students are disproportionately enrolled in two-year institutions (46% in community colleges and 3% in private two-year institutions; Excelencia in Education, 2015c). Transferring successfully to four-year colleges or universities has proven to be an elusive endeavor for most students from all backgrounds (Nora & Crisp, 2009). Successful transfers, especially for Latinx/a/o students, are crucial; if Latinx/a/os are to be developed for senior-level positions or faculty lines in higher education, academic preparation is critical.

To increase college completion for Latinx/a/o students, various elements of a college experience must be considered, one of which is the climate to which students arrive. Students arrive in their new surroundings on college and university campuses with a sense of hope and positive expectations, along with normal anxiousness and homesickness (Holloway-Friesen, 2016; Hurtado & Ponjuán, 2005; Watson et al., 2002). However, at predominantly White institutions, the lack of diversity and inclusive practices can negatively affect traditional and first-generation students of all backgrounds, and may hamper the feeling of inclusivity. This makes it more important to facilitate a successful transition through community building. Many colleges and universities provide residence halls that focus on academic majors and disciplines (e.g., engineering), special interests (e.g., leadership), or special studies (e.g., Honors College). Having a sense of community can help Latinx/a/o students to build such social capital as campus engagement (e.g., participating in events and programs, student organizations, leadership development) and practical knowledge (e.g., registration, success centers, financial aid, career services).

Many traditional Latinx/a/o college students also seek community, affirmation, spiritual experiences, and social interaction. Unfortunately, many colleges and universities are ill prepared to retain their Latinx/a/o students. During my 35 years in higher education, I have often heard students complain about the lack of knowledge and understanding that faculty and university administrators have concerning their culture and life experiences. This may result in distrust and lack of participation that, in turn, affects students' grades negatively (Anaya & Darnell, 2001; Holloway-Friesen, 2016; Hurtado & Ponjuán, 2005).

KEY CONSIDERATIONS FOR HELPING LATINX/A/O STUDENTS SUCCEED IN COLLEGE

More and more colleges and universities are developing initiatives to prepare Latinx/a/o and other underrepresented students for graduate and professional degrees. Some of these initiatives include federal TRIO programs, internships, study abroad, research, and shadowing. However, Latinx/a/o students are often the least informed, prepared, or encouraged to pursue such opportunities. First-generation students, especially, often just "don't know what they don't know." Hence, it is imperative to intentionally reach out to Latinx/a/o students and encourage them so that more students will take advantage of university resources, research opportunities, and faculty interactions.

Additionally, to help Latinx/a/o students succeed in college, they need to be engaged as leaders. To develop as leaders in the Latinx/a/o campus community and beyond, Latinx/a/o students must first know themselves well, including understanding their own cultural identity and intersecting identities. Learning to engage across cultural and ethnic differences is imperative to every person pursuing lifelong learning. Intercultural awareness and appreciation occurs both inside and outside the classroom and is heavily facilitated and influenced by student affairs professionals throughout the students' college experience. Appreciation and self-acceptance are also crucial as Latinx/a/o students begin to understand themselves and others. From the beginning, they need to have opportunities to build social capital through the development of networks and relationships and the identification of resources. This practice assists them in learning about not only resources and resourceful people but also the "unwritten rules" in both an academic setting and the world of work.

Indeed, with resources, acclimation to university and college life can be much easier and Latinx/a/o students can be set up for success as they enter their upper-class experiences and engage in research, internships, and mentorships. As students acclimate to the day-to-day rigor of studying, attending class, and completing assignments, it is equally important to expand their coping skills. Opportunities for growth may focus on such topics as time management, self-care, and getting out of their comfort zone to try new experiences. This new knowledge can enhance students persisting through college and in their graduate work and professional careers. In addition, self-promotion, assertiveness, and risk taking are characteristics that are not always associated with Latinx/a/o traditions and values. However, with coaching and mentoring, students can practice these skills by serving on committees, boards, and leadership teams. Students may be able to shadow staff and participate in activities that interest them, such as outdoor adventures, urban missions, event planning, and student government.

Both faculty and staff play a crucial role in Latinx/a/o student success. Faculty mentors can help students engage in research, participate in conference presentations, work in labs on special projects, and create their own academic and intellectual endeavors under their guidance. When students are able to interact with administrators, such as in student affairs departments, they gain rich experiences. Students who are able to attain such leadership roles as student body officers, student board or regent members, student organization officers, and so on, are much more likely to meet and work closely with the senior administration. These student leadership experiences expose students to the inner circles of dialogue, decision making, strategic planning, judicial matters, and financial considerations. The opportunities to engage directly with administrators give students insight to senior leadership as well as provide administrators a student's perspective.

However, to understand and help Latinx/a/o students to become successful future leaders in higher education and beyond, it is monumentally important that student affairs professionals, faculty, and other staff be interculturally competent and knowledgeable. Latinx/a/o students also need to develop a multicultural lens through which to see and engage the world as they learn to become comfortable with who they are. When students' uniqueness as well as commonalities are welcome, the climate becomes more inclusive and vibrant. Without the ability to look at Latinx/a/o students through a cultural lens, staff members could easily miss teaching opportunities. For example, it is important to understand key attributes of Latinx/a/o culture and how they vary across Latinx/a/o groups, including differences in language, experiences, and traditions for various countries of origin or heritage.

Education and learning are also key factors for building the intercultural awareness, knowledge, and skills of Latinx/a/o student leaders. Professional staff should be able to recognize when students are staying inside their comfort zones and need to be challenged. By being culturally aware, staff can understand that traditional cultural values sometimes impair students' ability to engage fully in an experience. Intercultural competency can also help faculty and staff to embed such deep Latinx/a/o cultural values as respect, trust, loyalty, and harmony into their classroom and programming. The absence of this cultural understanding can sometimes prevent Latinx/a/o students from developing the necessary skills of negotiation and even confrontation during turbulent or unjust situations. By being culturally aware, higher education practitioners and administrators will also be better positioned to encourage, motivate, and support students to pursue degrees beyond the undergraduate level.

PREPARING LATINX/A/O STUDENTS FOR GRADUATE SCHOOL

Latinx/a/o students also need to be prepared for graduate school. Latinx/a/os represent the lowest percentage of students enrolled in graduate programs. The disciplines most represented in the master's degrees earned among Latinx/a/os are education (26%), business (25%), and health professions (10%; Excelencia in Education, 2015a). According to the National Center for Education Statistics (2015), from 1995 to 2015, Latinx/a/o students ages 25 to 29 received 16.4% of bachelor's or higher degrees (White, 43%; Black, 21.3%); for the same period and population age, Latinx/a/

os made up 3.2% of master's or higher degrees (White, 10.1%; Black, 5%). In preparation for students to transition from undergraduate to graduate school, it is imperative to help Latinx/a/os begin the process of academic and social development.

Many undergraduate experiences forge the knowledge and skills required in graduate school. Some of these experiences include research projects, book clubs, project partnerships, committee work, professional conference attendance and presentations, and partnerships with faculty (Anaya & Cole, 2001). These experiences help students form their own foundation as leaders and scholars. Through these learning experiences, undergraduate Latinx/a/o students are able to build intellectual and social capital, which is especially crucial during the graduate school application process. In many cases, especially for first-generation Latinx/a/o students, the idea of attending graduate school never occurs until mentors begin to encourage them and help them to prepare for the admissions applications and standardized tests. Students should also be encouraged to participate in mission-driven programs like the NASPA Undergraduate Fellows Program, which is dedicated to increasing the number of underrepresented professionals in higher education, and post-baccalaureate achievement programs such as the McNair Scholars Program, which is designed to prepare first-generation undergraduate students for doctoral studies. However, even with assistance with the admissions process, intentional mentoring and coaching is needed to get Latinx/a/o students through graduate programs successfully.

Latinx/a/o students interested in pursuing a master's degree often also need assistance with the selection and application processes. This includes help preparing for required standardized testing, completing the application, practicing for phone and on-campus interviews, and understanding the institutional culture to which they are applying. Not only is preparation for the application process essential, but also the skills and knowledge necessary for successful completion of a graduate program (Luna & Prieto, 2009; Ramirez, 2013).

Once Latinx/a/o students successfully enter graduate school, there remains the challenge of learning and navigating a new set of unwritten rules, academic politics, and the cultural nuances of academia. Again, navigating unchartered territories can be an immense undertaking emotionally, intellectually, financially, and physically (Schlosser, Talleyrand, Lyons, Kim, & Johnson, 2011). Those pursuing degrees in higher education and student affairs should pursue assistantships that include working directly with students in specific service areas within Student Life, including housing and residential services, new student experience programs, multicultural affairs, community service, and so on. These assistantships provide much needed experience, opportunities to practice new knowledge and skills, and mentoring relationships with supervisors and other professional staff. In the classroom, Latinx/a/o students may learn about the foundations of the profession, including ethics and student development, and much more. However, outside the classroom is where students begin to build their portfolio of knowledge, skills, and talents.

PATHWAY TO A CAREER IN STUDENT AFFAIRS

As Latinx/a/o students graduate from student affairs master's programs across the country and begin their professional journey, they realize the vast array of career opportunities that await them. The prospect of looking for the first professional job can feel overwhelming, especially for first-generation Latinx/a/o students, even though they have managed to navigate college and graduate school successfully. It is important that Latinx/a/o students seek help and advice about their career development early. For example, it is important for candidates to select institutions that match their values, experience,

and passion. Because of general cultural values, Latinx/a/os specifically thrive in communities that value their contributions, expertise,
cultural traditions, and professional growth. However, many may not
be assertive or feel confident in seeking out the best fit. Therefore,
new Latinx/a/o professionals may benefit from guidance and support
in choosing what type of institution (e.g., public, private, faith-based,
community, or four-year) to apply to when considering new positions.
Other critical considerations include geographic area, salary, range
of responsibilities, opportunities to advance, family and community,
and the type of existing support for staff, faculty and staff of color,
and, in particular, Latinx/a/o professionals. Finally, because professional development is essential for advancement, job searchers should
know to ask about such opportunities as conferences and so on.

In addition to helping prepare new Latinx/a/o student affairs professionals to be successful in their first job search, they also need guidance
about building strong networks. Connecting with other professionals
across the country through national professional organizations, such
as NASPA–Student Affairs Administrators in Higher Education
and ACPA–College Student Educators International, enables new
professionals to build their knowledge base and professional skills.
Thus, although it is imperative for all higher education leaders to be
professionally engaged, it is especially important for Latinx/a/o professionals to engage in culturally specific organizations while learning
to navigate expectations that have been set by the dominant culture.
Such opportunities include the Hispanic Association of Colleges and
Universities (HACU) and the American Association of Hispanics in
Higher Education (AAHHE), among other national organizations.
Statewide organizations specific to Latinx/a/o faculty, staff, and students in higher education—such as the Texas Association of Chicanos
in Higher Education, the Connecticut Association of Latinos in

Higher Education, and the Arizona Association of Chicanos for Higher Education—can also aid professional development by facilitating networking, scholarly presentations, and research, as well as strategies for promoting Latinx/a/os in higher education. In turn, being knowledgeable can better position Latinx/a/o professionals to help higher education institutions close the gaps for Latinx/a/o students and open doors to senior leadership roles, as both faculty and administrators.

PURSUING DOCTORAL DEGREES AND EXPLORING SENIOR LEADERSHIP ROLES

Although the numbers of Latinx/a/o professionals in higher education continue to grow, as of 2013, less than 1% of Latinx/a/o adults had earned doctoral degrees, compared with Asian (4%), White (2%), and Black (1%) scholars (Excelencia in Education, 2015a). When reviewing the percentage of gains in earning doctoral degrees in the past 10 years, however, Latinx/a/os increased by 67% compared to Blacks (56%), Asians (49%), and Whites (32%; Excelencia in Education, 2015a). The two fields of study where the majority of Latinx/a/o doctoral students earned their doctorates were in the legal professions (39%) and health professions (32%; Excelencia in Education, 2015a). For an increase in leadership and faculty roles in higher education to occur, there must be intentional mentorship and coaching of Latinx/a/o students to consider pursuing their terminal degrees in an array of disciplines and professions.

Although more Latinx/a/o student affairs professionals need to be encouraged to pursue doctoral degrees, it is also important to help them understand that it is possible to enter and sustain a successful career with a master's degree. In fact, for most colleges and universities, a master's degree is required for entry-level positions in student affairs. Ample diverse career opportunities are also available within student affairs, including positions in housing, student activities, multicultural affairs, recreation, student development, and so on, and professionals may choose to spend their entire professional career in various areas or move to other institutions in search of promotions. However, when it comes to moving up into director, assistant dean, dean, and vice president roles, the terminal degree becomes more of an expectation, if not a requirement. When considering pursuing a doctorate, Latinx/a/o candidates have many variables to contemplate, such as family expectations, financial stability, location, academic support, and so on (Ramirez, 2013).

For many Latinx/a/os, it is difficult to relocate in order to pursue a graduate degree or in some cases, students choose not to leave their undergraduate institutions. Therefore, it is convenient for Latinx/a/o candidates to pursue a master's degree in the same or a nearby institution where employed or where they received their bachelor's degree. However, when it comes to pursuing a doctorate, moving locations or commuting is a common occurrence. Because of the importance of family and relationships in the Latinx/a/o culture, significant others, families, friends, coworkers, supervisors, and others all play an important role that may either impede or enhance success (Ramirez, 2013). Latinx/a/os should be encouraged to explore other disciplines and fields of study to complement their master's degree in higher education. If students in the student affairs field have a desire to teach, adding another academic field or discipline might be considered. In my own pathway, for example, there was no linear sequence into my education or career roles. My undergraduate degree is in business administration, my master's degree is in student affairs, my doctorate is in school psychology, and I am licensed in professional counseling. Despite the differences in these degrees, I use the knowledge and skills I acquired from my education every day in my role as dean for student development. For those wanting to pursue a doctorate, I strongly recommend choosing an area that will enhance the desired role in higher education that reflects personal passion and interests.

Owing to the complexity of the issues, it is critical for Latinx/a/o professionals to engage in intentional conversations with peers, family, faculty, and senior leaders. It is important for Latinx/a/os with doctoral degrees to help demystify the process for those considering the journey (Ramirez, 2013). Persistence and discipline are paramount to attaining the doctoral degree. Although intelligence is important, it is the capacity to endure that is essential. Characteristics such as independent thinking, creativity, curiosity, openness to critique and feedback, and persistence are important in academic development and growth. Conversations with colleagues and family are crucial, as is identifying a support community. Those with a significant other, children, full-time work, and other responsibilities have different pathways to attaining the doctoral degree. Too often, self-doubt or "impostor syndrome" can make it difficult to envision attaining professional goals (Multon, Brown, & Lent, 1991), so I often tell doctoral students to print their name with "Dr." before it and put it someplace they can see it every day.

Doctoral work brings yet another set of unwritten rules, politics, and cultural nuances of academia (Luna & Prieto, 2009). Once in a doctoral program, Latinx/a/o students should be encouraged to coauthor publications with their faculty, build their personal expertise in teaching and research areas, and continue to develop a network of colleagues who are in the positions they will be seeking upon graduation. As the recent graduate seeks faculty or mid-level to senior leadership roles, it is important to call on those networks to begin thinking about what type of role they want to pursue. Presenting at conferences, both national and regional, will also help doctoral students to hone their skills and knowledge, encourage broader networking, and even provide opportunities to publish their dissertation.

PURSUING THE FACULTY ROLE

Graduate school can serve to socialize doctoral students to academia and prepare them for the professoriate (Austin, 2002). In pursuing a faculty role, one must learn yet another set of cultural nuances and unwritten rules in academia as well as in the institution itself. This opens up a new set of obstacles for Latinx/a/os to overcome (Arredondo & Castillo, 2011; Contreras & Contreras, 2015; Delgado-Romero, Manlove, Manlove, & Hernandez, 2007). For those pursuing the faculty pathway after completing their doctorate, it is most helpful to reach out to someone they know from the institution where they would like to work to get a sense of the cultural climate, especially in the department to which they are applying. For example, a lack of women or ethnic minority faculty, especially tenured and full professors of color in that department, may be a red flag to consider before applying.

In examining the faculty search process itself, it is important to assess the level of commitment to diversity an institution, school or college, or department may demonstrate. The culture of the institution will affect the success of a prospective Latinx/a/o faculty member (Austin, 2002; Delgado-Romero et al., 2007; Ramirez, 2013; Torres, 2006). Consequently, candidates should consider where the position was advertised, how the position's responsibilities were described, the makeup of the faculty search committee, what was learned from interview questions and conversations with other faculty and students, and the level of commitment and support a new faculty member may expect to receive. As academia is mainly made up of White males, for Latinx/a/o faculty candidates (as well as those from other underrepresented groups) it is also important to discuss the tenure process and practice, teaching loads, service expectations, and research opportunities. Attention should also be given to the potential academic community. A support network should be evident both on campus as well as in the local community. In exploring the campus environment, candidates should ask hard questions, visit with faculty from the same school or college, and determine if the dean is proactive in and has a record of developing Latinx/a/o and/or minority faculty.

Additionally, communities are available that support doctoral students preparing to become faculty and newly hired faculty, including the Council of Graduate Schools' PFF Web (Preparing Future Faculty), National Center for Faculty Development and Diversity, Association of American Colleges and Universities, and so on. In addition to presenting at conferences within one's own discipline, another way to gain support from networking with other faculty is to attend and present at conferences specific to Latinx/a/os issues, such as those offered by AAHHE or HACU. Being successful as an academic is truly an art, and one must be adept in one's discipline while maintaining one's cultural perspective and values.

Nevertheless, Latinx/a/o faculty should also be aware of the cumulative impact of *cultural taxation* on faculty of color. This term was coined by Amado Padilla in 1994 to describe the burden placed, and sometimes assumed, by minority faculty (Joseph & Hirshfield, 2011). Often minority faculty are asked to serve on multiple committees for diversity's sake, or to work with minority students or serve as an advisor for minority student groups. Although it is a cultural value to give back to the community, spending more time on community service than on publishing may take a professional toll on the faculty member. Balance is the key to working toward tenure and full professorship status; therefore, authentic and culturally competent mentorship and community can help support and improve a Latinx/a/o faculty member's experience in the world of academia (Delgado-Romero et al., 2007; Joseph & Hirshfield, 2011; Ponjuán, 2011; Santos & Reigadas, 2002).

SENIOR LEADERSHIP IN HIGHER EDUCATION

When considering senior leadership roles in higher education, whether from the faculty or the student affairs perspective, the trajectory can prove challenging. As most higher education leaders would agree, leaders must develop, demonstrate, and adhere to their personal values, ethics, morals, and beliefs. This is important throughout one's entire professional career because steadfastness and trustworthiness in one's actions can speak volumes to how one leads and influences change. Senior leaders should be able to step outside their comfort zone and, at the same time, build a sense of trust by being consistent with their actions and words.

For many Latinx/a/os, working in higher education is an attractive and compelling career option because the field focuses on service, teaching, mentoring, and the idea of leaving things better than they were found. Many positive attributes of the Latinx/a/o culture and values naturally align with efforts to enhance success in student affairs. *Personalismo*, for example, promotes relationship building, which is the cornerstone of working with students. *Familismo* helps upward-moving professionals keep centered on life/work balance as well as integrate this concept when working with Latinx/a/o families of students. Faith and spirituality are other attributes that may help to build support and community. Thus, for Latinx/a/os thinking about a profession in higher education, a key consideration often relates to the hope of living out their commitment to education while draping it within their cultural values.

OVERCOMING HUMILITY AND EMPLOYING SELF-ADVOCACY

Although keeping close to one's cultural values is important for Latinx/a/os, it is also critical to overcome a traditional sense of humility and take on more responsibilities by volunteering on committees and task forces to help senior leadership recognize talents and potential contributions. Good senior leaders are always searching to mentor upcoming professionals, especially underrepresented professionals who bring multiple perspectives to the table. As aspiring Latinx/a/o senior leaders work to demonstrate their value at their home institutions, they must also continue to network, engage in and lead professional organizations, participate in discussions, conduct research, strategize for institutional transformation, and learn to articulate their talents and expertise.

Part of professional development should also include attending leadership conferences and institutes, both mainstream and culturally specific, such as the NASPA Escaleras Institute, which was specifically created for Latinx/a/o student affairs professionals aspiring to senior student affairs officer roles, including vice president positions. New knowledge and experiences enable Latinx/a/o professionals to build capacity in mainstream contexts. Demonstrating directness and self-promotion can sometimes feel counterintuitive to the traditional values of respect, sacrifice, and humility (Delgado-Romero et al., 2007; Ponjuán, 2011). In general, traditional Latinx/a/o values often contrast Eurocentric values of "branding" oneself, challenging authority, confronting problems, and making it to the top (Delgado-Romero et al., 2007). Demonstrating self-awareness is key to becoming a senior leader and for this reason, strong mentorship and sponsorship become critical to success (Delgado-Romero et al., 2007; Ponjuán, 2011).

Last, in considering senior-level positions in higher education, Latinx/a/os should consider the reality of external influences. In a study by Savala (2014), when Chicano administrators were asked what may have influenced their administrative appointments, the following were listed: (a) the political climate and the Chicano administrator's understanding of that climate; (b) existing affirmative action institutional plans; (c) the diversity of the institution and the community in which it is located; (d) pressure on the university to hire a Chicano administrator; (e) new university initiatives driven by incentive programs, cultural training, lawsuits, and so on; (f) the emphasis the candidate placed on maintaining their Chicano roots; and (g) advocacy from the governing board, screening committee, and search firm members.

In my own career path, I have benefited from mentors and advocates who have been able to open doors that later led to opportunities for me to move up to roles with greater responsibilities and spheres of influence. As a result, one thing that remains important to me is making sure to bring others along with me. This means that I serve as a coach, mentor, advocate, and cheerleader for others striving to attain leadership roles. It is also important for Latinx/a/o faculty, staff, and administrators to advocate for each other. I believe that the saying "it doesn't matter where you start, it matters how you finish" truly pertains to Latinx/a/o students aspiring to pursue higher education and become professionals, faculty members, and even university presidents!

CONCLUSION

As higher education continues to build capacity for Latinx/a/o student affairs and faculty roles, it is important to reach out to undergraduates early. Improving preparation for rigorous studies and developing skills for academic success are essential to Latinx/a/o students and professionals pursuing higher education. Unfortunately, many Latinx/a/o students navigate these pathways by happenstance, where one teacher or advisor might mention a scholarship to a student or ask what their plans are after high school graduation. Alternatively, perhaps, during the undergraduate experience, a student might catch the attention of a professor or staff member who may invite the student to apply for leadership positions, research team, or internships.

Mentoring and coaching are important components to facilitating both student and professional success within educational systems. In supporting and nurturing upcoming students, it is also essential that young professionals be mentored and advocated for in order to advance. As Latinx/a/o professionals then begin to work in the field, networking, peer support, mentoring, and guidance must remain integral factors to staying in the profession and advancing through tenure or promotion. When Latinx/a/o senior leaders experience success, their influence, knowledge, wisdom, and skills may have exponentially positive impacts on those around them. It is not easy to be the only Latinx/a/o at the table, and these experiences bring their own challenges. However, in the end, with commitment and support from professionals at all levels of the institution, upcoming Latinx/a/o students can find opportunities to develop as leaders and, in the process, help higher education address the needs of a growing Latinx/a/o student population.

REFERENCES

Anaya, G., & Cole, D. G. (2001). Latina/o student achievement: Exploring the influence of student-faculty interactions on college grades. *Journal of College Student Development, 42*(1), 3–14.

Arredondo, P., & Castillo, L. G. (2011). Latina/o student achievement: A collaborative mission of professional associations of higher education. *Journal of Hispanic Higher Education, 10*(1), 6–17.

Austin, A. E. (2002). Preparing the next generation of faculty: Graduate school as socialization to the academic career. *Journal of Higher Education, 73*(1), 94–122.

Bordes, V., & Arredondo, P. (2005). Mentoring and 1ˢᵗ-year Latina/o college students. *Journal of Hispanic Higher Education, 4*(2), 114–133.

Contreras, F., & Contreras, G. J. (2015). Raising the bar for Hispanic serving institutions: An analysis of college completion and success rates. *Journal of Hispanic Higher Education, 14*(2), 151–170.

Delgado-Romero, E. A., Manlove, A. N., Manlove, J. D., & Hernandez, C. A. (2007). Controversial issues in the recruitment and retention of Latino/a faculty. *Journal of Hispanic Higher Education, 6*(1), 34–51.

Excelencia in Education. (2015a). *Latino college completion: United States.* Retrieved from http://www.edexcelencia.org/sites/default/files/Exc2014-50StateFS-National.pdf

Excelencia in Education. (2015b). *The condition of Latinos in education: 2015 factbook.* Retrieved from https://www.nccpsafety.org/assets/files/library/The_Condition_of_Latinos_in_Education.pdf

Excelencia in Education. (2015c). *Helping or hindering: State policies and Latino college completion.* Retrieved from http://www.edexcelencia.org/gateway/download/26028/1484498330

Gonzalez-Figueroa, E., & Young, A. M. (2005). Ethnic identity and mentoring among Latinas in professional roles. *Cultural Diversity and Ethnic Minority Psychology, 11*(3), 213–226.

Holloway-Friesen, H. (2016). Acculturation, enculturation, gender, and college environment on perceived career barriers among Latino/a college students. *Journal of Career Development.* Advance online publication. doi:10.1177/0894845316668641

Joseph, T. D., & Hirshfield, L. E. (2011). "Why don't you get somebody new to do it?" Race and cultural taxation in the academy. *Ethnic and Racial Studies, 34*(1), 121–141.

Hurtado, S., & Ponjuán, L. (2005). Latino educational outcomes and the campus climate. *Journal of Hispanic Higher Education, 4*(3), 235–251.

Luna, V., & Prieto, L. (2009). Mentoring affirmations and interventions: A bridge to graduate school for Latina/o students. *Journal of Hispanic Higher Education, 8*(2), 213–224.

Multon, K. D., Brown, S. D., & Lent, R. W. (1991). Relation of self-efficacy beliefs to academic outcomes: A meta-analytic investigation. *Journal of Counseling Psychology, 38*(1), 30–38.

National Center for Education Statistics. (2015). *The condition of education 2015.* Retrieved from https://nces.ed.gov/pubs2015/2015144.pdf

Nora, A., & Crisp, G. (2009). Hispanics and higher education: An overview of research, theory, and practice. In J. C. Smart (Ed.), *Higher education: Handbook of theory and research* (Vol. 24, pp. 317–353). Dordrecht, Netherlands: Springer.

Pew Hispanic Center. (2016a). *Five facts about Latinos and education* [Data file and code book]. Retrieved from http://www.pewresearch.org/fact-tank/2016/07/28/5-facts-about-latinos-and-education

Pew Hispanic Center. (2016b). *Key facts about how the U.S. Hispanic population is changing* [Data file and code book]. Retrieved from http://www.pewresearch.org/fact-tank/2016/09/08/key-facts-about-how-the-u-s-hispanic-population-is-changing

Ponjuán, L. (2011). Recruiting and retaining Latino faculty members: The missing piece to Latino student success. *The National Education Association (NEA) Higher Education Journal, Thought & Action, 19*, 99–110.

Ramirez, E. (2013). Examining Latinos/as' graduate school choice process: An intersectionality perspective. *Journal of Higher Education, 12*(1), 23–36.

Santos, S. J., & Reigadas, E. T. (2002). Latinos in higher education: An evaluation of a university faculty mentoring program. *Journal of Hispanic Higher Education, 1*(1), 40–50.

Savala, L. A., III. (2014). *The experiences of Latina/o executives in higher education* (Doctoral dissertation). Retrieved from http://scholarworks.wmich.edu/cgi/viewcontent.cgi?article=12 95&context=dissertations

Schlosser, L. Z., Talleyrand, R. M., Lyons, H. Z., Kim, B. S. K., & Johnson, W. B. (2011). Multicultural issues in graduate advising relationships. *Journal of Career Development, 38*(1), 19–43.

Torres, V. (2006). Bridging two worlds: Academia and Latina/o identity. In J. Castellanos, A. M. Gloria, & M. Kamimura (Eds.), *The Latina/o pathway to the Ph.D.: Abriendo caminos* (pp. 135–159). Sterling, VA: Stylus.

Torres, V., & Hernandez, E. (2010). Influence of an identified advisor/mentor on urban Latino students' college experience. *Journal of College Student Retention, 11*(1), 141–160.

U.S. Census Bureau. (2015). *Educational attainment in the United States: 2015.* Retrieved from https://www.census.gov/content/dam/Census/library/publications/2016/demo/p20-578.pdf

Watson, L. W., Terrell, M. C., Wright, D. J., Bonner II, F. A., Cuyjet, M. J., Gold, J. A., Rudy, D. E., & Person, D. R. (2002). *How minority students experience college: Implications for planning and policy.* Sterling, VA: Stylus.

CHAPTER 15

FOSTERING NEW PATHWAYS THROUGH THE POWER OF COHORTS, MENTORS, PROFESSIONAL DEVELOPMENT, AND LEADERSHIP PARTICIPATION

Angela E. Batista and Shirley M. Collado

When we thought about what we wanted to share in this concluding chapter, the concepts of fostering new pathways through the power of cohorts, mentors, professional development, and leadership participation naturally came to mind. Consequently, we decided to root the chapter in something that we deeply value and that is core to broadening and deepening socially just pathways for Latinx/a/o individuals in higher education: authentic leadership.

Intentionally practicing authentic leadership, even when one must constantly negotiate who one is in varied spaces, is critical to the success of Latinx/a/o individuals in academia. Critical to this navigation of self in a variety of complicated higher education spaces is the ability to continue to grow as a professional and to identify cohorts, networks, and mentors that not only provide strong support along the pathway, but can sometimes influence the conditions along the way to increase the ability of Latinx/a/o individuals to thrive rather than simply survive. Ongoing learning, cohorts, networks, and mentors leverage the capacity of Latinx/a/os' social capital in spaces that were not historically created for them. They also provide cultural cues that help Latinx/a/o individuals feel more grounded as they recalibrate and adjust to the challenges and opportunities presented to them in professional, social, cultural, and political environments in academia.

This chapter presents a combination of personal narrative and best practices as illustrated by our educational and professional experiences. We hope to inspire Latinx/a/o professionals to reflect on their ability to lead and work congruently with their identity. We will briefly explore how various Latinx/a/o cultural dimensions naturally align values and norms with the experiences associated with cohorts, networks, and mentoring, and can therefore enhance the ability of Latinx/a/o leaders to practice authentic leadership and be their true selves. We will also share key elements of our individual journeys in higher education to illustrate the potential impact of providing innovative opportunities for Latinx/a/o students and leaders to join cohorts that will support their success as well as expand their educational and professional networks and access mentors. We seek both to empower Latinx/a/o professionals to shape and influence their own paths and to help allies and other leaders understand how to best support Latinx/a/o professionals who are striving to break barriers and advance from students to leaders and change agents. To that end, we will also discuss the importance of professional development and leadership participation as pathways to enhance professional success. We will conclude this chapter with a brief discussion of implications for the future as higher education continues to confront ongoing demographic changes that project Latinx/a/o students to become the majority within the next two decades.

SHARING OUR JOURNEYS

It is important to be who one is as one leads. The whole person. Accessible, real, open, and present. It's also important to be grateful, grounded, and humble, and to give credit where credit is due. For these reasons, we hope this chapter moves readers, opens them up, and inspires them to be who they really are in the company of others as they immerse themselves in the critical work of education. We invite readers to join us as we explore the power of cohorts, mentors, networks, professional development, and leadership participation and how they have helped to shape our success as leaders in higher education.

Shirley's Story

Back in 1989, I was about to finish high school in Brooklyn, New York, and was planning to continue my job stocking shelves and working the register at a local pharmacy in my neighborhood. I hoped to attend one of the institutions in the City University of New York (CUNY) because I thought that was the one option I could afford that would allow me to stay near family. As the eldest child, my family depended on me as a financial contributor and a major caregiver for my two younger brothers. I knew I wanted to work with young people and focus on education, so I hoped to become a social worker or high school teacher. I earned good grades at a mediocre high school and my

SAT scores were low like many other first-generation college students and Latinx/a/o youth in the United States. For me, there was no road map for college, no college tour, no guidance counselor telling me that I could do anything I wanted, no SAT prep classes, and no educational legacies in my family to help me navigate the road to college. All I knew was that I wanted an education and that somehow a degree would help me serve my community, make an honest living, and continue to support my family.

In 1989 the Posse Program began as a pilot, and I was a member of the inaugural class of Posse Scholars. This program was deemed "an experiment" at Vanderbilt University, where very few students like me had ever stepped foot on campus. Today, The Posse Foundation is one of the most comprehensive college access programs in the country. The foundation identifies and recruits talented urban youth with academic promise and leadership ability and sends them off in diverse teams— *Posses*—on full merit leadership scholarships to top colleges across the country. More than 25 years ago my alma mater, Vanderbilt University, took a chance on a simple, yet powerful idea, daring to believe that a group of five kids from New York City could thrive at a major university if they had the right support, even though many things about their academic and personal backgrounds would have pushed them out of traditional admissions processes. Today, Posses consist of 10 to 12 students each from 10 major cities in the United States attending top colleges and universities across the country. Posse Scholars persist and graduate at an impressive rate of over 90%—above the national average for all students in college and a rate that their high schools and SAT scores would have never predicted.

Picture this: The first five Posse Scholars started their journey to college on a 26-hour Greyhound bus trip from the New York City Port Authority down to Nashville, Tennessee. I had never been farther south than Washington, DC. What was most powerful about this trip was that my Posse and I decided to take that long bus ride because some of us could not afford to buy airline tickets and we wanted our moms to join us and still have a way to get back home to New York City. Veronica Rivera, Madeline Thomas, Paul Arguelles, and Mitos Gomez took the ride of a lifetime with me, and we began to lean on one another like family. We had no idea where we were going or what was waiting for us on the other side of that bus ride. All we knew was that we had a life-changing chance and that we needed to have courage. We knew we needed to rely on each other to cross the stage on Commencement Day so that many more Posse Scholars from all across the United States could come after us. Many reading this chapter may fully understand that sacrifice and know that journey all too well. That bus ride is symbolic of so many families in this country that take that chance with great courage when their child goes to college. Unfortunately, far too many students and families never get a chance to get on that bus in the first place. I chose to invest my career in expanding who gets to get on the bus on the journey to college and, most importantly, intentionally creating cohorts and networks that make sure that someone is sitting next to us on that bus to support us, to navigate the unknown with us, and to change with us.

My father drove a yellow cab in New York City for more than 30 years. My mother worked in the same factory that her mother and sister worked in when they arrived in the United States. As a Brooklyn-born daughter of Dominican immigrants, the older sister of two brothers, the granddaughter of a matriarch community activist, and the first person in her family to go to college, the experience of my liberal arts education was transformative. In fact, college allowed me to dream bigger than I ever thought possible. That experience critically shaped my love for the fields of psychology and human and organizational development and my deep passion for youth development. I felt called to serve as a leader in higher education and to do the work that The Posse Foundation instilled in me from inside the best institutions in the United States. I always stress one important point: Cohorts and mentors matter. I never would have gone to Vanderbilt University or remained there if I did not have my Posse with me and if I did not have the support of my Vanderbilt mentors and the Posse Program.

Angela's Story

I am a first-generation immigrant who came to the United States at the age of 12 from a rural village in the Dominican Republic. The eldest of four children, at the age of 9 I assumed a leadership role with my siblings when my mother departed as an undocumented immigrant for the United States. My parents were two of the lucky ones who had been given a chance to learn to read and write in our small community, completing third and fifth grade, respectively. In the Dominican Republic, Papi worked as a farmer and Mami was a seamstress. After arriving in the United States, Mami worked in a factory and Papi worked as a nighttime janitor. As a young child, before I left for the United States, I also took on leadership roles at school, tutoring other students and leading classes and study groups at our community church. My family's migration to the United States sharply shifted our access to education, and I understood that I had a great responsibility to take advantage of new opportunities. When I arrived in the United States, I set a goal of completing high school and perhaps working as a secretary. Achieving this goal would already represent a great advancement for my family and me.

When I started high school at age 14, I began to work as a volunteer in the Foreign Language Department (FLD) at my school. Truthfully, I did so to avoid going to the cafeteria, which terrified me because of daily fights and drug use, and because as a poor immigrant who was still learning English, I was a huge target for bullies. Through this volunteer opportunity, I learned many skills and built relationships with teachers in both the FLD and the Guidance Department. Although I did not know it then, they became my "posse" and I felt more at home at school than in my violent, poor neighborhood in Bushwick, Brooklyn. On my 16th birthday, the FLD chair walked me into the department's book room and told me to take a copy of any and all books I wanted. I left with 20 Spanish literature books that day—the first books that I ever owned (and many of them remain in my personal library).

Eastern District High School was a low-performing and low-resourced 4,000-student high school. The students were mostly African American, Caribbean Black, and Latinx/a/os from families who had arrived in the United States only a few years before. The majority of the faculty, on the other hand, were White, with most traveling from homes in the suburbs and New Jersey. I was an excellent student and argued with school administrators to move me out of the Bilingual Program. At first, they did not want to move me because they did not want to lose the funding associated with my good performance. However, I begged my mother to go to the school and I also asked the department chair to help me. Eventually the administrators consented, which resulted in my being transferred into honors classes because of my good grades. In my new English class, I met a new teacher, Anthony Calister, who told me that I was smart and simply had to go to college. He convinced me to pursue teaching, like him. No one in my family had graduated high school, let alone attended college. Yet with Mr. Calister's help, mentoring from the teachers in the FLD, and support from my guidance counselor, I applied to college. My part-time job at the Board of Education already contributed to my family's household income. Consequently, going away for college was not an option. I hoped to attend one of the CUNY colleges but applied to New York University (NYU) because my counselor, who graduated from NYU, encouraged me to apply. I did so without ever speaking to anyone at the schools or visiting the campuses.

I was accepted to NYU and waited patiently for the school to send a letter telling me what I needed to do to next. I received a letter on July 5, 1988, informing me that I had been awarded a full scholarship as part of the Higher Education Opportunity Program. The letter also said that I should report for the summer program the morning of July 5 or my admission and scholarship would be forfeited. As soon as I received the letter that afternoon, I borrowed a neighbor's phone to call the number on the letter to say that I planned to be there the next morning, but I was told it was too late. I did not question or challenge. Instead, I simply assumed that the person I spoke with must know better and moved to my second choice, Brooklyn College (BC). This was another life-altering shift. BC was, and is, an excellent school, and I completed my bachelor's degree, graduating cum laude, after attending the college for nine years while working full time and completed many developmental courses that used all my financial aid eligibility.

In 1996, I was nominated by my English professor, Richard Pearse, to the Institute for Recruitment of Teachers (IRT), a nonprofit organization that works to address the lack of diversity in education by recruiting qualified candidates of color, counseling them through the graduate application process, and advocating for funding with schools that were part of their consortium. About 30 students were chosen from the entire country that year, and I felt absolutely out of my league with Rhodes and Mellon scholars in this small group. Nevertheless, I persisted and wished to pursue a PhD in English literature. However, I was counseled out of that idea by the faculty at the IRT who did not think I could earn the GRE scores necessary for admission. Instead, they persuaded me to pursue a master's degree in counseling, and I eventually went on to attend the University of Vermont, where I was awarded an assistantship in the Office of Multicultural Affairs. Twenty years later, after successfully working in six institutions of higher education, I have returned to Vermont, where I am now serving in a vice president role.

There's much more to my story, of course, but the most important part of my message is that because of all these experiences and many others, I made it my life's purpose to work to increase access and success for underrepresented students and professionals in higher education. In addition to working at various institutions, I have also intentionally fulfilled leadership and service roles in local, regional, and national professional associations committed to supporting students like me to succeed, among them most notably at my professional home association, NASPA–Student Affairs Administrators in Higher Education. When I was a high school student, I felt that my teachers were my posse. In college, I did not have Shirley's experience of navigating the university experience with a group of peers; instead, I commuted three to four hours daily and went to campus only to attend classes or receive tutoring. I did not join any groups or clubs or participate in any student activities during my entire undergraduate career.

But I have found my posse in higher education as Shirley and many others have helped me to navigate my journey along the way. I have also benefited greatly from a big network of colleagues and mentors that stretches beyond the United States. I feel strongly that my story illustrates the importance of working to find one's own posse and doing so through the strategic pursuit of professional development and taking on leadership roles in professional organizations. It is precisely because of mentors like my high school teachers and college professors, and the sense of belonging and purpose I share with colleagues in higher education, that I have been able to reach higher than I could have ever dreamed as a 12-year-old, non-English-speaking immigrant.

THE IMPORTANCE AND BENEFITS OF PROFESSIONAL DEVELOPMENT AND LEADERSHIP PARTICIPATION

It is critical for Latinx/a/o professionals to engage in lifelong learning through professional development and to take on leadership roles in professional organizations as a pathway to enhance their success in higher education. We the authors have served in many key national service leadership roles for the Association of American Colleges and Universities, the National Association of Diversity Officers in Higher Education, the National Conference on Race and Ethnicity, NASPA, and many others. There are many ways and benefits to becoming professionally active and involved in the profession. It is possible to start small by signing up to receive information and updates through e-mail lists, submitting a conference presentation proposal with colleagues, attending affinity group events, and volunteering for smaller roles at the local or regional level. Getting involved can help Latinx/a/o professionals to build connections outside their home institution and cultivate a network of colleagues to consult with, get advice from, and discuss topics that are too sensitive to bring up with colleagues with whom they work daily. This network can also provide Latinx/a/o professionals with resources and referrals and help them to problem solve professional challenges.

It is important to keep learning to remain on the cutting edge of best practices and higher education trends, and professional organizations can offer a wealth of ongoing career development. Although professional associations require membership fees, members can take advantage of free or discounted publications, learn practical skills, attend programs focused on particular development goals, and meet with a mentor or coach to plan their next career steps. Latinx/a/o professionals may find it culturally challenging to put themselves forward and brag about themselves. Consequently, they can benefit from focusing on professional development because getting involved can serve as a way to earn recognition for their work. As Elizabeth Palacios noted in chapter 14, it is particularly important for Latinx/a/o professionals to connect to culturally relevant and affinity organizations that can affirm their identities and support their advancement and growth in a supportive environment. Furthermore, it is critical to be strategic about advocating for resources for professional development and to always bring back new knowledge to one's institution. Although it may also be worthwhile to invest one's own money strategically when the institution is not able to fund professional development, many options for virtual and online professional development are available, and it is not always necessary to travel to national conferences to serve in a leadership role.

IMPLICATIONS AND RECOMMENDATIONS FOR THE FUTURE

In her most recent book on meritocracy in higher education, in the chapter "No Longer Lonely at the Top: The Posse Foundation," Lani Guinier (2015) pointed out that The Posse Foundation has activated one of the most transformative solutions to address issues of retention, persistence, isolation, and talent cultivation with a very simple, but powerful idea: Everyone needs a posse. Everyone needs a mentor. Everyone needs to build social capital to fully participate and to leverage their capacity in academia and out in the world. It is critical for Latinx/a/o professionals to take responsibility and initiative to engage in lifelong learning through such professional development opportunities as collaborating with professional organizations.

Growing research strongly supports the added value, utility, and power of diversity in groups, networks, and communities where individuals work, learn, and live (Page, 2007). In chapter 8 of this book, Marta Elena Esquilin noted that the development of intentional intergenerational learning communities that honor authentic leadership, build inclusive cohort-based models, and cultivate talent in all forms is an essential part of expanding, deepening, and improving the pathways for Latinx/a/o students and professionals.

The future success of Latinx/a/o pathways in higher education will require a reshaping of how networks, cohorts, and social capital are formed in the first place. Cohort-based approaches and mentor models across sectors, disciplines, and identity groups are essential. Higher education must become comfortable with socially engineering these conditions along the pathway for Latinx/a/o students and professionals to fully participate in higher education.

As several scholars and practitioners have noted, the system of American higher education in both the public and private sector has repeatedly missed students who make up the significant emerging and future demographics of America (Bok, 2006; Bowen, Chingos, & McPherson, 2009). Our journeys are among many stories. Students like us need to be identified and supported so they, too, can live out their dreams. This is where the support of others comes in.

Why do Latinx/a/os need everyone's authentic leadership, and why do cohorts and mentors matter? As stated previously, everyone needs a posse and mentors. Everyone needs to build up social capital. Latinx/a/o professionals also need to be courageous during what is currently a very challenging time in the United States and in education especially. Higher education needs Latinx/a/o leaders, researchers, and practitioners who are willing to ask the hard questions and innovate in areas few dare to address; these individuals must have a willingness to build cohorts that can collaborate across sectors and disciplinary boundaries. Both higher education and Latinx/a/o leaders need to inspire others to build teams, collaborate, and innovate to solve some of the most pressing problems affecting Latinx/a/os in education: access, affordability, and the importance of all students and professionals to get a chance to be full-fledged members of their academic communities and to thrive through college completion. Higher education also needs to look at merit differently, in order to broaden the pathways for Latinx/a/o individuals, and to hold itself accountable for building the right set of conditions on the pathway in higher education that allows talented students and professionals from all walks of life to realize their dreams and maximize their talent in community with others.

Higher education will not successfully increase leadership success for Latinx/a/o professionals, or be able to effectively respond to impending student demographic changes, without developing more cohort-based models for supporting individual students and professionals. Although many programs are geared toward students, more initiatives and models are needed for Latinx/a/o faculty and staff professionals as well. It is critical that higher education develop cross-institutional and cross-sector networks and collaboration opportunities that go beyond a single institution. For example, a great deal can be learned from Hispanic-serving institutions, community colleges, and from more traditional and less diverse private colleges and research universities. Cross-institutional collaborations can also allow for more learning, innovation, and resource sharing; full participation in academia should be a core goal in supporting Latinx/a/o students and professionals. This goal will allow higher education to take advantage of the capacity of all students and professionals in academia.

CONCLUSION

Higher education must foster new pathways through the power of cohorts, mentors, professional development, and leadership participation. To do so, it is critical, as Sofia Pertuz shared in chapter 4, to both understand and honor how Latinx/a/o cultural values and norms inherently align with higher education practices and how cohorts, networks, and mentoring can enhance the ability of Latinx/a/o professionals to lead authentically. The ability to lead and work in ways that are congruent with one's identity can improve Latinx/a/os' success and simultaneously provide the diversity and new leadership that will be required for higher education to meet the demands of an increasingly diverse student population. As illustrated by our journeys, ongoing learning, professional development, and leadership participation should be pursued and supported to leverage capacity and success. While Shirley benefited from her Posse experience, Angela's experience has been less traditional. However, both of us were encouraged and guided by mentors and peers who helped us overcome barriers along their education pathways. We also both actively worked to grow through professional development and leadership participation opportunities that ultimately revealed clarity of purpose and a commitment to work toward changing the landscape of higher education.

There's no better time than the present for higher education to recommit to a more intentional and inclusive new kind of leadership, as the field adjusts to changing demographics, responds to complex national political issues, works to tackle existing retention and graduation gaps, and endeavors to prepare students for the most global society yet. All are invited to be part of the solution. Latinx/a/o individuals must be courageous in their intentional pursuit of new opportunities, and other higher education leaders should work every day not only to get Latinx/a/o students and professionals on the bus, but to ensure that they are welcomed, supported, and celebrated when they arrive at their higher education destinations.

REFERENCES

Bok, D. (2006). *Our underachieving colleges: A candid look at how much students learn and why they should be learning more.* Princeton, NJ: Princeton University Press.

Bowen, W. G., Chingos, M. M., & McPherson, M. S. (Eds.). (2009). *Crossing the finish line: Completing college at America's public universities.* Princeton, NJ: Princeton University Press.

Guinier, L. (2015). *The tyranny of the meritocracy: Democratizing higher education in America.* Boston, MA: Beacon Press.

Page, S. (2007). *The difference: How the power of diversity creates better groups, firms, schools and societies.* Princeton, NJ: Princeton University Press.

EPILOGUE

Kevin Kruger

The United States is changing. In virtually every corner of the country, racial, ethnic, and religious diversity has been increasing over the past 20 years. The 2016 presidential election underscored the impact of this increasing diversity through contentious debates about immigration, racial justice, the loss of middle-income jobs, and the ways in which government supports low-income Americans. All of these issues affect American colleges and universities. The aim of this book has been to put a clear focus on one aspect of this increased diversity—the significant increase in the Latinx/a/o population in the United States and, specifically, the increase in Latinx/a/o students at American colleges and universities. The individual journeys portrayed in this book across different professional levels and generations paint a vivid picture of the emerging Latinx/a/o community and culture within higher education and the potential this new diversity has for all of higher education.

The increasing diversity in higher education creates tremendous opportunities for student learning and the creation of diverse communities that support that learning. There is a significant opportunity to increase access from sectors of the population that have historically been underrepresented in colleges and universities. However, persistence and completion rates for Latinx/a/o students have lagged behind those for their White, non-Hispanic peers for the past 20 years. There are opportunities for the college student profile to reflect the diversity we see in our country and opportunities for all students to benefit from exposure to peers with very different racial and ethnic backgrounds and cultures. This exposure to different cultures is critical. As we move toward a truly global economy, one of the key competencies necessary for success will be advanced intercultural skills and exposure to different perspectives. A study of competencies highly desired by employers found that 96% of employers surveyed agreed or strongly agreed that college graduates should have educational experiences that teach them to solve problems with people whose views differ from their own (Hart Research Associates, 2015). In the same study, 78% of employers agreed that college graduates should gain intercultural skills and an understanding of societies and countries outside the United States (Hart Research Associates, 2015). Substantial evidence also shows that students who interacted with racially and ethnically diverse peers exhibited the greatest growth in active thinking, intellectual engagement, and intellectual and academic skills (Gurin, Dey, Hurtado, & Gurin, 2002).

Although this increased diversity comes with many exciting opportunities, it also presents a new set of challenges. Challenges related to access to and academic support for Latinx/a/o students, experiences of marginalization of Latinx/a/o students, a dominant culture that often undervalues Latinx/a/o students' experience, and low numbers of Latinx/a/o faculty all create significant obstacles for Latinx/a/o student success.

Higher education must address these challenges. As is discussed in this book, the Hispanic/Latinx population is the fastest-growing racial/ethnic sector in the United States. The Pew Research Center reported that Latinos "accounted for more than half (54%) of total U.S. population growth from 2000 to 2014" (Krogstad, 2016, para. 4). Throughout this book, the authors have discussed the need for expanded pathways for Latinx/a/o students, student affairs professionals, and faculty. It will be critical to build, nurture, and expand these pathways as the Latinx/a/o student population continues to grow.

PATHWAYS

Despite the significant demographic increase of Latinx/a/o Americans, progress has been slow in actualizing the same diversity in senior leadership positions in higher education. This is not only a higher education problem, it is an American problem. With a rapidly expanding population that accounts for "nearly half of all consumer spending growth . . . Hispanics are largely missing in action in the corridors of power in corporate America" (Guadalupe, 2015, p. 1). Although Latinx/a/os comprise an average of nearly 15% of the total reported employee base in Fortune 100 companies, fewer than 5% of executive officer positions were held by Hispanics and just over 7% of board seats were held by Hispanic leaders (Hispanic Association on Corporate Responsibility, 2016). In related research, a management consulting firm found that although "Hispanic managers reach mid-level management positions faster than their peers, they are slower to climb to higher levels within their companies" (National Hispanic Corporate Council, 2010, para. 2). This lack of representation in executive and senior leadership positions has led to the emergence of executive education programs that are designed to increase upward mobility for Latinx/a/o executives. Programs such as the Leadership Development Experience offered by the Association of Latino Professionals for America and the National Hispanic Corporate Council program at Southern Methodist University's Cox School of Business are designed to promote executive education for Latinx/a/o professionals and to expand the pathway to executive positions. These efforts to increase diversity in corporate leadership have a tangible payoff to the bottom line. Diverse companies make more money. Companies with greater gender diversity are 15% more likely to outperform their peers. The effect for ethnically diverse companies is even greater. Ethnically diverse companies are 35% more likely to outperform their peers (Hunt, Layton, & Prince, 2015).

It is no surprise that higher education faces similar challenges. It starts at the core function of a university—teaching. Latinx/a/o undergraduate enrollment (full time and part time) has increased from 15.2% in 2010 to 18.4% in 2014 (National Center for Education Statistics [NCES], 2016). Despite this growth, of all full-time faculty at degree-granting postsecondary institutions, only 2% identify as Hispanic (NCES, 2016). The small gains reported in faculty positions have largely occurred in nontenured, adjunct teaching roles. A recent TIAA Institute study found that underrepresented minority full-time tenure-track faculty increased only 1.7% in the past 20 years, while the full-time nontenure-track positions increased 2.9%. The gap is even larger for part-time faculty, where underrepresented minority part-time faculty increased 5% over the past 20 years (Finkelstein, Conley, & Schuster, 2016).

A similar gap exists in the administrative ranks within colleges and universities. The annual College and University Professional Association for Human Resources research on salaries and administrative roles found 86% of all college administrators were White; only 3% identified as Hispanic/Latino (Bichsel & McChesney, 2017). Figure 16.1 illustrates this racial/ethnic divide. Although the percentage of all minority administrators has increased slightly over the past decade, "the increase has not kept pace with the increase in the U.S. minority population or the increase in minority college graduates over this same period. Therefore, the gap between the representation of minorities in these positions and the population of minorities with graduate degrees is increasing rather than decreasing" (Bichsel & McChesney, 2017, p. 5).

Figure 16.1. Racial/Ethnic Composition of Higher Education Administrators, 2016

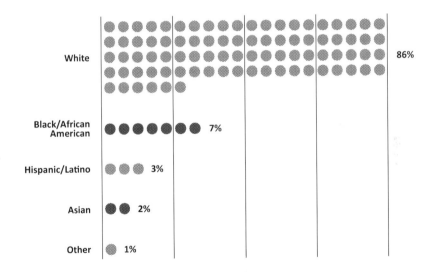

Note. Reprinted from "Pay and Representation of Racial/Ethnic Minorities in Higher Education Administrative Positions: The Century So Far," by J. Bichsel & J. McChesney, 2017, p. 4. Copyright © 2017 by CUPA-HR. Reprinted with permission.

The view from the top is not much better. Minority representation at the college presidency level has always been very low. "The profile of the typical college or university president remains largely the same since the first iteration of these data in 1986: an older white male" (Crandall, Espinosa, & Taylor, 2017, para. 1). In the most recent American College President Study, "30 percent of college presidents were women and 17 percent were members of racial or ethnic minorities—a slight increase from recent surveys" (American Council on Education, 2017, p. ix). The American College President Study data show that Hispanics/Latinos represented only 3.9% of college and university presidents (Crandall et al., 2017).

Data on student affairs leadership suggest slightly more diversity at the senior student affairs officer (SSAO) level. The 2014 NASPA–Student Affairs Administrators in Higher Education census of SSAOs found that, overall, 73% of SSAOs were White and 7% identified as Hispanic (Wesaw & Sponsler, 2014). The greatest representation was at two-year institutions, where 9% identified as Hispanic, followed by 8% at public four-year institutions. Only 3% of SSAOs at private four-year colleges were Hispanic (Wesaw & Sponsler, 2014).

It is clear from all these data on faculty, administrators, college presidents, and SSAOs that more attention needs to be paid to efforts to diversify key leadership positions within the academy. When speaking about college presidents, Alvin Schexnider, a former chancellor of Winston-Salem State University, noted, "The data indicate increases in diversity are unlikely without major efforts. Positions are held mainly by White males, and the need to diversify is self-evident. . . . Given the history, that's going to be a tough climb unless there are some aggressive steps" (Seltzer, 2017, paras. 14–15). The same statement could be made about other leadership positions in higher education. More needs to be done.

One of those major efforts is to create stronger pathway opportunities for professionals who would seek to work in higher education.

One such effort has been underway in student affairs for the past 30 years: the NASPA Undergraduate Fellows Program (NUFP). NUFP's mission is to increase the number of historically disenfranchised and underrepresented professionals in student affairs and/or higher education. Over the past five years, NUFP fellows who identify as Latinx/a/o have comprised the largest racial/ethnic group in the program, ranging from 30% of all NUFP fellows in 2012 to 26% in 2017. NUFP focuses on creating mentoring experiences that result in a wide range of positive educational outcomes. The Gallup-Purdue index reinforces this idea. Students who reported feeling supported and having someone who cared about them as a person and who encouraged them to pursue their dreams and goals were more engaged in their work after graduation and reported thriving in their overall well-being (Busteed, 2014).

One measure of NUFP's success is the increase in the number of Latinx/a/o professionals working in student affairs. Although there is no definitive data source for this, the number of student affairs professionals who belong to NASPA's Latinx/a/o Knowledge Community (LKC) is one measure. NASPA Knowledge Communities provide a forum for student affairs professionals to create a community of shared interests and disseminate knowledge and examples of effective practice. The LKC was formally established in 2002. In the past 10 years, membership in the LKC has grown 39%, from 738 members in 2007 to 1,029 members in 2017. One of the surest ways to increase representation of Latinx/a/o SSAOs is to increase the number of mid-level professionals working in student affairs.

One more example is worth noting. In 2015, a group of Latinx/a/o student affairs professionals designed and created the NASPA Escaleras Institute. The three-day institute was designed for Latinx/a/o student affairs professionals who aspire to SSAO roles. The program focuses on developing culturally relevant leadership skills that leverage the participants' unique ethnic heritages and histories. The Escaleras Institute was repeated in 2016 and will be offered next in 2018.

Although it is too early to see results from these two institutes, these kinds of pathway programs are critical to increasing Latinx/a/o representation in senior-level student affairs positions. It is vital that higher education make progress in diversifying leadership. With the increases in Latinx/a/o students entering colleges and universities, the lack of culturally identified role models and mentors will continue to have a hindering effect on Latinx/a/o student success, degree persistence, and degree completion.

SCHOLARSHIP

Beyond representation of Latinx/a/o professionals in higher education, it is also important to look at the scholarship that focuses on Latinx/a/o students and student affairs professionals. An examination of historical trends of scholarly journal articles, conference presentations, and published books can be used to develop insight into how these issues are emphasized and prioritized.

One example of this analysis is an article in the *NASPA Journal* that reviewed articles from 1967 to 1996 for content that focused on racial and ethnic issues. During those 30 years, almost one quarter of the articles had some kind of focus on racial and ethnic issues. Of those, 56% focused on broadly defined issues of race and ethnicity and 38% focused on Black issues. In the entire 30 years, only one article specifically focused on Hispanic issues (Banning, Ahuna, & Hughes, 2000). Since that article in 2000, the *Journal of Student Affairs Research and Practice* (formerly *NASPA Journal*) has published 13 articles that explicitly used "Latino," "Latina," or "Hispanic" in the title. Although not overwhelming, it does suggest a slow increase in scholarship focused on Hispanic/Latino issues and concerns. During that same period, the *Journal of College Student Development* published 17 articles that explicitly used "Latino," "Latina," or "Hispanic" in the title.

Presentations at national conferences are also a measure of the extent to which Latinx/a/o issues are prioritized and emphasized. An examination of the programs presented at the NASPA Annual Conference over the past five years reveals that although a significant number of conference programs focused on more broadly defined issues of race and ethnicity, only a small number of programs focused solely on Hispanic/Latino issues. As Table 16.1 illustrates, since 2014 the number of programs that focus on Hispanic/Latino issues, while small, has increased significantly. Also, the term "Latinx" was first used in a NASPA Annual Conference presentation title in 2016.

Table 16.1. **Number of NASPA Annual Conference Presentations Focusing on Hispanic/Latino Issues, 2013–2017**

Year	NASPA Annual Conference Presentations
2013	6
2014	7
2015	18
2016	16
2017	19

The relatively small number of journal articles and conference presentations reflects the relatively small body of research on the experiences of Latinx/a/o students. There is also limited research and writing on student development and identity models that focus on Latinx/a/o students. However, since 2001, there has been an increase in scholarship focused on the Latinx/a/o student experience. Ferdman and Gallegos (2001) were early pioneers in Latino identity development. They explored ways in which Latinos developed a "lens" or view of themselves as Latinos based on their experiences with family, college, and peers. They described six identity orientations based on the individual's lens—Latino Integrated, Latino Identified, Subgroup Identified, Latino as Other, Undifferentiated, and White Identified (Ferdman & Gallegos, 2001). This expanded view of Latino identity development and the identification of the multiple identities within the "Latino" world represented an important contribution to the scholarship on Latinx/a/o students. Other scholars such as Torres and Magolda (2004) and Guardia and Evans (2008) have examined the development of ethnic identity for Latino students and the ways in which the college experience can support those identities. It is particularly important that Latinx/a/o-specific research be advanced and to not assume that Latinx/a/o student development is covered under existing racial theory. "Latinos have had an uneasy relationship with the prevailing racial constructs in the United States. These 'either/or' notions, typically Black/White/not White, have not easily incorporated or allowed for the polychromatic (that is, multicolored) reality of Latinos" (Ferdman & Gallegos, 2001, p. 38). However, it is clear that more research and theory development needs to be done. The "multicolored" reality for the Latinx/a/o community referenced by Ferdman and Gallegos (2001) suggests much more scholarship is needed to fully understand the developmental experience of Latinx/a/o students.

A CHARGE FOR THE FUTURE

This book begins a conversation about equity and the compelling need to increase the work that is done across higher education to support the success of the millions of Latinx/a/o students who are enrolled in American colleges and universities. There is much to celebrate and there is much to do. I would like to close with some thoughts about what student affairs professionals must do to meet our obligations to support Latinx/a/o students.

1. We need to nurture and expand existing programs for Latinx/a/o professionals and faculty. The number of Latinx/a/o professionals must reflect the comparable diversity of the students enrolled at our institutions. We need more mentoring programs for young professionals that help them understand the pathways for professional advancement and that highlight the key skills necessary for that advancement. We cannot allow our Latinx/a/o colleagues to be "left behind" in consideration for leadership and executive positions. We must also enable and encourage challenging conversations about how Latinx/a/o professionals can incorporate their passion and advocacy into their work. Concurrent with this, we must challenge our institutions to embrace this type of advocacy when it is focused so clearly on creating conditions for Latinx/a/o student success.

2. It is not enough for higher education to continually express that Latinx/a/o students are the fastest-growing sector of students. A more focused effort is needed to develop programs that support the success of those students. New or reallocated resources, both fiscal and human, need to be identified to address the current state of Latinx/a/o student degree persistence and completion. As an industry, the attainment gap that currently exists for college completion can no longer be tolerated.

3. Renewed focus must be placed on increasing the amount of research that focuses on Latinx/a/o identity and development. Significantly more conference and workshop programs should highlight successful interventions and strategies that increase degree completion and career readiness for Latinx/a/o students. We need a new generation of scholars and practitioners to

conduct research, teach in graduate preparation programs, and develop evidence-based programs that highlight student success for the Latinx/a/o community.

4. Student affairs divisions should highlight staff development opportunities that increase the Latinx/a/o cultural competence for all professionals, but particularly for White student affairs professionals. This focus on increasing the cultural competence for all student affairs professionals is critical as the diversity of the student body continues to increase.

Finally, I would like to thank the authors of each chapter in this book for telling their stories and illuminating the emerging issues so critical to advancing and living the mission of student affairs work. Each of their contributions takes us one step closer to improving the experience for all Latinx/a/o students.

REFERENCES

American Council on Education. (2017). *The American college president study 2017*. Washington, DC: Author.

Banning, J. H., Ahuna, L. M., & Hughes, B. M. (2000). A study of the *NASPA Journal* (1967–1996): A 30-year reflection of scholarship in student affairs focusing on race and ethnicity. *NASPA Journal, 38*(1), 58–69.

Bichsel, J., & McChesney, J. (2017, March). *Pay and representation of racial/ethnic minorities in higher education administrative positions: The century so far*. Retrieved from College and University Professional Association for Human Resources website: http://www.cupahr.org/wp-content/uploads/2017/06/cupahr_research_brief_minorities.pdf

Busteed, B. (2014, September 25). The blown opportunity. *Inside Higher Education*. Retrieved from https://www.insidehighered.com/views/2014/09/25/essay-about-importance-mentors-college-students

Crandall, J. R., Espinosa, L. L., & Taylor, M. (2017, August 14). Looking ahead to diversifying the college presidency. *Higher Education Today*. Retrieved from https://www.higheredtoday.org/2017/08/14/looking-ahead-diversifying-college-presidency

Ferdman, B. M., & Gallegos, P. I. (2001). Racial identity development and Latinos in the United States. In C. L. Wijeyesinghe & B. W. Jackson III (Eds.), *New perspectives on racial identity development: A theoretical and practical anthology* (pp. 32–66). New York, NY: New York University Press.

Finkelstein, M. J., Conley, V. M., & Schuster, J. H. (2016, April). *Taking the measure of faculty diversity*. Retrieved from TIAA website: https://www.tiaainstitute.org/sites/default/files/presentations/2017-02/taking_the_measure_of_faculty_diversity.pdf

Guadalupe, P. (2015, November 30). More Latinos needed in corporate executive positions: Report. *NBC News*. Retrieved from https://www.nbcnews.com/news/latino/more-latinos-needed-corporate-executive-positions-report-n471466

Guardia, J., & Evans, N. (2008). Factors influencing the ethnic identity development of Latino fraternity members at a Hispanic Serving Institution. *Journal of College Student Development, 49*(3), 163–181.

Gurin, P., Dey, E. L., Hurtado, S., & Gurin, G. (2002). Diversity and higher education: Theory and impact on educational outcomes. *Harvard Educational Review, 72*(3), 330–366.

Hart Research Associates. (2015). *Falling short? College learning and career success*. Retrieved from Association of American Colleges & Universities website: https://www.aacu.org/sites/default/files/files/LEAP/2015employerstudentsurvey.pdf

Hispanic Association on Corporate Responsibility. (2016). *2016 HACR corporate inclusion index*. Retrieved from http://www.hacr.org/research_institute/cii

Hunt, V., Layton, D., & Prince, S. (2015). *Diversity matters*. Retrieved from McKinsey & Company website: http://www.mckinsey.com/business-functions/organization/our-insights/why-diversity-matters

Krogstad, J. M. (2016, September 8). Key facts about how the U.S. Hispanic population is changing. Retrieved from Pew Research Center website: http://www.pewresearch.org/fact-tank/2016/09/08/key-facts-about-how-the-u-s-hispanic-population-is-changing

National Center for Education Statistics. (2016). *Digest of educational statistics: 2015*. Retrieved from https://nces.ed.gov/programs/digest/d15/guide.asp

National Hispanic Corporate Council. (2010). *National Hispanic organization's executive leadership program develops Hispanic talent in corporate America*. Retrieved from http://www.nhcchq.org/nhcc-news/national-hispanic-organizations-executive-leadership-program-develops-hispanic-talent-in-corporate-america-2

Seltzer, R. (2017, June 20). The slowly diversifying presidency. *Inside Higher Education*. Retrieved from https://www.insidehighered.com/news/2017/06/20/college-presidents-diversifying-slowly-and-growing-older-study-finds

Torres, V., & Magolda, M. (2004). Reconstructing Latino identity: The influence of cognitive development on the ethnic identity process of Latino students. *Journal of College Student Development, 45*(3), 333–347.

Wesaw, A. J., & Sponsler, B. A. (2014). *The chief student affairs officer: Responsibilities, opinions, and professional pathways of leaders in student affairs.* Retrieved from NASPA–Student Affairs Administrators in Higher Education website: https://www.naspa.org/images/uploads/main/CSAO_2014_FULLREPORT_DOWNLOAD.pdf

THE AUTHORS

Lucy Arellano is an assistant professor in the College of Education at Oregon State University. As a Chicana from East Los Angeles, the granddaughter of a *campesino* (farm worker), the daughter of factory workers, and the first in her family to go to college, she strives in all aspects of her work to help those who seek a postsecondary education—particularly marginalized groups. Her research focuses on persistence, retention, and degree completion for emerging-majority students. She earned a doctorate in higher education and organizational change from the University of California, Los Angeles (UCLA).

Tracy Arámbula Ballysingh is an assistant professor of higher education and student affairs in the Department of Leadership and Developmental Sciences at the University of Vermont, and she is a Project MALES faculty affiliate. Her research focuses on Latinx/a/o college access and completion, educational outcomes for boys and men of color, first-generation college students, the first-year experience in college, and the role of Hispanic-serving institutions in the higher education landscape. She has served as an academic advisor, a mentor/instructor for first-year/first-generation college students, a director of student success programs, and a policy analyst for the chair of the Texas Senate's Higher Education Committee.

Angela E. Batista is vice president of student life and special advisor to the president for diversity and inclusion at Champlain College. She previously served as the associate vice provost for student affairs and dean of student life and interim chief diversity officer at Oregon State University; she was dean of students at the University of Southern Indiana and has also worked at the University of Vermont, Lynn University, and Mills College. Batista's expertise includes student affairs, institutional diversity planning, and student success and leadership development. A national award winner and international consultant, she is deeply engaged in national professional organizations. She has served as the national chair for NASPA–Student Affairs Administrators in Higher Education's Latinx/a/o Knowledge Community, as a member of NASPA's Equity and Inclusion Commission, as a member of the 2016 National Conference Leadership and Planning Team, and as a faculty member and co-director of NASPA's 2018 Escaleras Institute. She earned her doctorate in leadership from Nova Southeastern University and her master's degree from the University of Vermont. Her undergraduate work was completed at Brooklyn College in New York City.

Katherine Cho is a doctoral student in higher education and organizational change at the Graduate School of Education and Information Studies at UCLA. Her research interests include organizational theory, college retention, and the movement of knowledge within academic spaces. Concurrently, she is a research analyst at the Higher Education Research Institute. Prior to UCLA, Cho was a program manager in New York City, where she worked on student success and leadership programs. She holds an MA in sociology and education from Teachers College, Columbia University, and a BA in public policy studies from Duke University.

Shirley M. Collado was named the ninth president of Ithaca College in 2017; she is the first woman of color to serve as president of the college and the first Dominican American to serve as president of a four-year institution in higher education in the United States. Collado is an accomplished and transformational executive leader in higher education who is known nationally for designing and implementing innovative approaches to expanding access and student success. She is a national thought leader on developing successful cross-sector collaborations, building the capacity of diversity and inclusion in organizations, and strengthening the pathway to the professoriate and to leadership in higher education. The Brooklyn-born daughter of Dominican immigrants, Collado is the first person in her family to attend college and the first Posse Foundation Scholar to receive a doctoral degree. She led the Posse Foundation as its executive vice president for several years, was the executive vice chancellor and chief operating officer at Rutgers University–Newark, and served as the vice president for student affairs and dean of the college at Middlebury College.

Anthony Cruz is vice chancellor of student affairs at St. Louis Community College in St. Louis, Missouri. During his 21 years of higher education experience, Cruz has used his expertise to provide leadership—primarily in the areas of enrollment management, student support services, and retention. Before joining St. Louis Community College, Cruz worked as a student affairs administrator at several colleges and universities, including Sinclair Community College, Cincinnati State Technical and Community College,

Broward College, Kaplan University, and Florida International University. Cruz has a BA in political science from Florida International University, an MA in public administration from Florida State University, and a doctorate in education from Florida International University.

Jacob L. Diaz is the dean of students/director of housing and residence life at the University of South Florida St. Petersburg. A first-generation college and transfer student, he grew up in a bilingual home in San Diego, California. His research and professional interests focus primarily on multiculturally competent leadership, key factors that contribute to student success, and college student identity development. Diaz also served as vice president for student development, assistant vice president, and dean of students at Seattle University, and he was assistant dean of students and director of the Center for Student Ethics and Standards at the University of Vermont. He received his EdD in educational leadership and policy studies from the University of Vermont.

Melissa L. Freeman is the Title V Promoting Post-Baccalaureate Opportunities for Hispanic Americans project director at Adams State University. She is the founding director of Adams State University's Higher Education Administration and Leadership program, which was funded by a Fund for the Improvement of Postsecondary Education (FIPSE) grant. Her areas of expertise include college access and success among historically marginalized students, transfer issues, policy and politics, history of higher education, Hispanic-serving institutions, quantitative and survey methodologies, and entrepreneurship in higher education. In 2006, Freeman received the Charles I. Brown National Fellowship for dissertation study from the National Center for Education Statistics/Association for Institutional Research. She holds a doctorate in higher education administration from Ohio University in Athens, Ohio.

Marta Elena Esquilin is the associate dean of the Honors Living-Learning Community and an assistant professor of professional practice in the American Studies Program at Rutgers University–Newark. She also serves as the lead consultant for the BOLD Women's Leadership Network and board chair for CLAGS (Center for Lesbian and Gay Studies). In 2005, under the leadership of Derald Wing Sue at Teachers College, Esquilin coauthored the seminal article "Racial Microaggressions in Everyday Life: Implications for Clinical Practice." Her work focuses on creating educational environments that encourage the positive development and success of all students, with a particular emphasis on raising awareness about how microaggressions create hostile environments for marginalized social identities within work and school settings.

Mildred García is president of the American Association of State Colleges and Universities. She previously served as president of California State University (CSU), Fullerton. A recipient of myriad awards and honors—from receiving the American Council on Education's Reginald Wilson Diversity Leadership Award to being named a Distinguished Alumni Honoree of Columbia University—García was appointed by U.S. President Barack Obama to the President's Advisory Commission on Educational Excellence for Hispanics and has served with distinction since 2011. García previously served as president of CSU Dominguez Hills; she was the first Latina president in the largest system of public higher education in the country. García earned an EdD from Columbia University, Teachers College.

Nichole M. Garcia is a postdoctoral research fellow at the University of Pennsylvania. In 2016, she received the Inter-University Program for Latino Research–Andrew W. Mellon Dissertation Fellowship to complete her comparative study on Chicana/o and Puerto Rican college-educated families to advance narratives of intergenerational achievement. She employs mixed methods to examine inaccurate portrayals of educational outcomes for communities of color. In doing so, institutions of higher education can select the appropriate programs and evidence-based interventions to meet the growing needs of Latinx/a/o students. She received her PhD in social science and comparative education from UCLA.

Claudia García-Louis is an assistant professor at the University of Texas San Antonio, a Project MALES (Mentoring to Achieve Latino Educational Success) faculty affiliate, and a research associate with the AfroLatin@ Forum. Her research seeks to disrupt deficit thinking about communities of color, disadvantaged populations, and underrepresented students. Her goals are to expand the definitions of *Latinidad* and *Blackness* in higher education, to make a critical contribution to newly formed lines of inquiry that explore the educational experiences of AfroLatinx/a/os, and to conduct research that highlights Latinx/a/o heterogeneity through an asset-based lens.

Ignacio Hernández is an assistant professor in the Department of Educational Leadership at CSU Fresno. Hernández turns to minority-serving community colleges as a source of inquiry within the broad institutional landscape of higher education in the United States. His research seeks to highlight the experiences and lessons learned by Latinx/a/o leaders in community colleges that may serve to re-imagine normative definitions of community college leadership and the social practice of leadership in higher education. Hernández earned his doctorate from Iowa State University. He served on the boards of NASPA's Community Colleges Division and the National Community College Hispanic Council.

Sylvia Hurtado is a professor in the Graduate School of Education and Information Studies at UCLA, where she also served as director of the Higher Education Research Institute. She is a past president of the Association for the Study of Higher Education, and she has served on the boards of the Higher Learning Commission and initiatives of the Association of American Colleges and Universities. Her research has focused on how colleges are preparing students to participate in a diverse democracy, the pathways of underrepresented students in scientific research and professional careers, and student and institutional outcomes of diverse and broad-access institutions in higher education. She obtained her doctorate from UCLA.

Lorena Michelle Jirón is a child of immigrants from Nicaraguan and Dominican descent and grew up in a single-parent household in Miami, Florida. She attended Miami Dade College and earned an undergraduate degree from Middlebury College in Vermont. She graduated with a law degree from the Fordham University School of Law in New York City in 2017. Jirón is passionate about improving the experiences of the Latinx/a/o community and plans to continue to work to improve the lives and experiences of Latinx/a/os in her community.

Kevin Kruger is an accomplished speaker, leader, and educator who joined NASPA in 1994 and became its first executive-level president in 2012. In his capacity as a national advocate for students and the primary spokesperson for student affairs administrators and practitioners, he draws on more than 30 years of experience in higher education. Prior to NASPA, Kruger worked for 15 years at the University of Maryland College Park and the University of Maryland Baltimore

County. Kruger has also served as an adjunct faculty member in the Student Development in Higher Education program at Trinity College in Washington, D.C.

Anesat León-Guerrero is a Chicana from a farm-working immigrant family and was raised in Oregon, Arizona, and Michoacán (Mexico). She was an undergraduate at Oregon State University (OSU) where she studied sociology, Spanish, and ethnic studies. She served on the board of the Oregon Students of Color Coalition and on Oregon's Cultural Competency workgroup for the Higher Education Coordinating Commission. She also served as executive director of diversity programs for the Associated Students of OSU, where she focused on advancing diversity, inclusion, and social justice on campus. She is currently pursuing a master's degree in student affairs at Indiana University–Bloomington.

William Luis is the Gertrude Conaway Vanderbilt Professor of Spanish at Vanderbilt University, where he also directs Latino and Latina studies and edits the *Afro-Hispanic Review*. He has taught at Dartmouth College, Washington University in St. Louis, Binghamton University, and Yale University. Luis has authored, edited, and coedited 14 books and more than 100 scholarly articles. Luis was the recipient of a 2012 Guggenheim Fellowship. Born and raised in New York City, he is widely regarded as a leading authority on Latin American, Caribbean, Afro-Hispanic, and Latino U.S. literatures.

Edward F. Martinez is the assistant dean of student services at Suffolk County Community College and serves as a member of the board of trustees at Five Towns College in Dix Hills, New York. He has diverse administrative, academic, and program development experience in higher education and in student affairs. Martinez holds several leadership positions within NASPA, including serving as a member of the Community Colleges Division (CCD) board, chairing the CCD Latinx/a/o Task Force, and serving on the Leadership Team for the Latinx/a/o Knowledge Community. Martinez earned his doctoral degree in educational administration and leadership from Dowling College.

Eligio Martinez Jr. is a visiting assistant professor in the Educational Leadership Doctoral Program at California State Polytechnic University, Pomona, and a Project MALES Research Affiliate. His research focuses on the intersection of race, class, and gender for Chicano/Latino males throughout the P–20 educational pipeline. Martinez has experience working with and conducting research in urban middle school, high school, community college, and four-year college contexts. His main research interest focuses the middle school experiences of young men of color and the stratification they encounter during this stage that limits their future opportunities.

Magdalena Martinez is an assistant professor in the Department of Public Policy and Leadership, College of Urban Affairs, and the director of education programs with the Lincy Institute at the University of Nevada, Las Vegas. Her areas of expertise include education policy, leadership, access and equity for underrepresented student populations, and the role of higher education in a diverse society. Martinez is a New Leadership Academy Fellow through the National Center for Institutional Diversity at the University of Michigan and an Equity and Policy Fellow through the Ford Foundation, University of Southern California, and Western Interstate Consortium in Higher Education. Martinez holds a doctorate from the University of Michigan.

Juan Carlos Matos is the assistant vice president of student affairs for diversity and inclusion at Fordham University. He was born in the Dominican Republic and grew up in Brooklyn. He is passionate about diversity and inclusion, which has energized his work with students, faculty, and staff at Fordham and beyond. His work has resonated with the Jesuit ideal of *cura personalis*, which translates to "care for the whole person." A doctoral student at Fordham, Matos is studying administration and supervision within the Executive Leadership Cohort. His research interests connect to how experiences of LGBTQIA administrators of color have shaped their career trajectories within higher education.

Gerardo Ochoa is assistant dean for diversity and community partnerships at Linfield College. Prior to his current position, he served as a financial aid administrator for 10 years. In addition to his role at Linfield, he is the coauthor of *Path to Scholarships: College Edition* and consults with colleges, high schools, and nonprofits to increase student college affordability. Ochoa has extensive experience working with underrepresented youth in higher education, primarily Latinos at the middle school, high school, and undergraduate levels. He graduated from the University of Oregon, where he majored in sociology and minored in Latin American history.

Tonantzin Oseguera is the associate vice president for student affairs at CSU Fullerton. A first-generation college student born and raised in Mexico City, she is a student affairs professional dedicated to the retention, care, and persistence of high-risk student populations. Oseguera has served in student affairs administration—advising on matters of student government, evolving campus activities, and developing student leadership programs—for more than 14 years. Oseguera earned her doctorate in higher education at the University of Southern California. Her research focuses on underrepresented students and underserved populations in higher education.

Elizabeth (Liz) D. Palacios is the dean for student development, the special assistant to the president on diversity, and a faculty member in the Higher Education and Student Affairs Graduate Program at Baylor University. In 2017, she became president-elect of the Texas Association of Chicanos in Higher Education. Palacios has authored several publications and presentations, and she wrote a book chapter in the National Association of School Psychologists' primer on training and research on multiculturalism in schools. She served as an inaugural faculty member for the NASPA Escaleras Institute and on various national, regional, and local boards of higher education. Palacios earned her doctorate in school psychology from The University of Texas at Austin.

David Pérez II is an assistant professor of educational leadership at Miami University in Oxford, Ohio. His research focuses on increasing the success of Latino undergraduate men in higher education, and he has been recognized by both NASPA and ACPA–College Student Educators International as an emerging scholar for his contributions. His publications are featured in top-tier journals, including the *Journal of College Student Development, Journal of Diversity in Higher Education*, and *International Journal of Qualitative Studies in Education*. In 2014, he launched The National Study on Latino Male Achievement in Higher Education to elucidate how students employed different forms of capital to thrive at 20 selective public and private universities. This study was supported by grants from the ACPA Foundation, Miami University, NASPA Foundation, and the National Resource Center for the First-Year Experience and Students in Transition. Pérez is a Project MALES faculty affiliate and a NASPA Emerging Scholar. Pérez received his doctorate in higher education with a concentration in sociology from The Pennsylvania State University.

Joel Pérez is vice president and dean of students at Whittier College, where he oversees the departments of residence life, student activities, student conduct, and orientation; the Office of Equity and Inclusion; the Counseling Center; the Health Center; and the Center for Career and Professional Development. He has more than 19 years of experience in student affairs. Prior to arriving at Whittier College, Pérez served as dean of students for the Department of Community Life at Seattle Pacific University and in a variety of roles that encompassed residence life, student activities, and student leadership. He was a chief diversity officer at George Fox University in Oregon and at Pomona College and Chapman University in California.

Sofia B. Pertuz serves as assistant vice president and dean of students at Hofstra University. Born in the Dominican Republic and raised in the Bronx, Pertuz has experience in strategic planning, assessment, and critical incident management in student affairs. She is an adjunct in the higher education program at Hofstra and has been an invited speaker on contemporary issues in leadership, diversity, social justice, and LGBTQIA advocacy at national conferences and myriad institutions. Pertuz is actively involved in NASPA and has received several awards for her service. She is the founder and moderator of an online doctoral support network with nearly 4,000 actively engaged members. Pertuz attended SUNY New Paltz and earned master's and doctoral degrees in higher education leadership, management, and policy from Seton Hall University.

Joseph Ramirez is a doctoral student in the Graduate School of Education and Information Studies at UCLA; he is also a research analyst in the Office of Institutional Research and Planning at Fullerton College. He earned his AB in anthropology from Princeton University and his MA in higher education and organizational change from UCLA. His research focuses on how institutional resources, structures, and staff are organized to advance student goal attainment and achievement.

Brianna Carmen Sérráno is a Latinx, Chicanx, non-binary, queer transperson working in cultural and LGBTQIA centers within higher education. They currently serve as the co-chair for the People of Color Constituency Group for the National Executive Board of the Consortium of Higher Education: LGBT Resource Professionals. Sérráno has also served in NASPA leadership roles in the Latinx/a/o, Gender and Sexuality, and Undocumented Immigrants and Allies Knowledge Communities. They are also a published author on topics related to gender and sexual identity. Sérráno earned a Master of Education degree in college student affairs from The Pennsylvania State University and is currently pursuing a doctorate in higher education leadership at Colorado State University.

Daniel G. Solórzano is a professor of social science and comparative education at UCLA. He has authored more than 100 research articles and book chapters on issues related to educational access and equity for underrepresented student populations in the United States. Solórzano is a recipient of the UCLA Distinguished Teacher Award, the American Education Research Association's (AERA's) Social Justice in Education Award, and the Critical Race Studies in Education Association's Derrick A. Bell Legacy Award. In 2014, Solórzano was selected as an AERA fellow, and in 2017, he received the inaugural Revolutionary Mentor Award from the Critical Educators for Social Justice within AERA.

INDEX

Figures and tables are indicated by "f" and "t" following the page numbers.